EARLY CHRISTIAN EXPERIENCE

new
Test
ament
lib
rary

THE NEW TESTAMENT LIBRARY

Advisory Editors

GÜNTHER BORNKAMM

EARLY CHRISTIAN
EXPERIENCE

SCM PRESS LTD
BLOOMSBURY STREET LONDON

A selection of articles translated by Paul L. Hammer
from the German
Das Ende des Gesetzes (fifth edition, 1966) and
Studien zu Antike und Urchristentum (second edition, 1963)
published by Christian Kaiser Verlag, Munich

334 01561 8
FIRST ENGLISH EDITION 1969
© SCM PRESS LTD 1969
PRINTED IN GREAT BRITAIN BY
W & J MACKAY & CO LTD, CHATHAM

CONTENTS

Abbreviations   vii

Translator's Preface   ix

   I   God's Word and Man's Word in the New Testament   1

  II   Christ and the World in the Early Christian Message   14

 III   Faith and Reason in Paul   29

 IV   The Revelation of God's Wrath (Romans 1–3)   47

  V   Baptism and New Life in Paul (Romans 6)   71

 VI   Sin, Law and Death (Romans 7)   87

 VII   The Praise of God (Romans 11.33–36)   105

VIII   On Understanding the Christ-hymn (Philippians 2.6–11)   112

 IX   Lord's Supper and Church in Paul   123

  X   On the Understanding of Worship   161
       A The Edification of the Congregation as the Body of Christ
       B The Anathema in the Early Christian Lord's Supper Liturgy

 XI   The More Excellent Way (I Corinthians 13)   180

ABBREVIATIONS

BOOKS

CR	*Corpus Reformatorum* (1834ff.)
DEdG	Bornkamm, G., *Das Ende des Gesetzes, Ges. Aufs.* I (1963⁴).
HzNT	*Handbuch zum Neuen Testament*
NTT	Bultmann, R., *Theology of the New Testament* I, trans. by K. Grobel (1951)
RGG	*Religion in Geschichte und Gegenwart* (1957³ff.)
StrB	Strack, H. L., and Billerbeck, P., *Kommentar zum Neuen Testament aus Talmud und Midrasch* (1956²)
SzAuU	Bornkamm, G., *Studien zu Antike und Urchristentum, Ges. Aufs.* II (1963²).
TDNT	*Theological Dictionary of the New Testament*, trans. by G. W. Bromiley, 1964ff.
TNT	Bultmann, R., *Theologie des Neuen Testaments* (1961⁴)
TWNT	*Theologisches Wörterbuch zum Neuen Testament* (1933ff.)

PERIODICALS

EvTh	*Evangelische Theologie*
JTS	*The Journal of Theological Studies*
NTS	*New Testament Studies*
TLZ	*Theologische Literaturzeitung*
TR	*Theologische Rundschau* (new series)
ZNW	*Zeitschrift für die neutestamentliche Wissenschaft*
ZTK	*Zeitschrift für Theologie und Kirche*

TRANSLATOR'S PREFACE

It is the privilege of the translator to share in bringing these essays of his *Doktorvater* to the English-speaking world. Except for the occasional transliteration of necessary Greek words and phrases, all non-English languages have been translated in both the text and the footnotes. The notes usually refer to the latest editions of cited works and include also the titles and page numbers of English translations where they exist. Quotations from the Bible generally follow the Revised Standard Version and translations of classical writers utilize the Loeb Classical Library where available.

I wish to express here my deep gratitude to Professor Bornkamm, as well as to Dieter Georgi, Richard Jeske, Karl Donfried and Calvin Steck for their valuable suggestions, and to librarians and secretaries at United Theological Seminary of the Twin Cities, Harvard Divinity School and Colgate Rochester Divinity School/Bexley Hall for their cheerful help.

PAUL L. HAMMER

Spring 1969
Colgate Rochester Divinity School/Bexley Hall

I

GOD'S WORD AND MAN'S WORD
IN THE NEW TESTAMENT*

I

THE CONCERN IMPLIED by our topic is one which our ancestors of three to four hundred years ago and earlier would not have raised—at least not in the way in which it troubles people today. To the fathers of our church, Holy Scripture was for centuries and millennia so clearly and indisputably the Word of God that the question of God's word and man's word in Holy Scripture could not arise at all. Scripture as a whole, down to the last word and letter, was considered to be an unassailable domain of the divine truths of revelation. It was regarded as *the* Scripture, *the* Book of books, set apart from all other documents of the world and of history. It was distinguished by an incomparable authority—a direct, infallible dictation of the Holy Spirit.

But then another time came, a time in which the human spirit and man's reason awoke to their freedom. The previously undisputed and valid foundations of the church's traditions and dogmas began to totter and were no longer accepted without investigation. This was the period of the Enlightenment. It was a time of great scientific discoveries in all fields—the natural sciences as well as the historical sciences and the humanities—in which reason began its critical work and no longer stopped short of the previously sacred domains of church dogma and teaching. Today we often look back to that epoch of the human spirit with a certain contempt and estrangement, for since then the unshakable faith in reason and optimistic assurance of conquest typical of that time have in turn become deeply questionable. Yet it was an epoch which has strongly determined and shaped the thinking and questioning of the modern period down to our own time. However one may judge the details of the revolution—the

---

* Address given at the Kirchentag an der Ruhr in Essen in September, 1957; first published in *Kirche in der Zeit XII* (1957), pp. 301–5.

powerful change in human thinking with its profound consequences—that began then and still continues; whether one admires its conquests, discoveries and achievements or complains of its destructive might, this much is certain: since that time all of us, believers or non-believers, are faced with questions that earlier generations did not ask, questions that are still alive today and have not yet been silenced. None of us, even if he wants to, can simply return with a somersault to the unshaken perspective of our fathers. Not a few Christians seek to make this leap back into the past, considering all the questions that vex us in our faith since the rise of the modern scientific period merely as insinuations of the devil, to be condemned in a lump. But our faith must be in bad shape if we do not want to meet these questions; or if, as Christians, we cannot deal with the issues in any other way than like ostriches, sticking our heads in the sand of pious tradition. A Christianity which so fears for its faith that it avoids the questions that the truth-seeking mind must ask, no longer needs to wonder why the message that it owes to the world now is disposed of as always an outdated word of the past, having no power to conquer and convince. Of course, and this must now be said with the same or even greater emphasis, we are very ominously burdened even today —especially in our thinking about the question of God's word and man's word in the Bible and particularly in the New Testament— by the spirit, or better the spiritlessness, of the critique of reason which has challenged our Christian faith since the days of the Enlightenment. It was then that people first began to put the question about God's word and man's word in the Bible in the sense of "either-or". Strictly speaking the question was: Is the Bible God's word *or* man's word? To this question unbelief very quickly gave a clear answer—we all know it well enough: the Bible is nothing more than man's word, a product of the intellectual and religious and literary history of mankind—perhaps an especially worthy document with an historical impact like no other book of mankind, but still nothing more than a voice or a choir of voices from the manifold confusion of the religious voices of the world. God's revelation? The Book of books, Holy Scripture, God's own word? What strange expressions of an antiquated faith!

Yet it would be unjust and untrue were we to mention only the answers of unbelief. Even the fathers of the Enlightment and of rationalism were already for the most part genuinely and in their own way piously concerned to honor the Scripture as God's word. For them that meant that the Bible is the great textbook of mankind about eternal, divine truths; that there is *one* God and that his providence governs men; that the soul of man is immortal and that man is called to a life of virtue and reason. Of course, this belief in the eternal, religious and moral truths in the Bible tied itself more and more firmly to the opinion that the Bible is at the same time a very human book. It is bound to the language, thoughts and concepts of definite times, countries and cultures, and therefore it is largely imperfect, fallible and archaic. How primitive the Bible's world-view often is! How childish and antiquated its belief in miracles! How imperfect, especially in the Old Testament, are many of its religious conceptions about sacrifice and cult, about spirits and powers, about life and death! It is this twofold view of seeing both the eternal, divine truths in the Bible and the human, the all too human, way of its witnesses and testimonies that shaped the form in which the question about God's word and man's word troubles the thinking and believing of men today. Now repeatedly we ask: What in the Bible is God's word and what is *only* man's word? What is eternal, binding and valid, and what no longer concerns us, because it is the bygone word of man? Where does the one begin and the other leave off? What must one believe, and what may one confidently give up as obsolete and archaic?

Question after question arises, to which answers are given with unending variety. We cannot silence the controversy about them. What one person challenges, another defends as a holy article of faith. How can there still be clarity and decision? Where are the criteria, and who can handle them confidently? To a certain extent the thoughts of all of us move quite obviously and frequently in this direction, and we even go a good bit of the way confidently and calmly. Obviously when we read something in the Old Testament, we decide between an eternally valid word of God and a mere outdated word of man. In our Bible-reading we all proceed more or less according to the tried method which the Bible itself presents, with some of its passages in ordinary print and some in bold-face type. Passages like: "Fear not, for I have redeemed you. I have called you by name; you are mine!" or: "Those who sow with tears shall reap with joy," we accept as God's word; others we abandon as a human, an all too human word, such as the terrible passages in the psalms of revenge, e.g. the curse on Babylon's children in Psalm 137: "Happy shall he be who takes your little ones and dashes them against the rock!" Thus quite unconsciously we decide between passages in the Old Testament, and obviously also between passages and words of the New Testament. In fact, to some extent we are able to succeed with this method, and therefore it is not to be regarded as wholly bad. None of us could do without it.

And yet I think that under the influence of this "either-or" question of God's word or man's word in the Bible we entangle ourselves in hopeless uncertainties from which we no longer are able to emerge. To solve and answer these questions one must bring along as it were an already finished dogmatics, i.e. a doctrine about what in the Bible is valid as God's word and must remain intact, and what we may confidently view as the mere outdated word of man from an antiquated era. However, by such a procedure we circumvent the best that contact with the Scripture yields to us: the hearing, amazement and discovery of that about which we knew nothing. In other words, we miss a real and living encounter with God in his word. For how is such an encounter with God's word still to occur if, either from a rigid, orthodox dogmatics or from what reason accepts as valid, we already know from the start what is God's word and what is merely man's?

So we ought to learn a thoroughly different approach. First and foremost we ought to direct our thoughts to what the New Testament itself has to say to our question and how it answers it. The following considerations seek to introduce this.

II

Anyone who opens the New Testament and reads will see very soon that our question about God's word and man's word is a central one in the early Christian message and that we are given a clear and definite answer there. Of course, and this must be said at the outset, in the New Testament the question is formulated in an entirely different way. We no longer meet it there in the unsound form of the "either-or" of which we spoke earlier. To be sure, the New Testament also contains this "either-or" question, for instance in Jesus' sharp attack against the Pharisees and scribes. They had made God's word powerless and had substituted human tradition for it (Matt. 15; Mark 7). The apostles also battle against the corruption of the divine word through human ordinance and human tradition (Col. 2). But the primary and intrinsic secret to which the New Testament message directs us is that God's word has become *one* with man's word, that it has come to us and become understandable in a human word. In this light it pays to ponder thoroughly Jesus' own message in the gospels. We all know that one word summarizes the manner and impact of his preaching in the gospels: "He preached as one having authority and not as the scribes." "Authority" most certainly means his direct, divine power and authority. It is this that is present and effective in the words with which he proclaims the will of God: "You have heard that it was said to the men of old, but I say to you!" It is present and effective also in the words with which he promises the kingdom of heaven to the poor, the forgiveness and joy of the heavenly Father to the lost, and life to those bound by death. There is no parable, no word to the disciples, no controversy, no healing word of Jesus in which this sovereignty, this kingly sovereignty, does not issue forth to enrage one person and to save and bring joy to another. But always this authoritative word of Jesus sounds fully human, God's word in the simplest human word. If one considers how all religions, and particularly the Jewish religion in the time of Jesus, had first to set in motion as it were a powerful apparatus of sacrifice and cult, of hierarchical ordinances and holy traditions, of theology and scriptural learning, in order to bring God and man together and to order their relationship to each other, one perceives with astonishment and wonder how different everything is in the gospels where Jesus meets men, delivers his message and accomplishes his deeds. Under his word, the whole ironclad social structure in which all—Jews and Gentiles, religious and irreligious, Pharisees and sinners—have their inexchangeable place, becomes null and void; it collapses. Now all that applies is God's will and reality, and man—man as he is in his un-disguised truth, man whom God himself judges and saves and calls out of the manifold chains of his guilt, his pretended piety, his dreams and illusions. Again and again there is this amazing thing: God's word is directly present; it has arrived and arisen in the simplest word of man. He who has ears to hear, let him hear! God is present as Lord and Helper, as Creator, Father and Judge. What validity is there now in the distinctions between religious and irreligious, between scribes and people, between righteous and unrighteous? God's reign breaks in, it dawns, and the repeated "Blessed are" applies to the poor, the sorrowing, the hungry, the humble and insulted. God is present—God is present for you! And you stand in his light, in his joy, his forgiveness and promise. God is present in his entire reality and truth; man is as he really is, stuck fast in his guilt, desperate in his anxiety, in his fear and in death's distress; and yet just so sought and found and surrounded by God and sheltered in his love. One cannot present radically enough this wonder and mystery of the encounter between God and man in all the encounters of Jesus with men. Every word of Jesus to the Pharisees and scribes, to sinners and tax collectors, to the sick, to the disciples, is filled with it. Here no toilsome dogmatic instructions need be given, no trial take place, no examination of faith be conducted, no presuppositions first be established, in order that the one hearing it may receive the message. But at the same time there is nothing of empty promises, wishes, vague hopes for some uncertain future. "Take heart, my son; your sins are forgiven!" "Well done, good and faithful servant, enter into the joy of your master." God's word has become one with the simplest human word—that is, in fact, the mystery of the entire message of Jesus. Humanity plainly has become the seal and sign of the word's divinity. That is Jesus' unique authority.

III

What we have just learnt from the gospels about Jesus' word has also retained its powerful and decisive effectiveness in the message of his witnesses. None of the New Testament witnesses has reflected upon the relationship between God's word and man's word so thoroughly as the Apostle Paul, and none has spoken so unmistakably and helpfully as he. We can select only a few examples. I think especially of a remark from the oldest letter of Paul that we possess. In I Thessalonians, the Apostle closes his thanksgiving with the words: "And we also thank God constantly for this, that when you received the word of God which you heard from us, you accepted it not as the word of men but as what it really is, the word of God, which is at work in you believers" (I Thess. 2.13). For a moment one must consider the context in which this passage occurs and the situation from which it comes. Paul looks back—the entire previous part of the letter speaks of this—and he can only marvel and give thanks for what has resulted from his proclamation. For to all appearances the presuppositions for what actually happened were not present there at all. Paul entered Thessalonica (Saloniki) as a poor stranger and eked out a bare living among them by working night and day, having been driven from Philippi—the first congregation of Paul on the European continent—in insult and disgrace. And this man proposed to be the bringer of a divine message, that calls men to turn from their idolatry to the true and living God and to make the ultimate decision about life and death? To all human comprehension, it is a grotesque claim! What kind of a God and Lord can that be, who lets his messenger move through the world so wretchedly, without equipping him with impressive authority and all the marks of divine, miraculous power?

If one wants to assess correctly how astonishing this acceptance of the Apostle and his message in Thessalonica was, one must realize that in that period, in Thessalonica, too (as we can see from the Apostle's own allusions), there were various rivals of the gospel: roving apostles, heralds of other gods, who made a quite different appearance. They were well versed and eloquent, inspired and inspiring, slick and showy in technique, praising the powerful deeds of their gods and bewitching their hearers. And as we know from II Corinthians, at that time there were also plenty of persons among the Christian missionaries who tried to vie with such pagan apostles, praising their Lord Jesus Christ, too, as such a power-god and letting him speak in exalted, ecstatic language. But Paul wants to have nothing to do with all this: "For our appeal does not spring from error or uncleanness, nor is it made with guile; but just as we have been approved by God to be entrusted with the Gospel, so we speak, not to please men, but to please God, who tests our hearts" (I Thess. 2.3f.); or, "For we are not, like so many, peddlers of God's word; but as men of sincerity, as commissioned by God, in the sight of God we speak in Christ" (II Cor. 2.17). For Paul, that means a renunciation of exalted words of wisdom and of any portrayal of his own spiritual power or private revelations; although, given the understanding of that time and setting, by their use he might have assured his appearance and impact as the true man of God. For Paul, God's word is the word that he can declare only in the reality of his own humanity. Therefore Paul boasts only of his weakness (II Cor. 12.9) and presents to men only the crucified Christ as God's power and wisdom (I Cor. 1.24). God's word, incomprehensible in its richness and wisdom, is still always a word that applies to every man and is to be understandable to everyone. Therefore to the Greeks he becomes a Greek and to the Jews a Jew (I Cor. 9.19ff.). So, too, when discussing speaking in worship he instructs his congregation not to revel in its own full possession of the Spirit, but to speak understandably and reasonably, so that the unbeliever and the one who still stands entirely on the fringe can also understand it, be encountered, become aware that God himself calls him, and come to confess: "God really is in your midst!" (I Cor. 14.25).

Thus God's word is intended to be delivered humanly, and its divinity is to be proclaimed and grasped in its humanity. The Apostle had already understood his task in Thessalonica in this way, at an earlier date. For that very reason, as we saw, he had not behaved as one of the miracle-men who at that time filled the world—as one who had at his disposal divine revelations and powers. Rather, he had delivered his word and done his work—very simply—as a servant of Christ, as Christ's prisoner who is simultaneously freed by Christ, a steward of God's mysteries who wants to be judged before God and man only by the extent of his faithfulness (I Cor. 4.1f.). For God's word does not come to us except in the garb of this humanity, and this is just what the people in Thessalonica understood (cf. also Gal. 4.13f.). This is the reason for the thanks of the Apostle, that in spite of his ever so human, yes, all too human, appearance, they accepted his word for what it truly is: not man's word but God's.

All these words of Paul, which we could amply multiply from his letters, are—who can evade this impression?—certainly a moving witness to the sincerity with which Paul did his work and to the passion of a heart and life totally dedicated to the service of Christ. But we should wrest still more from them, for at the same time they are intended to help and instruct us in the question about God's word and man's word that troubles us. If it concerned only the Christian virtues of the Apostle's humility and faithfulness, only the sincerity of his disposition, then certainly there would be justification for the question: Should not all that be obvious for a servant of Christ? Is it necessary to speak so much of that? But truly the Apostle only spoke of this in order to open to the congregation, unmistakably and clearly, the real mystery of the divine word. In fact, from the manner in which Paul understands his commission, it becomes clear once and for all what the true marks of the divine word are. This is now worth considering further.

Paul once summarized in Romans the miracle and mystery of the divine word in the simple, powerful sentence: "The word is near you," so near that you can "believe with your heart and confess with your lips" (Rom. 10.8f.). Paul can speak of the divine word in this way only because for him the mystery of Christ, God's miracle and grace in Christ, has dawned. The *word* is near. That means simultaneously that in this word *Christ* is completely near to us. From now on, the despairing and presumptuous effort by which our human questions about God and the manifold attempts and efforts of all human religion are so deeply and hopelessly marked, moved and directed, should come to an end: an end to that effort of wanting to force God and his word to come near, as it were by arranging a flight into the dizzy heights of the stratosphere or by plunging into the abyss of the divine in order to bring information from those unattained worlds. Indeed, all religions of mankind are such an unceasing attempt to outdo each other in such high flights and deep plunges in order to force God himself and his word to come near. They are a gigantic effort by which great and sublime discoveries are indeed made and great performances accomplished in religious readiness for involvement and sacrifice! And yet—they are an aimless movement, despairing and presumptuous, that leads only ever deeper into illusions and hopelessness.

All this aimless running is over, says Paul. Christ is here. You do not need first to bring him down out of heaven or up from the realm of the dead. The word of God is near you; you do not need to bring it here from the heights or depths (Rom. 10.6f.). Such attempts in the world may again and again bewitch and fascinate, and appear to be the newest of the new, but they always come too late. For long ago God has accomplished what we cannot accomplish. He has come near to us, in the form of him about whom it is said: The word became flesh (John 1.14). God's word has arrived once and for all in the word of man and become audible for each of us. God himself has accomplished the miracle of this nearness of his word; and he himself has seen to it that the hearing and perception of his word is now possible for all. Therefore in Rom. 10 Paul speaks of a fixed chain that binds God's word and our hearing, believing and confessing with one another: How are men, he asks, to call on God without believing? How are they to believe without hearing his word? How are they to hear without a preacher? How are there to be preachers unless they are sent (Rom. 10.14f.)? It is a chain in which no link may be missing without breaking the entire chain. If one of these links is missing a catastrophe results. Indeed, the history of the church and of faith unfortunately knows all too many examples. In that case, one prays and calls on God, but without real faith; one means to believe, but without the readiness first to hear God's word; one hears, but only what one wishes to hear and without the presence of messengers whom

God himself has sent; one speaks vainly, but without inquiring about God's commission. Therefore it is worth being on guard and examining keenly. But it is no less important to open eyes, ears and hearts to the fact that God has allowed nothing to be lacking in order to make his word known and to identify himself firmly with us in his word.

IV

Wherever this word becomes audible, it can only speak of what God has done to us and the world, of the story of his grace and his judgment, culminating in and summed up in the story of Jesus Christ. Therefore the gospel always has one and only one indispersable content for all time: Christ the crucified one, Christ the living one, Jesus Christ our Lord. And yet this story of God with the world and with us is not a story that one can recount with only dates and facts, as for example the historical dates and deeds of Caesar Augustus were recorded in monuments and history books. The real mystery of God's story is much more, that into this story the story of our own life is written. Above all and unique in this way, God's story has become the word to us and for us. So in their message the apostles are not content to impress upon us a series or chain of mere facts or even saving facts. Mere facts, yes, even mere saving facts, are never language and word in themselves. At the most they can be compiled into sacred formulae. They do not become language for us and God's word to us until we also express ourselves in this word. In this way the divine word becomes a human word. Precisely in its humanity, it receives its nobility and its convincing and redeeming power as divine word. For this reason, while they are proclaiming the divine acts, the apostles never tire of speaking of us ourselves in our unveiled reality as man before God: man in his lostness before God, bound in guilt and illusion; man in the body of death; man in his godlessness, who still does not get rid of God. But now more than ever it is man surrounded by God's love, acquitted, redeemed, delivered from his own terrible and hopeless history and dedicated now as a new creature to Christ the Lord and presented with a new life-history. All history unfolds in the irreversible course of past, present and future. Our entire life is enclosed in it. Behind us is the past, from which we are never free and which we always drag behind us like a slave's chain; between past and future lies the present, crucial for decision and yet hopelessly transient; and then there is the future, enticing and terrifying at the same time, precariously withdrawn from our grasp. Wherever God's word sounds forth, our life and our history is, as it were, discussed with us, disclosed and illuminated. Nothing better can happen to us than this. But it always happens in such a way that in place of our hopeless and forlorn history a new history is opened and presented to us in Christ. Now the past from which we come no longer means guilt and death, but bears the name of Jesus Christ. God has given him up for us all! God did not spare his own son. Now the present also is no longer marked by that fatal transience but by the great certainty: If God is for us, who can be against us? And now also the future, earthly and eternal, no longer has the deceitful appearance of our own dreams and wishes, nor the ghostly grimace of a gruesome threat. Rather, the future belongs to him, Jesus Christ, and therewith also to us, so far as we in faith belong to him. "Therefore, we are more than conquerors through him who loved us." For: "Who can separate us from the love of God in Christ Jesus our Lord?" (Rom. 8.31–39).

Now do we comprehend what it means that in the New Testament God's word meets us in the form of a human word? Do we really still want to continue the foolish effort to separate God's word from man's word? No, we say it once more: humanity is the seal and insignia of the divine word itself. To pay attention to and grasp this—that is what the New Testament summons us to do. God became man for your benefit—that gives even God's word its form.

In this way his word is to be understood, received, believed, preserved and confirmed. For in its humanity, again and again the divine word is threatened by our unbelief, our apathy, our deafness, blindness, stubbornness. What is it but a mere human word, fallible, weak, transient? says our reason. Why does God not speak in loud, booming language and split the heavens? says our presumption. Why is it as insignificant as the miserable grain of wheat that the birds fetch from the path, that sends down no roots on rocky ground and is choked by thorns? says our impatience. But thanks be to God that he does not speak to us other than in the form of this poor human word. For this insignificant word is pregnant. It bears the kingdom of God in itself and accepts us into life from God, into God's joy and freedom.

Anyone who lets the New Testament itself ask and answer the question of God's word and man's word encounters, as we said, God's miracle and grace, from which we alone can live. He meets God himself and learns to thank him for speaking to us so humanly. The ancient questions with which we started were: What in the New

Testament is God's word and what is only man's? What in it is eternally valid and what is outdated and transient? All these questions, on which theologians and laymen rub their hearts and minds raw, still may be asked. But all at once they are set right. They have lost their barbs. They have become very secondary questions, if we have learned to find the mystery of his grace in the humanity of the divine word.

V

It may be appropriate to conclude these reflections by recalling a New Testament story in which, I think, the question and mystery of God's word and man's word is made visible and answered in an incomparable way. We all know the story of the meeting of Jesus with the Samaritan woman (John 4). In his travels, the thirsty Jesus sits at Jacob's well and requests a drink of water from the Samaritan woman. What happens in this meeting? In the story Jesus is nothing more than a poor stranger who, as it appears, does not fit into the world around him. It is a world in which the controversy about God's word and man's word is dreadfully in progress, visible and tangible in the deadly hostility between Samaritans and Jews. Both think they have the true word of God, and they brand the faith of the others as heretical and their teaching as merely a perverted word of man. *We* have the true tradition, the true worship on Mount Gerizim, the sacred history of the fathers, said the Samaritans. And not otherwise, the Jews said: *We* have the true word of God, the temple, the right place of worship; we have and keep the places of his revelation. We— not you!

In the middle of this world, which even now has not changed in appearance, Jesus stands as a stranger whom the Jews call a Samaritan and the Samaritans a Jew. But look, the stranger begins to speak, and as he speaks those barriers and insurmountable hostilities are shattered. He speaks God's word and awakens a new thirst and a new longing that all those traditions of belief are unable to fulfill: "Whoever drinks from the water which I shall give him will never thirst." And what happens in this pledge and promise? All at once the woman to whom he speaks this word has to perceive that her whole life lies uncovered before him. Her own tangled life with its wild, unbridled passion; the tragedy of her marriages; the unresolved guilt of her days and nights. How relentlessly and yet how mercifully this happens. No indictment, no sentence of judgment! Only this one pledge and promise: For you the source of genuine, real life, the life from God, is here. Whoever thirsts, let him come. And in this way she receives the great promise and instruction: she is to worship God in spirit and in truth, to receive his word from the lips of one who in men's eyes is nothing but a poor stranger and yet who alone can bring a man home and make him at home in the Father's house. God is spirit! That means that once and for all he is here; he is present; he waits for us; yes, he not only waits but runs to meet us, like the father of the prodigal son, with open arms. The Father's joy receives us. It was for this that his Son became man; it was for this that his word has entered into man's word and should forever be sought and found nowhere else.

Our story ends with the Samaritan woman running back to her village and bringing to her people news of her strange meeting with this foreigner. And they come to where he is and remain with him. Then, as they meet with him themselves, they say a striking word to the woman: "We no longer believe because of what you say, but we have heard and known ourselves that truly this is the Savior of the world." Critically and helpfully at the same time, here again the mystery of man's word and God's word becomes visible. In fact, in the presence of his word all of our witness becomes really man's word. This word *must* and *should* be delivered, and yet it only can guide us to hearing him in whom alone God's word and man's word truly have become one. Only in this way shall we be led to confess "that truly this is the Savior of the world."

II

CHRIST AND THE WORLD IN THE
EARLY CHRISTIAN MESSAGE[1]

I

IT IS A STRANGE historical juncture that the history of the gospel of Jesus Christ had its beginning on the soil of the European continent in a place that was also of supreme significance for the history of the Roman Empire and thereby for the history and culture of the West. Not quite a hundred years before the Apostle Paul entered Philippi, the outcome of the battle between Caesar's murderers and Antony and Octavian (autumn, 42 BC) had been assured here. Eleven years later, Antony and Cleopatra had also been defeated. With the victory at Actium (September 2, 31 BC) the history of the Roman Empire begins. Augustus confirmed the reputation in world history of the city of Philippi, whose name also preserved the memory of the founder of the Macedonian kingdom, the father of Alexander the Great. He settled veterans in it and granted it (*Julia Augusta Victrix Philippensium*) the *jus italicum*, that is, the privileges of a Roman city subject only to the imperial government. The history and favor of the emperor spread their splendor over the little city.

Here, too , as Acts tells,[2] began the history of Christ's reign and his gospel on Roman soil proper, and thus also on European soil. Of course, the narrator certainly is quite unconscious of the historical significance of the place, but he does not fail to emphasize the special character of the city as a Roman "colony."[3] Here Paul and Silas experience their first denunciation before a Roman authority. They were reported to the officials as Jewish agitators and destroyers of Roman custom and were publicly whipped and arrested by them, in spite of the protection which the law guaranteed to Roman citizens, an injustice whose reparation Paul demands for the first time with reference to his rights as a Roman citizen. Just as Acts had already marked the new period of Pauline missionary activity by the introductory vision in Troas (a call for help is the first word with which the new continent comes forward), so in his own words, too (Phil. 4.15), Paul was conscious of a new beginning occurring here.

As the gospel proclaimed by him reached this new soil, the Apostle, we may assume, had already included the entire empire in his missionary plans.[4] Philippi lies on the great imperial road, the Via Egnatia, which connected the empire's western and eastern parts. For Paul, his commission as a world missionary was no longer uncertain. He had set foot upon the way to Rome. His missionary course and goal are determined and guided by the faith and confession that Jesus Christ is Lord and the world belongs to him, the Lord.

For early Christianity this commission and will to world mission was anything but a foregone conclusion. Of course, the gospels report a series of words of the Risen Lord in which he gives the commission for world mission to his disciples.[5] But they were written at a time when the question of the meaning and justification for world mission had been decided. There can be no doubt that in the gospels there is an unhistorical compression and shortening of the space of time in which the knowledge of the lordship of Christ over the world and of the way in which the gospel encompassed both Jews and Gentiles made itself felt. The fact is that the first community in Jerusalem did not at first see itself as called to such a commission. The conversion of individual men who were not of the Jewish people was a surprising wonder and a disturbing problem,[6] but it was certainly not as yet an event of major significance.[7] It dawned on the representatives of the first Jerusalem community only years later at the Apostolic Council, after a hard struggle, that Paul was entrusted with the gospel to the Gentiles as they were for the Jews.[8] Only with troubles and conflicts, jolts, reverses and special revelations did the knowledge of the rightful lordship of Christ over the world make its way. It was against their own will, against their sacred traditions, indeed against the word of Jesus himself, who still limited his messengers in their mission to the lost sheep of the house of Israel and had forbidden them to go on the streets of the Gentiles and into the cities of the Samaritans.[9] As Luther said, it was like a blind horse, yes, often like a very shy and stubborn horse, that early Christianity found the freedom and the way to this knowledge and this commission.

The path of the world mission was not ventured first from Jerusalem but from Antioch. It was Paul, embarking from Antioch, who first worked theologically through the decision made there and who set forth on the path with the full, passionate thrust of his person. Of course, his commission to go to the ends of the inhabited world appears to have occurred to him only on the so-called second missionary journey.[10] Starting from Troas, he left behind Asia in the west and Bithynia in the north, and moved on to the northwest by way of Samothrace to Macedonia. From now on he was guided by the definite intention to cross the world as far as Rome, indeed even as far as Spain. In Rom. 15.22f., he himself says that the plan to push forward as far as Rome did not occur to him only after the conclusion of his mission in the eastern half of the empire, but had concerned him for years.[11] Even when the work in Corinth, the tie to Antioch and Jerusalem, and finally Ephesus held him back for years from the realization of his plans, he did not lose sight of Rome. His final return to Jerusalem from the so-called third missionary journey apparently happened not only to assure the delivery of the collection, but, as earlier at the Apostolic Council, in order to defend there again his repeatedly challenged apostolic commission to the Gentiles and the rights and freedom of the Gentile church. Then, after what he hoped would be an agreement with the Jerusalem people (Rom. 15.28–32) there in the city, historically determined as the original place of Christ's church, he wanted as it were once more to close the circle more firmly[12] and this time to extend the sphere of his missionary activity to the boundaries of the inhabited world. His hopes remained unfulfilled. He reached Rome only as a prisoner (cf. the last chapter of Acts).[13]

Faith in the lordship of Jesus Christ over the world, established in the resurrection and exaltation, characterizes the course and goal of the Pauline mission. But it was also characterized by the haste with which the Apostle moved on from one congregation to another, leaving the extension and care of the congregations to his fellow workers and looking after them himself only by letters and, where demanded, by occasional visits. It was especially characterized also by the peculiar way in which, for him, each city stands directly for a whole district.[14] He himself in his proclamation had only to carry out, to realize historically, to extend and to declare what had happened long ago in the resurrection and exaltation of Jesus Christ as Lord. "Their voice has gone out to all the earth, and their words to the ends of the world" (Rom. 10.18). "They shall see who have never been told of him, and they shall understand who have never heard of him" (Rom. 15.21). The praise of all Gentiles, of all peoples should now praise the Lord (Rom. 15.9–12).

II

What we have said so far about the connection between the confession of the Kyrios and mission, between the lordship of Christ and his claim to the inhabited world, is still exposed to a profound mis-interpretation as to its basis and meaning. One could be tempted to conclude that the early Christian mission, especially the Pauline mission, secretly or openly, was guided by a strange anti-political political conception; that the picture of Jesus Christ as the Lord of the world had received its contours from the contrasting "Caesar as Lord." In this way the reign of Christ would in the end be only the reflection of the empire.

If this were so, then here already, in the early Christian confession of the Kyrios and understanding of the world, there would be the beginnings of the idea of a Christian empire and the presuppositions for a later theology of Christian rulers. Initially this would then have to be preserved and defended in bitter and sacrificial battle against the pagan empire and its powers, until three hundred years later the time came when Christ the Victor, Christ the Ruler of the world, had conquered the enemy powers and established his lordship. There is no question that these ideas displayed an extraordinary power in the first centuries, and that out of them grew a self-contained picture of history and a new relationship between Christ and emperor, the reign of Christ and the empire.

This history comes most impressively to the fore in the various interpretations given to Virgil's famous Fourth Eclogue at the beginning and end of the period of the ancient Caesars.[15] Composed in the horrible time after Caesar's murder, it proclaimed prophetically the birth of a divine child whose lordship would usher in a new, blissful age over the world, and this age appeared to be fulfilled in Augustus's kingdom of peace. Thus the Augustan period glorified the figure of the Caesar with divine titles and honors, even if against Augustus's own will, erected a temple to him and to Rome, and with powerful pathos praised his birth as "gospel" and the blessings of his reign as the new beginning of the world's history. What still was held within the limits of ancient Roman faith in the times of Augustus,[16] grows rankly beyond these limits under his successors, rejected only by a few.[17] The homages paid earlier to Augustus are exaggerated beyond measure; the titles freely given to the Caesars or demanded by them are marked with an increasing exuberance, even if these successors are named Caligula, Nero or Domitian, and are despatched with daggers after a terrible reign of terror.[18] At its end stands Constantine,[19] himself still celebrated by one of his panegyrics as *deus praesentissimus*, as the image of Apollo, deified by his soldiers, honored by the Romans as the appearance of the deity after his victory at the Milvian Bridge by a colossal statue, and glorified repeatedly as the earthly appearance of the unconquerable, almighty sun-god. However, the same Constantine, who submitted to these homages and is even portrayed as Helios on a porphyry statue in the forum of his new world-city, there bears the globe of the world in his hand, adorned with the cross. And in a Good Friday address to the Christians, added by Eusebius to his *Vita Constantini* and probably going back to the emperor, at least in its basic ideas significantly enough once again in an extended interpretation of Virgil's Fourth Eclogue, he gives the honor and title of the promised savior of the world finally to Christ, the divine Logos.[20]

Since then there has been a metaphysics of the Christian empire and the idea of a Christian emperor. The kingdom of Christ and the political empire, after the overcoming of the unfortunate conflict, now by the providence of God stand in an ordered relationship to each other. As we read in Eusebius, the most important[21] of theologians of Constantine's empire, God's wisdom had indeed, with deep foresight, made Christ and Augustus contemporaries. The foundation of the earthly monarchy now prevails as a symbol of the monarchy of the one God proclaimed by Christ, the appearance of the earthly prince of peace as a symbol of the divine prince, the earthly victory over the rebellious peoples as a symbol of the divine victory over idols and demons. The earthly emperor is now the preparer of Christ's way, a new Moses, a servant of Christ; but he is still at the same time his earthly ruler and his image, and he receives his position and his incomparable status in this co-ordination to God and Christ.

With due solemnity, the basic ideas of this Constantinian theology of the empire have been renewed and repeated most recently by E. Stauffer. They are most strongly active in his *New Testament Theology*, and are the leading theological motifs of his historical sketch, *Christ and the Caesars*. According to the presentation given there, the ancient myth of empire and ruler—in its greatness as well as in its limits and tragedy—was first shaped in the empires and rulers of the ancient orient, and was associated with Rome and its emperors after the victory of Augustus. It took a horrifying form in its apotheosis and its cult. Here, it is claimed, in this myth, was the historical foundation on which faith in the lordship of Christ was built up—as an attack and a fulfillment at the same time. It is not by chance, therefore, that a section in Stauffer's *New Testament Theology* on "The historical commission and temptation of the Empire" opens the large second main part, "Law and Promise," which is then followed by the third, "The Christ-event." There the function of the forerunner of Christ[22] is explicitly ascribed to the emperor—and this in the framework of a New Testament theology!—who, like Moses,[23] is to lead mankind up to the borders of "what the imperial man is able to do to bless mankind," and still the fulfillment must be left to him who, like Joshua earlier, is first to lead the way into the promised land.[24]

Language and world-view change. Above all, political conceptions change. Nobody today, for instance, would feel easy about using exalted words about the "imperial man." But even today, the conception of the Constantinian myth of the empire and the christianization of the ancient idea of the emperor is by no means past. They also present themselves in altered forms of the state and in sober and modest political passwords, where once again attempts are made to encompass the reign of Christ and the area of political life in a comprehensive world-view and to associate them harmoniously with each other. Such attempts will always repeat themselves when, as in our time, men have perceived with terror the terrible sundering and conflict of both kingdoms and become tired of them, and then, having experienced with horror the audacity and fragility of the deification of political powers, again pose the question about the metaphysical and religious foundation of political life. In such a time the expectation necessarily appears that "Christianity" could bring in the solution for the unmastered questions of political life and that with its help we could successfully break out of the enclosure of the secular that has become a prison. In this situation, theology is understandably tempted to look upon the confession of Christ as the Lord of the world in terms of a basically political analogy and no longer to ask the question whether Jesus Christ the Lord really submits to that metaphysical alliance with Augustus.

III

If we turn back to the confession of the Kyrios in early Christianity, we must say with all certainty that the idea of the empire and the

myth of the emperor were surely not the forge and torch from which
the Christian faith was kindled, by way of contrast. Of course, nobody
may overlook the tension that existed between the exalted, honorific
titles of Christ and the splendid titles of the political ruler. The only
powerful evidence within the New Testament of this opposition
between faith in the "king of kings," the "ruler over the kings of
earth," Jesus Christ, and the apotheosis of political might is the
Revelation of John. How strongly it is determined in the detail and
entirety of its view of history by this interaction, and how faith
expresses here that the deified power of the empire has found its
conqueror and judge in Jesus Christ, need not be shown in detail
here.[25] But we would not understand the essential character of the
early Christian message if we sought to derive it in its origin and
basis from this antithesis to the political myth of the empire and
emperor. It has not received its contours from this opposition, however much it has made its way by virtue of it. Is it by chance that
Augustus is no more than a marginal figure in the Christmas story and
that the names and persons of the Roman emperors in the New
Testament are hardly to be found, and then only on the periphery?
Is it by chance that we learn so little in the New Testament of what
was then the political shape of the world, of the provinces of the
empire, its officials, its culture, its religion, its philosophy, its history,
its army, its economic and social relationships? Where we learn something, it is only of the world in which the gospel is announced, the
language in which one must speak, which does not determine the
gospel in its substance.

What does this express? Apparently it expresses something entirely
different from contempt of the political world, with which, for
instance, the Stoics occasionally raised themselves above the small-
ness of earthly limits and goals to the world of the spirit: "a little
point is the whole, in which you travel to the sea, make wars, order
kingdoms—disappearingly small, even if it is washed on both sides
by the ocean. High above are mighty spaces to whose possession the
spirit has access" (Seneca, *quaest. nat., praef.* 11). Nowhere in the
New Testament outside the Revelation of John do we find the scorn
and hostility against the empire as they were known in the gloomy
political predictions of the so-called Sibylline Oracles and in the
threatening prophecy of late Jewish apocalyptic from the east, and
also on Roman soil in the latter period of the Republic and in the time
of the emperors.[26] Nowhere do we hear anything of the voices of

oppressed peoples, who gave vent to their rebellion against Rome's rapacity and unsatisfiable destructive fury in the manner of the King of Britain in Tacitus (*Agric.* 30). Nowhere do we hear the voice of loathing with which the educated Greeks scorned the cultureless, snobbish and noisy activity of Rome, nor the voice of painful boredom with which Rome's own writers and poets now and then in the time of the civil war weighed and recommended to the prudent the surrender of the capital city and the flight to the country or even to the blessed stillness of distant islands.

Faith in the lordship of Jesus Christ over the world, therefore, does not fit into the contrasting pattern of political enthusiasm and anti-political scorn of the world, because the world in early Christian thought is understood in a completely different way. For early Christian faith, the world is not just the essence of what exists, as the Stoics[27] defined it, nor in the narrower sense the structure of political orders and human areas of life. Rather, in an entirely non-Greek and non-Roman way, the world is understood in the early Christian message in terms of its movement to and from its basis, from which it receives its essence.[28] Its basis and essence, however, is man, God's creation and yet simultaneously lost before God because of sin, subjected to death. It is man, continually reminded of his destiny and called to his destiny by God's Law, for the Jew written on his stone tablets and for the Gentile in the heart, and yet simultaneously man who is hopelessly lost in relation to this call of God. For just as we are, the Law of God is not able to break open the prison of man, whether he lawlessly offends against God's will as the Gentile or with a dogged legalism is as zealous about it as the Jew. It only confines him more and more securely. That is man, Adam, in whom we are and who is in us, who gives his nature to all history and all the world, to this age as a whole. At the same time, that means man about whom one cannot speak as about an observable object of the world or a naturally destined fate. Rather, one rightly can speak of him only in the personal confession of one's own guilt.[29] Rom. 7.24 says: "Wretched man that I am! Who will deliver me from this body of death?"

Into this world over which as it were the gigantic shadow of guilty man lies, and which has marked the vanity of its coming and going by this guilt, even to the sighing of the creature;[30] into this world, which has become the sphere of power of the forces which, though exalted on the throne by man himself, reproach him in his imprisonment in guilt;[31] into this world, which I am myself, God has sent his Son in

the form of sinful flesh, in the form marked and disfigured by sin—
made sin for us (Rom. 8.3; II Cor. 5.21). He bears the flesh, sin and
death. Here, of course, the deed of sin does not determine the form of
the guilty, but the obedient bearing of sin determines its form. What
makes the world this world, what makes man this man is borne and
conquered by Christ. On the cross which the world sets up for him
and on which he dies, the world itself finds its end. Therefore, the
word of the cross is not only foolishness in the eyes of the world's
wisdom, but it means especially that God has made the wisdom of the
world into foolishness and has chosen what does not exist to destroy
what does exist (I Cor. 1.28).

In that in the resurrection of Jesus Christ, God himself acknowledged him and exalted him as Lord, he has unlocked and opened a
new life for the believers. It is a life that no longer bears the chains
of the past, but is open for God's future; that no longer is enslaved to
sin, but obedient to righteousness; that no longer has condemnation
before it, but acquittal behind it and before it. "If anyone is in Christ
he is a new creation" (II Cor. 5.17). Or, better translated (Paul
almost always means by "creation" the creation as a whole): "If
anyone is in Christ, then it means that the new creation is here! The
old has passed, behold it is become new." What late Jewish apocalyptic
prophecy expected of the messianic future,[32] what was also expressed
in the oracles and poems of the Gentile world in hopes for the great
advent of a divine bringer of salvation, the arrival of a kingdom of
peace and the end of all earthly suffering and trouble—as in Virgil's
Fourth Eclogue—that, says the early Christian message, is fulfilled,
already present, resolved and opened in the one who bears the name
above every name: Jesus Christ is Lord (Phil. 2.11). Presence and
fulfillment here are, of course, in suffering, trouble, tears and death,
a hidden reality, salvation in hope, not yet revealed. And yet they are
present reality, because the way to God is open and in Jesus Christ
the word of forgiveness has sounded, the act of redemption has been
performed, God's history, which transplants us into the position of
freedom and sonship, has happened.[33]

From this event and only from this can we understand what the
early Christian message means by the lordship of Jesus Christ, yes, by
his lordship over the world. To put it very simply: The message of the
lordship of Jesus Christ is the gospel of justification, the word of
reconciliation. As such, it is not a message that would have nurtured
itself on the political myth of the emperor and the empire. It is at the

same time the message of Jesus Christ as the end of the world and as the Lord of the world. Although this message is directed to man, who must speak the "I" of Rom. 7, the event of which the Gospel speaks concerns the world just as much: "In Christ God was reconciling the world to himself, not counting their trespasses against them" (II Cor. 5.19);[34] "God so loved the world . . ." (John 3.16). Through the lordship of Jesus Christ it receives its limits and its end. The "principalities and powers," the "elemental spirits of the world" have been robbed of their weapons and made prisoners who must testify to his triumph.[35] Anyone who still wants to remain or to become anxiously or enthusiastically obedient to them, or who by a world-view or religious activity seeks by force to obtain from the world itself true life, life in God's presence, thereby dishonors the head, the Lord who is exalted over the world.[36]

Thus in faith and witness to the lordship of Jesus Christ, the world is forced into its appropriate form, the "form" of the transitory. "The time is short—the form of this world passes away!" (I Cor. 7.29, 31.) Of course, for early Christian faith that is more than a melancholy, resigned statement of the transitoriness of all that is earthly, more so to say than a cosmic *memento mori*. It is understood in the light of the future, of God's eternity, and of the redeeming lordship of Jesus Christ, who sets limits for the world, but precisely thereby leads it back to its basis and nature as creation. Therefore in opposition to all Gnosticism, which gives up the world, the idea of creation in the early Christian message is firmly maintained and witnessed to with new energy.[37] In Christ the world is illuminated as God's creation; in Christ its lostness is revealed; in Christ it has its limits and its time; for the sake of Christ, whom God has placed as its lord, it comes to an end, since the world itself with all that is in heaven, on earth and under the earth will offer confession to him, the Lord, to the glory of God (Phil. 2.9–11).

So for early Christian faith the here and now becomes a sphere of obedience and testing. How that is intended, in what multiple ways it is used and developed, need not be explained here (cf. the household codes of the New Testament letters!). Here it need only be pointed out that the early Christain message, however much it places all its directives under the "in the Lord" (Col. 3.18ff., *passim*), still directly and intentionally avoids conferring on the orders and tasks in the world a metaphysical dignity based on faith in Christ. We must emphasize that today, especially in contrast to a modern mythologizing of the Pauline expressions about the state that has made angelic powers of the "authorities," the ruling powers of Rom. 13, which— as in the expressions in Col. 2 about the defeat of the cosmic "rulers" and "powers" through Christ—are conquered by Christ and incorporated into his kingdom.[38] In contrast to this, it must be said most emphatically that in Rom. 13 Paul really means simply the political authority, and subjugates believers to the order that is binding for all (Jew and Gentiles, Christian and non-Christian) and is obvious for "everyman," —or should be. [39] Thus he understands the state as a constituent not of the kingdom of Christ, but of the old aeon, in which the Law applies, and according to God's will is and should be judicially executed, a pointer to God's judgment toward which we all move. What the Christian is responsible for doing in this sphere is nothing special, but only this: he must promptly and properly fulfil what he in conscience owes to the state in the face of God's "order." In the sphere of political life there ought to be no unfinished obligations; the reason is that the Christian is called to the unending obligation of love, an obligation that exceeds the realm of life of the old, dying aeon and the valid duties in it. Here Paul does not differ at all from Jesus' remark in the story about the tax,[40] in which a man's relationship to the state is similarly given a disconcertingly simple, unproblematic form which is often so problematic for us because it pushes all complex reflections, and ifs and buts to the side, in order that the eschatological demand (give to God what is God's) may receive and retain full emphasis. Put in Pauline terms, it represents the call to love and to preparedness for the approaching day of Jesus Christ.

What characterizes and differentiates believers is just that in their ties and obligations to the world they stand as the children of freedom,[41] no longer as the enslaved who seek life in it, but as those in Christ, liberated by Christ by his dying and rising and transplanted into the lordship of his love.[42] As those at home with a heavenly citizenship,[43] they recognize the time and know that the night is retreating and the morning approaches.[44]

With all that we have said, we have only tried to express in other words that the early Christian message of the lordship of Jesus Christ over the world is nothing other than the word of reconciliation, the gospel of justification. Today there is a widespread opinion that this message of justification is a time-bound and situation-bound doctrine that has lost its actuality for us. Our time is challenged and summoned by new questions. To these new questions is supposed to belong, among many others, the task of political service. But once the message of justification has been displaced from the middle and has sunk to becoming a matter of course and a concern of pious inwardness, the search begins for a metaphysical foundation for political service, a general synthesis of the kingdom of Christ and the empire, and the myth of the world-ruler reappears in Christian form, albeit as a bad copy. But Jesus Christ does not let himself be subjected to this metaphysical alliance with Augustus. Therefore, the question to the church is especially this: whether it decides, as the Apostle, to know nothing other than Jesus Christ, which is to say the crucified (I Cor. 2.2); that means to deliver the word of reconciliation, nothing else. And this precisely in a time when an abundance of unresolved questions and tasks of political, social and cultural nature rush upon us—I emphasize: *upon us*—and must be taken hold on by us. In all, we must not only not forget the One, but let that One become all, and that means in ways that are quite concrete, new, present; not at all in the mere recitation of conventional, churchly formulae that wound nobody and heal nobody—in word and in deed, in involving oneself and in denying oneself. In this way it will be shown whether what Paul says is still true about us, too: "as poor, yet making many rich; as having nothing, and yet possessing everything" (II Cor. 6.10).

For the early Christian message, this "all" means: Christ the end of the world—Christ the Lord of the world. Therefore, in John's gospel the two sentences appear: "God so loved the world that he gave his only Son" (John 3.16), and the saying of Jesus: "In the world you have tribulation; but be of good cheer, I have overcome the world" (John 16.33). Both sentences describe the same event: The love of God toward the world, becoming an event in Jesus Christ, is fulfilled and completed in the world's conquest.

What John says in his language is also the gospel of which Paul is not ashamed as the way to Rome lies before him. Rome—that is indeed more than a beloved world-city and capital. It is the essence and embodiment of the empire, representative and symbol of the politically shaped world. Rome—that is the world with its intelligence and stupidity, its gods and demons, its culture and barbarity, its humanity and cruelty.[45] Rome—that is man in his incalculable possibilities. But where man is, only man, there is no salvation. Therefore, Paul must also proclaim the lordship of Jesus Christ there, as one indebted to the Greeks and non-Greeks, the wise and the

foolish. The question whether the gospel of Jesus Christ will stand
the test in contrast to this summons of the world and of man and not
come to nought is decided for Paul; for this gospel is "the power of
God for salvation to everyone who has faith" (Rom. 1.16).

NOTES

[1] The essay reproduces an address given in Göttingen, Heidelberg, and
Stuttgart. (First published in *ZTK* 47 (1950), pp. 212ff.)

[2] Acts 16.12–40.

[3] Acts 16.9f.

[4] A. von Harnack, *Mission und Ausbreitung* (1923[4]) I, pp. 79ff. (ET, *The Mission
and Expansion of Christianity*, 1908, pp. 74ff.).

[5] Matt. 28.18–20; Luke 24.47; Acts 1.8; cf. also Mark 16.15; 13.10.

[6] Acts 8.26ff.; 10–11.18.

[7] Of course, Luke with quite deliberate technique has imprinted this general
meaning on the Cornelius story and made Peter the standard witness of the great
turn of events. Cf. M. Dibelius, "Die Bekehrung des Cornelius" and "Die Reden
der Apostelgeschichte und die antike Geschichtsschreibung," both in *Aufsätze zur
Apostelgeschichte* (1957[3]), pp. 96ff. and pp. 120ff. (ET, "The Conversion of Cornelius" and "The Speeches in Acts and Ancient Historiography" in *Studies in the
Acts of the Apostles*, 1956, pp. 109ff. and pp. 138ff.).

[8] Gal. 2.9f.

[9] Matt. 10.5f.

[10] v. Harnack, *op. cit.*, pp. 8off. (ET, pp. 74ff.).

[11] Cf. also Rom. 1.10–13.

[12] The phrase in Rom. 15.19, "from Jerusalem and as far around . . .", in my
opinion points to this meaning. It does not seek to say that "Paul includes Jerusalem
in the areas to which he is to be an apostle according to God's will" (G. Sass,
Apostelamt und Kirche, 1939, p. 129), but designates Jerusalem as the salvation-
historical center of the inhabited world, whose eastern part Paul traversed before
his departure for Rome and Spain (Rom. 15.23f.).

[13] Sass, *op. cit.*, pp. 122ff.

[14] *Ibid.*, pp. 129ff.

[15] In the following I take up some basic ideas of my essay, "Christus und
Augustus," *Deutsche Universitätszeitung* IV/24 (1949), pp. 3f.

[16] Cf. C. Koch, "Gottheit und Mensch im Wandel der römischen Staatsform,"
Das neue Bild der Antike II (1942), pp. 133ff., esp. pp. 152ff.

[17] Suetonius, *Vespasian* 23. 4; E. Stauffer, *Christus und die Cäsaren* (1960[5]), pp.
155ff. (ET, *Christ and the Caesars*, 1955, pp. 142ff.).

[18] Stauffer, *op. cit.*, pp. 224ff. (ET, pp. 205ff.).

[19] On what follows, see: J. Straub, *Vom Herrscherideal in der Spätantike* (1939),
pp. 99ff.; also his "Konstantins christliches Sendungsbewusstsein," *Das neue Bild
der Antike* II (1942), pp. 374ff.; E. Stauffer, *op. cit.*, pp. 290ff. (ET, pp. 264ff.);
H. Lietzmann, *Geschichte der Alten Kirche* III (1938), pp. 126ff. (ET, *From Constantine to Julian*, 1950, pp. 137ff.).

[20] Cf. A. Kurfess, "Kaiser Konstantins Rede an die Versammlung der Heiligen,
eine Karfreitagsrede vom Jahre 313," in *Pastor bonus* (1930), pp. 115ff.; Stauffer,
op. cit., pp. 301ff. (ET, pp. 274ff.).

[21] References in H. Eger, "Kaiser und Kirche in der Geschichtstheologie Eusebs von Caesarea," *ZNW* 38 (1939), pp. 97ff., esp. pp. 105ff.; H. G. Opitz, "Euseb von Caesarea als Theologe," *ZNW* 34 (1935), pp. 1ff.

[22] E. Stauffer, *Die Theologie des Neuen Testaments* (1948⁴), p. 67 (ET, *New Testament Theology*, 1955, p. 85).

[23] Stauffer, *Christus und die Cäsaren*, p. 120 (ET, p. 111). The comparison of the emperor with Moses is characteristic of the Constantinian theology of the empire. Cf. for example Eusebius, *Vita Const.* I, 12. Further particulars in J. Straub, *Vom Herrscherideal in der Spätantike*, p. 124; also his "Konstantins christliches Sendungsbewusstsein," p. 374.

[24] It is understandable that such a christological beginning must be of decisive significance for the presentation of New Testament theology as a whole. I cannot go further into this here. Stauffer's "theology of history" leads, as can be shown in detail, to a resulting "mythologizing" of the early Christian message. Not by chance, its assertions appear only as intermediary members in the train of a salvation-historical drama, whose elements are obtained from the mythological expressions of late Jewish apocalyptic and the theological expressions of patristic writings up to the Constantinian period. Thus one gets an imposing picture and sees unrolling a drama of the primordial foreknowledge of God about creation and fall, promise and fulfillment, church and world events up to the *recapitulatio omnium*, in which everything has its place. But the theological fact of highest importance, that the New Testament witnesses repeatedly supply only fragments, rudiments and splinters to this whole (when they are not completely silent on it) and just do not draw out the lines drawn out by Stauffer, that the stresses and accents in the New Testament are distributed characteristically otherwise and that the special interest of the early Christian message apparently is placed otherwise, meanwhile becomes completely obscured. One can make this clear very simply from the proportions of Stauffer's *New Testament Theology*: in the astonishingly wide space given there, e.g. to satanology and the doctrine of the angels' fall, the *descensus*-idea, the doctrine of the next world (purgatory!) and the individual phases of the consummation, and in the narrow space that remains for the treatment of, e.g., the concept of faith or the Pauline doctrine of justification.

[25] Cf. R. Schutz, *Die Offenbarung des Johannes und Kaiser Domitian* (1933), esp. pp. 33ff.

[26] Abundant references in H. Fuchs, *Der geistige Widerstand gegen Rom in der antiken Welt* (1938).

[27] Chrysippus in *Stoicum Veterum Fragmenta* (ed. H. F. A. Arnim, 1864) II, 528.

[28] Sasse, article '*Kosmos*' in *TWNT* III, esp. pp. 892ff. (ET, *TDNT* III, pp. 892ff.).

[29] See the essay on Rom. 7, "Sunde, Gesetz und Tod," in *DEdG*, pp. 51ff. (ET in this volume, pp. 87ff.).

[30] Rom. 8.20.

[31] Col. 2.14f.

[32] Rev. 21.5. Jewish material in StrB III, pp. 840ff.

[33] Rom. 8.17ff., 31ff.; Rev. 12f., etc.

[34] Cf. also Col. 1.20, etc.

[35] Col. 2.9–15.

[36] See the essay, "Die Häresie des Kolosserbriefes," in *DEdG*, pp. 139ff.

[37] Cf. R. Bultmann, *TNT*, pp. 167ff. (ET, *NTT* I, pp. 168ff.).

[38] For a critique of this widespread interpretation cf. H. van Campenhausen, "Zur Auslegung von Rom. 13: Die dämonistische Deutung des *exousia*-Begriffes," *Festschrift für A. Bertholet* (1950), pp. 97ff.

[39] It is high time finally to make an end of the clouds of "popular angel

mythology" which allegedly is supposed to stand behind the Pauline view of the state (also according to the opinion of W. Schweitzer, *Die Herrschaft Christi und der Staat*, Beitrag z. Ev. Theol. 11, 1949). In addition to the convincing evidence brought by von Campenhausen, that the theory of the simultaneous political and metaphysical interpretation of the "authorities" in Rom 13.1 and the "double character" of the powers which are to be subjugated by Christ but nevertheless still have in themselves the inclination to rebel against him go against the early Christian view, the following exegetical reasons speak against the angelological interpretation (some have been asserted already by others, esp. G. Kittel and Dibelius. I add further ones):

1. There can be no doubt about the frequent purely political meaning of *exousia* (in singular and plural).

2. In Rom. 13 the term *exousiai* is parallel to *archontes*, which, used without closer definition, describes simply the authorities, the rulers. Only with an explicit addition can it describe the demonic powers (prince of the world, chief of demons, etc.) in the New Testament.

3. *exousiai* appears with the meaning "angel powers" in the New Testament only in explicitly christological contexts (and there always in connection with other designations for these angel-powers).

4. Not a single word of Rom. 13.1–7 refers to the enthronization of Christ; indeed, his name is not mentioned at all, although Paul, of course, gives an explicit theological foundation for the position of authority and the Christian's duty to obey.

5. Elsewhere, too, in this directive that applies to "everyman," Paul intentionally avoids specifically Christian expressions and uses the same terms and arguments that are also to be found abundantly (here and there almost verbatim) in the non-Christian, Hellenistic-Jewish sphere. References in M. Dibelius, *Rom und die Christen im ersten Jahrhundert* (1942), pp. 6ff.

[40] Mark 12.13ff., parallels in Matthew and Luke.

[41] Cf. also Matt. 17.24ff.; I Cor. 7.20ff.

[42] Col. 1.13.

[43] Phil. 3.20.

[44] Rom. 13.11.

[45] K. Barth, *Kurze Erklärung des Römerbriefes* (1956), p. 22 (ET, *A Shorter Commentary on Romans*, 1959, p. 20).

Additional literature: O. Cullmann, *Der Staat im Neuen Testament* (1961[2]), pp. 68ff. (ET, *The State in the New Testament*, 1956, pp. 95ff.). On Virgil's Fourth Eclogue cf. F. Altheim, *Römische Religionsgeschichte* II (1953), pp. 144ff. On the so-called Good Friday Sermon of Constantine cf. further H. Dörries, "Das Selbstzeugnis Kaiser Konstantins," *Abhdlg. der Akad. der Wiss. in Göttingen*, Phil.-hist. Klasse, 3. Folge, 34 (1954), pp. 129ff., esp. p. 161; H. Kraft, *Kaiser Konstantins religiose Entwicklung* (1955), pp. 271f.

III

FAITH AND REASON IN PAUL[1]

I

THE QUESTION ABOUT the relation of faith and reason in Paul appears to be a very barren one. From the first chapter of I Corinthians each of us knows that the Apostle, as preacher of the message of the cross, fought just as sharply against the wisdom of the world as against justification by one's own works. Both the world's wisdom and righteousness from works characterize the man who seeks to establish himself before God and fails. Just as Christ is the end of the law (Rom. 10.4), by the same token he is also the end of this world's wisdom. God has destroyed it through the cross (I Cor. 1.18ff.). From now on the same rule holds for Jews and Greeks: "Let him who boasts, boast of the Lord" (I Cor. 1.31). No one may weaken the importance of this phrase and say that it is only an overexaggerated occasional remark. No, Paul formulates it fundamentally, comprehensively and quite consciously as an offense. The message of the crucified one is a stumbling-block to Jews, a folly to Greeks (1.23); and vice versa, the wisdom of the world is foolishness to God (3.9). In fact, with these words Paul offended people repeatedly, and aroused the indignant protest of Christianity's opponents. They prompted Celsus and Porphyry to engage in their furious ridicule of the irrational belief of Christians and their scorn of reason, their superstition, even their downright idiocy, the charge that they know only blind faith and glorify irrationality and ignorance.[2] This open or secret critique has remained through the centuries. Goethe still openly protests against these Pauline phrases: "It would not be worth the trouble to become seventy years old if all the wisdom of the world were foolishness to God" (*Maxims and Reflexions*, 2). Certainly one must give heed to the fact that in I Cor. 1–3 the Apostle speaks about the wisdom of the world and not immediately about reason. But does this differentiation really help us further? Does there still remain room somewhere for the reason of man? Certainly one must raise such a question when in II Cor. 10.3–5 Paul sharply answers the opponents who challenge his legitimacy as a real Apostle and man of the Spirit: "For though we live in the world we are not carrying on a worldly war, for the weapons of our warfare are not worldly but have a divine power to destroy strongholds. We destroy arguments and every proud obstacle to the knowledge of God, and take every thought captive to obey Christ." So it appears that the question about the relation of faith and reason can be answered only in the sense of an uncompromising opposition. In any case, this judgment seems valid in view of Paul's undisputed, genuine letters. This means excluding especially the Areopagus speech in Acts 17, which for adequately expressed reasons cannot be regarded as Pauline and therefore initially cannot be considered here.[3]

However, such a succinct solution of the problem would be a short circuit and a radical misunderstanding of Pauline thought. This is true even in view of the passages cited from the Corinthian letters. For the objection just referred to, that one may not simply equate the wisdom of the world (or of this age) with reason, is indeed justified. The "wisdom of the world" is a very definite way of thinking, qualified by its content. It has always run aground on *God's* wisdom and plunged man into lostness. From this lostness God has resolved to save him through the foolishness of the message of the cross (Cor. 1.21). It is only of *this* wisdom of the world that II Cor. 10 speaks. At this very point the Apostle energetically appeals to the *reason* of man—we mean by this his elementary understanding. It is not by chance that the phrases in I Cor. 1.18ff. occur in a carefully reasoned relationship: "For since, in the wisdom of God, the world did not know God through wisdom, it pleased God through the folly of what we preach to save those who believe."[4] The paradox of divine action is to be understood! It is not by chance that the picture of the destruction of the bulwark of reason in II Cor. 10.3ff. is also a well-known typical theme in the battle of the sage elsewhere.[5]

II

But it would be certainly a very un-Pauline endeavor, if from a few scattered passages we sought only to convey apologetic evidence that the Apostle was after all not so wicked a disdainer of reason as could appear at first glance. In fact, he makes very powerful use of reasoned arguments in his letters, and the rich terminology of our theme already shows how important this motif is for Paul.[6] And yet it is very characteristic of Paul that the problem of "reason and revelation" widely raised, in later theology, does not concern him as a theoretical problem at all.[7] In a certain sense one may say that he does not *yet* know it. The apologists of the second century later attacked it. But it would still be wrong to think that this problem first arose in early Christian apologetics. The problem itself is to a large extent only the continuation and legacy of Hellenistic Judiasm. There the appropriation of popular philosophical thought from the Greeks that already had occurred, and the clothing of Jewish articles of faith with the garment of Greek ideas, belong to the essential marks of the theology, apologetics and propaganda-literature of the Hellenistic synagogue long before Paul. Here, in addition to the Greek translation of the Old Testament, the Septuagint, it suffices to cite only the names of Philo,[8] Josephus and the Wisdom of Solomon, and to remember that countless writings of Hellenistic Judaism adorned themselves with the ringing names of Greek philosophers, seers and poets: Heraclitus, Sophocles, Phocylides, Menander, Orpheus, the Sibylline Oracles. It is important in this context to note that the reasoned theology of the Hellenistic synagogue appropriated and developed a fixed type of missionary preaching, which in its basic concepts could also be taken over by the early Christian missionary preaching.[9] The first and most important of the typical themes[10] which recur repeatedly is the doctrine of the one, true God, in contrast to the multiplicity of the pagan gods. This involved the praise of his oneness, his creative power, his wisdom, goodness and providence. It further involved the call to conversion away from idols to the true, reasoned knowledge of God, a sharp critique of idol and sacrificial worship, and finally the announcement of divine judgment on the pious and the impious.[11] All these basic concepts, in part already conceived by the late classical pagan philosophy and critique of religion but now bound together with new theological motifs by Judaism, were appropriated by early Christian missionary preaching and made to serve the Christian proclamation of salvation. This occurred even though, of course, Jewish material was excluded (especially the Jewish understanding of cult and law and the Jewish concept of election). Greek-Jewish concepts, however, still occupy the widest space in the Christian sermon and retain to such an extent their own thematic independence that, important though the place is that remains for it, the intrinsic Christian message can curiously recede.

In this regard the Areopagus speech in the New Testament is especially instructive. Only in its conclusion is mention first made of "one man" through whom God will judge and whom he has attested through the resurrection. Of course, for the Christian sermon this is the decisive point toward which all moves. For the sake of this One, God has now overlooked the time of ignorance and allows the hour of repentance to be announced for all men and all places (Acts 17.30). Nevertheless, the scheme of Hellenistic-Jewish missionary preaching, previously presented, remains, and the independence of its theological motif is kept unchanged. What Jewish preaching had already said has received its very legitimacy and actuality through the Christian message.

We know, especially from the first two chapters of Romans, how very much Paul, too, was rooted in the tradition of this Greek-Jewish theology. Many of its motifs and concepts confront us again in these two chapters: the idea that although God is invisible to human senses, still his works can be seen with the eyes of reason; that the true knowledge of God means at the same time knowledge of his demand, his law, and includes a life of obedience; that the worship of self-made idols is foolishness. All this Philo, the Wisdom of Solomon and many other writings of Hellenistic Judentum know also.[12] The many abstract concepts in Rom. 1 and 2 are of *Greek*, not of Old Testament-biblical origin, such as God's "invisible nature," God's "eternal power and divinity," the term "immortality," the ethical term "proper conduct" known from the Stoics, the list of vices in ch. 1 to depict decadent moral life, the terms "nature," "conscience" in ch. 2, and many others. Of course, Paul has combined all these concepts from Greek tradition with Old Testament-Jewish thought and precisely in so doing shows the influence upon him of Hellenistic-*Jewish* theology: the motif of the divine judgment of wrath, which dominates Rom. 1–3; the emphasis on the ideas of creator and creation; clear allusions to Old Testament passages and many a peculiarity in anthropological terminology, as for example the displacement of the Greek term "mind" by the biblical word "heart" (1.21)—all this shows that the theology of Hellenistic Judaism is also the direct root of some Pauline concepts. Not a small number of significant motifs stem from it, and without question Paul, just as other early Christian missionaries, appropriated them in his preaching.[13] He himself briefly summarizes the central thoughts of the typical missionary sermon in I Thess. 1.9f.: "You turned to God from idols, to serve a living and true God, and to wait for his Son from heaven, whom he raised from the dead, Jesus who delivers us from the wrath to come."

Yet it is just the first chapter of Romans which shows Paul making a completely different use of the basic thoughts of this apologetic-rational missionary sermon, and giving to reason, too, an essentially different function from that which it has in the Hellenistic-Jewish and Hellenistic-Christian type of sermon about which we spoke. To be sure, he employs the same motifs of natural revelation and a knowledge of God as does, for instance, the Wisdom of Solomon. Indeed, he does it even more radically than that document. Broadly and laboriously Wisdom deals with the possibility of knowing God from his works: "From the greatness and beauty of the creation its creator is to be seen analogically" (13.5). But, of course, men have fallen into error. They have given to the creation the honor which is due the creator, an understandable if not also an entirely excusable error. For "If delighted by the beauty of some (elements and stars) they supposed gods to be in them, so indeed they should have known how much better than these (their) Lord is, for the originator of beauty had established them" (13.3). This is, as one sees immediately, tuned to nearly the same tone as the Areopagus speech: "What therefore you worship as unknown, this I proclaim to you" (Acts 17.23).

But the Paul of Rom. 1 and I Cor. 1 speaks in an entirely different way. The question about the *possibility* of a reasoned knowledge of God is not an open question for him at all. When one considers what place such reflections already occupy in Stoic theology, in Philo, in the *Corpus Hermeticum* and later in Christian apologetics, and what lofty titles they attach to the "mind" or to the "reason" of man in the context of a rational or mystic-gnostic anthropology, then one first notices the peculiarity of Pauline thinking and speaking. Not that he challenges the knowability of God from his works through the eyes of reason. On the contrary! This is not an open, theoretically given possibility for him, but *the reality* with which he begins. Therefore, he does not need only to clarify it pedagogically and apologetically, as does the Wisdom of Solomon. In the Wisdom of Solomon it is the goal and climax of a doctrine of wisdom that climbs higher and higher from the earth. For Paul, on the contrary, it is placed most definitely at the beginning and is grounded very simply and definitely in the sovereign decision of God: "Because God has showed it to them" (Rom. 1.19). Furthermore, it is not a past reality of paradise. No, it is and remains present. But precisely in its contemporaneity it is now the valid basis for the judgment: all are without excuse. It is true precisely because they knew God and *not*, as Wisdom 13 has it, because "All men were by nature void; for them the knowledge of God *was lacking*." Thus in the Wisdom of Solomon "vanity" is the expression and result of their *ignorance*. For Paul, on the contrary, it is based on their *knowledge* of God. They have not praised him nor thanked him. Therefore their thoughts have become void and their heart is darkened.[14]

This is the thrust of Pauline thought. It is so vehement that it shatters the well-woven pedagogy of the Wisdom of Solomon and all the well-assorted systematics or typical missionary and apologetic themes in Hellenistic-Jewish and Hellenistic-Christian practice. Naturally one must keep in mind the difference between a missionary sermon to the pagan and a letter which the Apostle writes to Christians, and one may not without further consideration interpret Rom. 1 and 2 as an authentic document of Pauline missionary preaching. Yet it is true that, if any text does so, surely Rom. 1 and 2 permit conclusions as to the manner of the Pauline missionary sermon. Thus we need to note well the difference between the proclamation of Paul and the apologetic and pedagogical missionary preaching of the synagogues of the dispersion, as well as of early Christianity. It appears to me to consist of this, that the thoughts of Pauline preaching do not allow themselves to be divided into well-ordered individual pieces of teaching like the other missionary preaching referred to: about one God, about the knowledge of his works, about man and his endowment with reason and conscience at creation, about the written and unwritten laws of God, etc. It is not a coincidence, but very characteristic, that there is *not* a single sentence in Paul like the well-known article of faith of other Jewish and Christian missionary preaching: "First above all believe that there is one God, who created and ordered the universe" (*Herm. M and I;* The Letter of Aristeas; The Preaching of Peter, *passim*). It is not as if Paul presupposes that all this is well known and completely forgoes the topics of former Jewish-Christian preaching and theology; for him, rather, all is immediately woven into the great *general theme of the meeting between God and man* that means either judgment or grace. Characteristically, therefore, the judgment motif in Rom. 1 does not stand at the end, as it does everywhere else in Jewish and Christian texts, but at the beginning: "For the wrath of God is revealed from heaven against all ungodliness and wickedness of men who by their wickedness suppress the truth"

(1.18). This is already a present eschatological event, visible and active in the imposed penalty from God, namely in the fallenness of men sealed by God himself in the perversion of their moral life: "Therefore God gave them up" (1.24, 26, 28). In contrast to the texts of Hellenistic-Jewish literature Paul speaks of reason, therefore, not with an apologetic and propaedeutic intent but—to put it in the language of early Protestants dogmatic—with an elenctic purpose, i.e. in order to convict the hearer of his guilt before God. The same is true of the Pauline understanding of conscience (Rom. 2.15).[15] Both reason and conscience rightly do not have as their principal function the task of disclosing to man the being and essence of God and his law and thus of leading man toward his own destiny and dignity, but rather, in face of the divine will already revealed, that of holding and enclosing him in his lostness. The sentence about the law of my reason (Rom. 7.23) clearly expresses this state of affairs, that the law in my members lies in conflict with the law of sin. While Hellenistic theology cannot do enough to praise the bond between God and man as a rational being, for Paul the mind manifests to man his separation from God, precisely because he assents to God's law. The godless man cannot escape God. It is true of him: "Wretched man that I am! Who will deliver me from this body of death?" (Rom. 7.24).

III

What we have discussed up to this point concerns the functions of reason with regard to the *unredeemed* man. For the most part we are accustomed in an analysis of Pauline theology to deal with reason on this plane. However, it is no less important to keep in mind the positive meaning which reason has for Paul in the proclamation of the *message of salvation* itself and in the unfolding of *Christian* existence. It appears to me that scholarly research has considered this aspect far too little. And yet it is entirely clear that Paul allots to reason and to the rationality of men an exceedingly important role for the self-understanding of the Christian and for all areas of his life.

It is self-evident that Paul does not derive the message of salvation in Jesus Christ from what man already knows by virtue of his reason. Here it can only be the resounding proclamation of what God has done in his grace. This is and remains a miracle for all human understanding. But the manner and method of this proclamation is still most characteristic in Paul.

We shall seek to clarify this for ourselves again through a contrast. Up to this point we have distinguished the Pauline proclamation from the rational-apologetic type of Hellenistic-Jewish and Hellen-istic-Christian missionary speech. Now we must distinguish his pro-clamation from still another type of missionary preaching. We shall name it shortly the revelation-speech type. In terms of religious phenomenology, we may surely reckon the missionaries of this kind as falling within the category of the "divine men," widespread in the syncretistic period. The "divine men" present themselves as the agents or even the representatives of a divine being, bring heavenly information, call to repentance, and promise salvation. We know many of them from late-classical paganism:[16] Apollonius of Tyana, Alexander of Abunoteichos, Peregrinus Proteus and many nameless prophets, seers, miracle-workers and bringers of salvation. However, there is no question that countless missionaries of ordinary Christianity, especially in a Hellenistic setting, also belonged to this type, and the Christian community had trouble in coming to grips with these "mes-sengers of salvation." Celsus and Lucian mockingly depict them as typically Christian phenomena.[17] However, our concern is not with the extreme eccentricities of such pagan and Christian enchanters, but rather with the type of missionary speech that confronts us here. The characteristic marks of these prophets are the hierophantic style of their message, the apodictic character of their sacred speeches, and not least the titles with which they also introduced themselves or with which they allowed their divine masters to speak. We know especially from the Gospel of John what possibilities this type of revelation-speech also offered to the Christian proclamation, and how this type was utilized by it.[18] But it is still very characteristic that Paul thoroughly avoids such a style of revelation-speech. He almost never introduces the Lord himself as speaking directly.[19] In no place does he utter anything like a *"hieros logos"* (sacred word). Nor does he ever treat as a sacred text the kerygmatic formulae which he appropriated and passed on; he always immediately interprets and develops them. The style of the Pauline sermon is just not that of the revelation-speech but of the diatribe[20] with its pointed sentences, questions and counter-questions—a manner of speaking which regards the hearer as a partner in a dialogue and does not forget him even for a moment. Furthermore, the wonder, the incomprehensibility of the mes-sage of salvation which Paul proclaims, is to be *understood* in its incomprehensibility. Therefore, he uses new thought-forms, analogies, pictures, even when they are inadequate, insufficient, and unsuccessful, and not infrequently they shatter his sentences—as Rom. 5.12ff. most impressively demonstrates. The Pauline *anakolutha* (sentence interruptions) are themselves instructive examples of this manner of thinking and speaking.[21]

In order to assess the meaning of this assertion, one must bear in mind that Paul had to distinguish his own work sharply from the common itinerant preachers, as his oldest letter (I Thess.) already shows and II Corinthians completely demonstrates.[22] In II Corinthians they clearly appear as spiritualists, who challenge his legitimacy as a true apostle because he is lacking in the manifestations of divine power.[23] The situation is so difficult for Paul here because he also understands himself as one commissioned and claims for himself the authority of the exalted Lord (II Cor. 5.20).[24] He, too, is a spiritualist and indeed could speak to the mature in the language of wisdom (I Cor. 2.6ff.). Nor are prophecy and speaking in tongues foreign to him. If his opponents so desire, he foolishly can boast of these things himself (II Cor. 11.12). And still he avoids such behavior. "For if we are beside ourselves, it is for God; if we are in our right mind, it is for you" (II Cor. 5.13).[25] For Paul, the *renunciation* of such foolish boasting and all mystagogical conduct belongs to the true legitimacy of his apostolate. Instead of that, he boasts of his weakness, in which alone the power of God is perfected (II Cor. 12.9). Therefore, he seeks to exercise his office with the sincerity of God and to be known to the conscience of all (II Cor. 1.12; 4.2). "As men of sincerity, as commissioned by God, in the sight of God we speak in Christ" (II Cor. 2.17). The other spiritual behavior he calls a falsification of the divine word (II Cor. 2.17; 4.2).

With the renunciation of all parading of his own "spiritual" gifts and apocalyptic revelations, which could have established him as an ecstatic and divine man (II Cor. 12.1ff.),[26] and indeed in certain circumstances could even have demonstrated his apostolic authority (I Thess. 2.6f.), is connected a further trait, which marks the conduct of Paul as missionary and preacher just as decisively. This is his adaptation, in different ways, to Jews and Gentiles, to win both those under the law and those without law: "I have become all things to all men, that I might by all means save some" (I Cor. 9.22).[27] The solidarity with his hearers, in which the Apostle so radically places himself, shows that he always seeks them where they really are, so that the gospel can do its liberating work on them. The sentences of I

Cor. 7.17–24 are intended to agree completely. The term "calling" used here in fact means something like "position," "occupation,"[28] i.e. not the calling *through* which the Christians became Christians, but rather the concrete life-situation *in* which they have been confronted by God's call. In this, the position in life in which slaves and master find themselves becomes peculiarly relativized—the slave becomes a freedman of Christ and the master becomes a slave of Christ —but at the same time it is most meaningful: the very place where a change is to occur through Christ is in one's concrete situation. Thus there is no need for a prior change of "conditions." As the Christian does not need to realize his Christian existence initially through the reception or the annulment of circumcision, so, too, he does not need a new social position. Again it is clear that for Paul the real, natural life-situation of the hearers of the message is all-important. That situation is to be *understood* anew by believers in Christ.

What we have said thus far about Paul's defense of his proclamation has its exact parallel in the manner and method in which he treats the question of spiritual gifts in worship in I Cor. 14. There he places prophecy and speaking in tongues in rugged opposition to each other. Without doubt, in the ordinary Christian understanding in Corinth the spiritual gifts of prophecy and speaking in tongues were most closely related. Both were ways of speaking, through which the exalted Lord or the Spirit communicated directly. Here the speaking in tongues was regarded simply as an exalted form of prophecy. In no way did speaking in tongues and prophecy oppose each other. This corresponds to the picture of the prophet and giver of oracles which existed so plentifully in the syncretism of the Hellenistic period. In the portrayal of the "enthusiasm" of seers, ecstasy and raving were often made explicitly prominent.[29] The Acts of the Apostles teaches how closely speaking in tongues and prophecy belonged together in ordinary early Christian understanding. This already occurs at Pentecost, when Peter interprets the speaking in tongues by the witnesses, which many of the listeners regard as signs of drunkenness (Acts 2), with reference to the promise in Joel 3.[30] It is also to be found especially in the short description of those filled with the Spirit in Acts 19.6: "they spoke with tongues and prophesied." The Christian prophets described by Celsus still connect their message with the outburst of speaking in tongues.[31] This is certainly not to be attributed only to a later period. It is much more an ordinary Christian expression of prophecy, certainly already presupposed by Paul. Indeed, he himself names both gifts, speaking in tongues and prophecy, in close connection with each other: "If I speak in the tongues of men and angels . . . and if I have prophetic powers and understand all mysteries and all knowledge . . ." (I Cor. 13.1f.).[32]

Hence it is all the more noteworthy that in I Cor. 14 Paul so sharply differentiates between the two and designates the "speaking with the mind" as the mark of prophecy, in contrast to every "speaking with the spirit,"[33] so that it could appear that for him prophecy was no expression of the Spirit at all.[34]

This antithesis, one may therefore say, is original with Paul and has no parallels in early Christian literature. If one asks why this understandable, rational speaking is so important to the Apostle that in the congregation he would rather speak five words with his mind than ten thousand words in tongues (14.19), the answer certainly cannot be that he wanted to extinguish the Spirit and reduce all expressions in the life of the congregation to the standard of a general rationality. Paul knows all too well that the Spirit of God is an overwhelming power, and in I Cor. 12.2 he does not hesitate to place the stirring of the Spirit parallel to that enthusiasm which the Corinthians knew from their pagan past and environment. Thus the standard by which he judges is not *reason as such*. For him, the all-important thing is that even the least—the unbeliever and the stranger—are to be able *to understand* the word spoken in worship. They are to be convinced, so that they confess: "God is really among you" (14.25)! It is highly instructive that in I Cor. 14.24f. verbs appear which Paul can apply just as well to "conscience" in Rom. 2.14f. ("convict," "call to account," "disclose the secrets of his heart"), although his concern in the context of I Cor. 14 is not the particular one of the encounter with God's law, but the general one of the resounding proclamation of the word in worship. The term "convict" seems to me to be especially characteristic, for its primary and intrinsic meaning is not to become theoretically convinced of the correctness of a doctrine. Rather, it aims at the man himself who hears the word, that confronted by the truth and reality of this word, his innermost being may be revealed. Only in this way, according to Paul, does the "edification" of the congregation take place. For its sake speaking with reason is so exceedingly important and the admonition of the Apostle applicable: "In thinking be mature" (I Cor. 14.20). For only when the Word of God is proclaimed intelligently and intelligibly will the hearers, rightly understand both the divine word and also at the same time themselves, too, in their situation before God.[35]

It is in this connection too that Paul similarly does not forgo "rational" argument in the establishment of his instructions for law and order in the congregation. Of course, the main motif again and again is the appeal to the believers' new existence which they have received through Christ. But it is instructive that Paul here avoids the apodictic style of the law-giver and does not hesitate to support his regulations with generally rational grounds as well, thus appealing to the natural understanding of his hearers. For this reason there is a remembrance of nature and custom in the directions about the veiling of women in worship (I Cor. 11.13, 15), and we find examples from what was self-evident, valid usage everywhere—for instance I Cor. 11 and Paul's defense of his right to be supported by the congregation like the other apostles (I Cor. 9.7), and the reference that incest was not tolerated for a moment even in paganism (I Cor. 5.1ff.).[36]

Finally, we still have to show that the *motif of reason* also plays a not insignificant role in the ethical directives of the Apostle. Paul had to wage an especially sharp battle in this very area against the spiritualists, for here the temptation threatened to erupt in multiple forms of spiritual enthusiasm. Each of these eruptions means that man skips over the reality and truth of his existence before God and thereby simultaneously becomes guilty in relation to his brethren. That is the mark of the spiritualists in Corinth and Rome, in contrast to those who are weak, who boast of their strength and freedom in the question of eating meat offered to idols. Of course, they *also* have their "rational" grounds. "All is permitted" is well known already as a basic principle of the Cynic-Stoic sages.[37] And the proposition that there are no idols, and that therefore there is also no offering of meat to idols, appears to be a rational proposition of Christian Gnosticism following directly from faith. Paul cannot and does not want to challenge this. But he very quickly relativizes *these* rational bases, declares them unimportant and substitutes for them a question of conscience: What helps the other person? For "knowledge puffs up, but love builds up" (I Cor. 8.1). Only love supplies the true, supporting rational ground, which no longer regards only its "own" but also "the interests of others" (Phil. 2.4). In I Cor. 8–10, just as in Rom. 14–15, Paul very carefully makes this understandable and convincing to the congregation. Here the rational argument of his opponents, "all things are lawful for me," also receives its necessary limitation in Paul's mind: "but I will not be enslaved by anything" (I Cor. 6.12).[38]

The spiritualist who boasts of his freedom is indeed not only blind to his brother but also deceives himself. For in the ecstasy of his enthusiasm he thinks that he is already with God, that he has the limits of time behind him and already has come to share in the resurrection of the dead (I Cor. 4.8f.). Therefore, in Corinth the future resurrection of the dead is denied (I Cor. 15; cf. II Tim. 2.18). Paul calls the congregation back from this spiritual fanaticism to common sense and to the true knowledge of God (I Cor. 15.34; cf. I Thess. 5.6, 8). This means simultaneously the right intelligence with regard to the situation of man before God and the sensible, rational examination of what is "good and acceptable and perfect" (Rom. 12.2) before God and neighbor. For Paul, rational, spiritual worship[39] means the sacrifice of the *whole* life, not the agreement of reason with the general Logos of the world, as the Stoics taught, and not the mystical elevation of the mind into divinity as in Hermetic theology. These admonitions of Paul contain in each case an appeal to reason. Thus in his admonitions he makes rich use of concepts and moral directives already long familiar to the rational ethics of paganism. "Finally, brethren, whatever is true, whatever is honorable, whatever is just, whatever is pure, whatever is lovely, whatever is gracious, if there is any excellence, if there is anything worthy of praise, think about these things" (Phil. 4.8).

IV

Our reflections have shown that for Paul there is an emphasis, for a long time insufficiently considered (as it seems to me), on the rationality of man, on his being rational, becoming rational and remaining rational; and this motif is not only in the expressions which are to *prepare* for the proclamation of the gospel (as Rom. 1 and 2), but also carries through where Paul develops the gospel itself and where the nature and conduct of the Christian are the theme of his statements. In fact, it returns many times in repeatedly new variations and applications to the life of the *Christian*. In almost classical form, Paul shows this even at the beginning of the admonitions in Rom. 12.3, where, following the sentences we cited earlier, he once more begins and succinctly formulates: "For by the grace given to me I bid every one among you not to think of himself more highly than he ought to think, but to think with sober judgment, each according to the measure of faith which God has assigned him." The whole context shows that for Paul this concerns the *new* life of Christians. Hence the admonition not to be conceited (Rom. 12.16; 11.25). But it is just as characteristic that in Rom. 12.3, in the pointed formulation of a play on words—"not to think of himself more highly than he ought to think but to think with sober judgment," the ancient Greek term "sober judgment" occurs and the admonition to observe moderation stands first. Thus it is not something new, something more in the sense of a fantastic enthusiasm, but holding to the old that is decisive. The old has become new for the Apostle in that now it stands in the light of God's grace and on the plane of responsibility before him. So for Paul, the call to be rational and discreet means the same as the challenge to renew the mind (Rom. 12.2).

NOTES

[1] A lecture given at the Heidelberg Academy of Sciences at a session of the Philosophical-Historical Seminar on October 7, 1957, and at the General Meeting of the Studiorum Novi Testamenti Societas in Birmingham on November 9, 1957. Published in shortened form and without footnotes in English in *NTS* 4 (1957–8), pp. 93–100.

[2] Cf. C. Andresen, *Logos und Nomos. Die Polemik des Kelsos wider das Christentum* (1955), pp. 167ff.

[3] Cf. M. Dibelius, "Paulus auf dem Areopag," in *Aufsätze zur Apostelgeschichte* (1953²), pp. 29–70 (ET, *Studies in the Acts of the Apostles*, 1956, pp. 26–77). I need not enter here into the numerous more recent treatments of Acts 17.

[4] On this understanding of the passage cf. especially H. Schlier, "Die Erkenntnis Gottes bei den Heiden," *EvTh* (1935), pp. 9–26; "Kerygma und Sophia," in *Die Zeit der Kirche* (1956), pp. 206–32, esp. pp. 209f. Note the *sophia*-doctrine of late Judaism: God has poured out his wisdom on all his works of creation (Sir. 1.1–9; Prov. 8.27, etc.). Similarly Bachmann, J. Weiss, Kümmel, *loc. cit.*: "in the wisdom of God . . . the world has not known him." Whatever happens, one may not understand it as "due to the wisdom of God . . . the world has not known him." Lietzmann's paraphrase is also to be rejected: "in the time of wisdom's activity . . ." Paul does not place the revelation in creation and the revelation of salvation in the gospel in a relationship of temporal sequence. Like Schlier, U. Wilckens, *Weisheit und Torheit* (1958), pp. 32ff., understands this correctly.

[5] Cf. Prov. 21.22; Philo, *conf. ling.* 129–31, etc.; Epictetus III, 22.94, 96; IV, 1.86f. Additional material on II Cor. 10.4 in H. Windisch, *Der Zweite Korintherbrief* (1924), pp. 296f.

[6] Note the numerous concepts from the stem *no-* (*nous, noein, noēma, anoētos, katanoein, metanoia, nouthetein*), from the stem *phre-* (*phrenes* = understanding in I Cor. 14.20; *phronimos, phronēma* and others); further *eidenai, suneidenai, suneidēsis, gignōskein, gnōsis, sunesis, sunienai, krinein, dokimazein, peirazein, logizesthai* and others.

For Paul the term *nous* seldom designates "reason" in the full sense; so it is in Rom. 7.23, also *nooumena kathoran* (see with the eyes of reason) in Rom. 1.20; in both cases it is the reason that perceives and understands the work and will of God. Otherwise the general and original meaning clearly dominates: *nous* as "the knowing about something, the understanding and judging that belongs to man as man and determines his attitude" (R. Bultmann, *TNT*, p. 207; ET, *NTT* I, p. 211), in no way only as a considering but also as a striving, willing attitude. As therefore God's (or sometimes Christ's) *nous* is spoken of as the mark of the divine, saving will (Rom. 11.34; with the same meaning as *pneuma* (spirit) in I Cor. 2.16), so one can speak of the human *nous* as the will and disposition of man (I Cor. 1.10) or also concretely of his conviction (Rom. 14.5). The *nous* (mind) of man can be debased (*adokimos*, Rom. 1.28). His mind (will, disposition) is called to renewal (Rom.12.2). Cf. Bultmann, *op. cit.*, pp. 207ff.; ET, pp. 211ff.

[7] Nowhere does one find reflections about the indwelling divine *nous* in man, as for instance is characteristic for Philo.

[8] Positively though Philo can speak of reason, only the ecstatic *enthousiasmos* leads to the true knowledge of God. Cf. W. Bousset-H. Gressmann, *Die Religion des Judentums* (1926[3]), pp. 448ff.; W. Völker, *Fortschritt und Vollendung bei Philo von Alexandrien, Texte u. Unters.* 49, 1 (1938), pp. 279ff.; H. Jonas, *Gnosis und spätantiker Geist* II/1 (1954), pp. 77ff.; H. Thyen, "Probleme der neueren Philo-Forschung," in *TR* 23 (1955), pp. 240ff.

[9] H. Thyen, *Der Stil der jüdisch-hellenistischen Homilie* (1955), deals instructively with the form and style of the Hellenistic synagogue-sermon, which most strikingly is patterned after the Cynic-Stoic diatribe and which influenced early Christian preaching. On what follows cf. also C. H. Dodd, "Natural Law in the Bible," in *Theology* 49 (1946), pp. 113f.; 130ff.; 161ff., and also his *Gospel and Law* (1951).

[10] E. Norden, *Agnostos Theos* (1913 = 1956[4]), esp. pp. 3ff. and pp. 125ff., first showed the stereotyped motifs and the dissemination of a fixed scheme in pagan-philosophical literature and then in the writings of Hellenistic Judaism and early Christianity. Additional references in W. Nauck, "Die Tradition und Komposition der Areopagrede," in *ZTK* 53 (1956), pp. 11ff. Especially important in Nauck is the evaluation of two fragments of a Sibylline writing (p. 26, lines 32ff.).

[11] As an especially characteristic example from the Sibylline fragments treated by Nauck, I select: 1. "God is only one, he alone ruler, the eternal, greatest . . ." (I, 7; cf. I, 32; III, 3). 2. The call to repentance: "O desist, you fools, from wandering about in lightless, gloomy night and darkness; at last flee from the darkness of night and grasp the splendor of light! See, it beams so brightly and, fail not to recognize, for all. Come and walk not continually in the darkness of gloomy error . . ." (I, 25ff.). 3. The foolishness of idol worship: "Indeed, be ashamed to worship crocodile and cat as gods!" (III, 20), "Pray, you foolish, also to snakes, cats, dogs; worship the birds of the air and the creeping animals of earth, pictures and signs of stone, made by human hands . . ." (III, 27ff.). 4. The announcement of judgment: "Therefore the heat of consuming fire will grasp you and the blazing flame will eternally burn you, perishing daily in disgrace on account of the false, empty gods. But the faithful worshippers of the true and eternal God will inherit life . . ." (III, 43ff.). German translation by A. Kurfess, *Sibyllinische Weissagungen* (1951); the English translation above by H. C. O. Lanchester in *The Apocrypha and Pseudepigrapha of the Old Testament*, ed. R. H. Charles, vol. II (1913). An additional example is offered by the fragment of Pseudo-Sophocles, not yet included by Nauck (handed down by Clement of Alexandria in his *Stromata* V, 14: 113; ET in *The Ante-Nicene Fathers*, vol. II, 1956; and by Eusebius in *Praeparatio Evangelica* XIII, 13.40, 48; ET, *Eusebius' Preparation for the Gospel*, by E. H. Gifford, Part II, 1903; German translation by P. Riessler, *Altjüdisches*

Schrifttum, p. 1046; ET follows that by A. C. Coxe in *The Ante-Nicene Fathers*, vol. II, pp. 470, 472): "Sophocles, as Hecataeus, who composed the histories in the work about Abraham and the Egyptians, says, exclaims plainly on the stage:

> One in very truth, God is One,
> Who made the heaven and the far-stretching earth,
> The Deep's blue billow, and the might of winds.
> But of us mortals, many erring far
> In heart, as solace for our woes, have raised
> Images of gods—of stone, or else of brass,
> Or figures wrought of gold or ivory;
> And sacrifices and vain festivals
> To these appointing, deem ourselves devout . . .

And with this agrees the tragedy in the following lines:

> For there shall come, shall come that point of time,
> When Ether, golden-eyed, shall ope its store
> Of treasured fire; and the devouring flame,
> Raging, shall burn all things on earth below,
> And all above."

[12] Cf. my essay: "Die Offenbarung des Zornes Gottes," in *DEdG*, pp. 9ff. (ET, "The Revelation of God's Wrath" in this volume, pp. 47ff.).

[13] W. Nauck, *op. cit.*, p. 38, enumerates the fixed motifs of the Jewish and early Christian missionary preaching which have their parallels in Rom. 1–2: creation (Rom. 1.20, 25), knowledge of God (1.19f.), worship of God (1.23, 25), repentance (2.4), judgment (2.5f., 8f.), salvation (2.7, 10).

[14] His sharply negative judgment of idol worship puts Paul on the side of the Sibylline fragments, while Aristobulus, the Wisdom of Solomon and Acts 17 agree in the judgment of a positive connection. Cf. W. Nauck, *op. cit.*, pp. 40ff.

[15] Cf. my essay: "Gesetz und Natur," in *SzAuU*, pp. 111ff.

[16] Cf. the characteristics of these "divine men" in L. Bieler, *THEIOS ANER. Das Bild des göttlichen Menschen in Spätantike und Frühchristentum* I/II (1935/36), in addition K. Deissner, "Sendungsbewusstsein der Urchristenheit," in *Zeitschrift für systematische Theologie* 7 (1930), pp. 772ff.; H. Windisch, *Paulus und Christus* (1934), pp. 24–89; and especially D. Georgi, *Die Gegner des Paulus im Zweiten Korintherbrief* (1964). Cf. also G. v. d. Leeuw, *Phänomenologie der Religion* (1956²), pp. 764f.

[17] Cf. Origen, *contra Celsum*, VII, 8f.; Lucian, *de morte Peregrini*, c. 11.

[18] The style and dissemination of these revelation-speeches is dealt with by H. Becker, *Die Reden des Johannesevangeliums und der Stil der gnostischen Offenbarungsrede* (1956), pp. 14–59, with plentiful examples from the prophetic sayings that have been transmitted through Celsus in Origen, from the Odes of Solomon 33, Hermetic texts, Pseudo-Clementine writings, apocryphal acts of the apostles, Mandaean literature and others. Becker names as fixed elements of style (pp. 53ff.): 1. "The self-given titles, often further developed as 'autodoxology' of the revealer with the dimension of a 'report' about his nature and origin. Thus the description of the world situation that motivates his coming is closely connected." 2. "The invitation or in some instances the call to decision. In the profane sphere of the world the call comes from without to acknowledge the depicted situation and further to complete the turning away from the cosmic to the real, the spiritual origin." 3. "The promise for those who follow the call of the revealer, and very often connected with a threat against the unbelievers." One acknowledges that this type of revelation-speech is largely not to be differentiated from the apologetic-pedagogical. The motif of the one also penetrates the other. The mark of the

revelation-speech is, however, the hierophantic clothing and the claim to bring divine revelation from the beyond. Becker rightly speaks of a "dualistic" style (p. 55).

[19] The only exception is II Cor. 12.9, but this, too, is not directly proclamation but the answer of the Lord to the Apostle's prayer.

[20] Cf. R. Bultmann, *Der Stil der paulinischen Predigt und die kynisch-stoische Diatribe* (1910). Concerning the non-Christian and Christian diatribe, cf. H. J. Marrou, *Reallexikon für Antike und Christentum* 3 (1957), cols. 990ff.

[21] Cf. my essay, "Paulinische Anakoluthe im Romerbrief," in *DEdG*, pp. 76ff. On Rom. 5.12ff., cf. pp. 8off.

[22] Hence the extended apology in I Thess. 2.1–12. M. Dibelius rightly says in his excursus to I Thess. 2.12 (*HzNT* 11, 1937³, p. 11): "The Christian missionaries, like the most serious itinerant teachers of philosophy, were early obliged to distinguish their work from the activity of false miracle-workers as they traversed the Greek world and later also the Christian congregations. See *Herm. Mand.* XI; *Didache* 11, 12." "The nearer the apostolic mission stood to the style of presentation and to certain formulations of the public philosophical preaching of the time, the more necessary it was to emphasize the differences." In the non-Christian literature, too, we meet scorn for the self-seeking and pretentious behavior of the enchanters (references in Dibelius, *op. cit.*, pp. 7f.). Thus it is not necessary, as Dibelius establishes, to seek an actual occasion for the apology of I Thess. 2.1ff. Still II Corinthians especially shows that Paul very soon had to come to grips concretely with such itinerant apostles and even those of Christian origin (cf. D. Georgi, *op. cit.*). Neither should we overlook the fact that nowhere in the early Christian literature does this polemic meet us as in Paul. On the theological meaning of I Thess. 2.1ff. cf. my essay, "Gotteswort und Menschenwort im Neuen Testament," in *SzAuU.*, pp. 223ff. (ET in this volume, "God's Word and Man's Word in the New Testament," pp. 1ff.).

[23] On this cf. E. Käsemann, "Die Legitimität des Apostels," *ZNW* 41 (1942), pp. 33ff. (printed in the series "Libelli" of the Wissenschaftlichen Buchgesellschaft) and D. Georgi, *op. cit.*, pp. 72ff. (see n. 16 above).

[24] On this cf. my article "*presbeuō*," *TWNT*, VI, pp. 681f.

[25] *eite gar exestēmen, theō; eite sōphronoumen, humin.*

[26] This thoroughgoing peculiarity in the self-understanding and bearing of the Apostle is completely misunderstood by H. Windisch, *Christus und Paulus* (1934), where Paul is designated directly as a "divine man."

[27] How important this trait of his missionary activity is for Paul is shown by the care and rhetorical mastery in the formulations of I Cor. 9.19–23. Verse 19 comprehensively formulates the basic thought; vv. 20–22a formulate it with variation in a triple application: (*a*) to the Jews (v. 20) in two parallel sentences, where the second explains the first; (*b*) to those without the law (v. 21); (*c*) to the weak (v. 22a). Verses 22b/23 summarize the whole, again in two sentences, the first of which is directly connected, also in form, to the three previous theses, and aims at affecting men with whom the Apostle identifies himself, while v. 23 speaks of the hope which concerns his own future and his own bliss. The sentences in vv. 19–23 have a similar construction throughout. They all contain (1) an emphasized verb, placed either at the end or the beginning, which describes the Apostle's behavior ("made a slave" in v. 19, "became" in vv. 20, 22a, b, "do" in v. 23); (2) a concessive participial phrase which in contrast paraphrases the right that belongs intrinsically to him, and thus provides the background for what he does (though I am free . . . not being under the law . . . not being without the law); (3) a *hina*-clause, i.e. "in order to" or "that" (7 *hina*-clauses!). All expressions have a fixed direction toward the goal. The uniform monotony of the sentences

(note the use of "I might win" five times) impressively shows the goal to which the will of the Apostle is consistently directed in the multiplicity of his own changing role.

²⁸ Cf. K. Holl, *Gesammelte Aufsätze zur Kirchengeschichte*, III (1928), p. 190; H. Lietzmann, *loc. cit.*; non-Christian references in W. Bauer, *Wörterbuch zum Neuen Testament* (1958⁵), col. 862 (ET, *A Greek-English Lexicon of the New Testament*, trans. of 4th ed. by W. F. Arndt and F. W. Gingrich, 1957, p. 437).

²⁹ Examples in J. Behm in the article, "*glōssa*," *TWNT* I, p. 722 (ET, TDNT I, pp. 722ff.); and E. Fascher, PROPHÉTÈS (1927), *passim*. Cf. also R. Reitzenstein, *Hellenistische Mysterienreligionen* (1927³), pp. 236ff., and H. Kramer in the article, "*prophētēs*," *TWNT* VI, pp. 784ff. (esp. pp. 789, 793ff.).

³⁰ It is unnecessary here to enter in detail into the problems of Pentecost. It holds without question that the account also recognizes the early Christian phenomenon of speaking in tongues. Cf. E. Haenchen, *Die Apostelgeschichte* (1956), p. 143.

³¹ Cf. Origen, *contra Celsum* VII, 8ff. Montanist prophecy offers the same picture; on this cf. H. Lietzmann, *Geschichte der Alten Kirche* II (1953²), pp. 195ff. (ET, *The Founding of the Church Universal*, 1938, pp. 255ff.).

³² Cf. also I Cor. 12.10 and on this E. Fascher, *op. cit.*, pp. 184f.

³³ One ought to note that *Didache* 11.7 characterizes precisely the prophet as "speaking in the spirit;" he is therefore not subordinate to "examination"! Cf. also *Herm. Mand.* XI, 5.

³⁴ Indeed, this strange fact of the case is to be understood from the simple fact that Paul here proceeds from the common understanding of "spirit," in which his own "spirit"-concept does not appear at all.

³⁵ Very clearly, the Apostle's concern allows itself to be recognized also in the use of *peithein*. The word means "persuade," and in a hostile sense "talk a person into," "speak to please" (Gal. 1.10; I Thess. 2.4). Indeed, Paul uses the word in a thoroughly positive way, but characteristically connects it with the parallel expression: "known to your conscience" (II Cor. 5.11). In this sense it aims at the obedience of the hearers (*peithesthai*) and at the trust (*pepoithenai*) grounded in God.

³⁶ Cf. H. v. Campenhausen, "Die Begründung kirchlicher Entscheidungen beim Apostel Paulus," *Sitzungsberichte der Heidelberger Akademie der Wissenschaften*, philos.-hist. Klasse 1957, Abh. 2; and his *Kirchliches Amt und geistliche Vollmacht* (1953), pp. 32ff.

³⁷ Cf. J. Weiss, *Der Erste Korintherbrief* (1910⁹), pp. 158f., on I Cor. 6.12.

³⁸ The word actually could occur also in Epictetus.

³⁹ *logikē latreia* can be translated "rational" worship, when it is understood as an antithesis to Stoic-philosophical thought. But it is more natural to think of the contrast with mysticism, for we find the phrase almost verbatim in *Corpus Hermeticum* I, 31, and XIII, 17–19 (cf. Lietzmann, *loc. cit.*), and the following expressions, "be transformed," "renewal of mind," ostensibly take up the language of the mystery religions, even if in polemical usage.

IV

THE REVELATION OF GOD'S WRATH[1]
Romans 1–3

I

IT IS A GENERALLY observed fact that in Rom. 1.17f. Paul describes the revelation of God's righteousness in the gospel and the revelation of wrath on all godlessness and unrighteousness of men with parallel phrases: "For in it the righteousness of God is revealed through faith for faith . . . For the wrath of God is revealed from heaven against all ungodliness and wickedness of men," etc. The chain of sentences in vv. 16–18 is joined together by a fourfold use of "for" and connected to v. 15, which speaks of Paul's readiness to extend his service of the gospel to all the world: v. 16a gives the personal basis of his readiness; vv. 16b and 17 go on to define the characteristic designation and to give the first thematic development of the revelation of God's righteousness that occurs in the gospel; and v. 18 introduces the first major section, extending to 3.20, the proclamation of the revelation of God's wrath over the world, on which basis the message of the gospel as a message of salvation rests.

Verse 17 certifies the gospel as the revelation of God's righteousness "from faith to faith," that is, as making present the event of salvation which God has brought to the world in Jesus Christ and that is actualized in the spread of the gospel (cf. 3.21ff.). Thus the term "is revealed" describes the message itself as an eschatological salvation-event. It is not simply an imparting of certain truths and not just a report of significant events, but the word in which God's will is accomplished in the present. The description of this revelation as the "power for salvation" (v. 16) makes this character of the revelation as an event fully clear, just as the terms "salvation," "righteousness of God" (1.17) and "wrath of God" (1.18) definitely establish the eschatological meaning of the whole.

But how, then, are the two apparently opposing revelations in vv.

17 and 18 related to each other? The "revelation" of God's righteousness as eschatological event, as the explicitly emphasized "but
now" of 3.21 indicates, is bound to the definite hour in which God
allows time to be fulfilled and brings a new age in Jesus Christ (Gal.
4.4). It is made present as "the acceptable time, as the day of salvation" (II Cor. 6.2), to those who hear at any time, by the proclamation
of the gospel. But that means that at the same time it is the hour of
judgment for unbelievers (II Cor. 2.15f.; 4.3; I Cor. 1.23f.). The "is
revealed" of Rom. 1.17 thus has an "actually present" meaning. But
how is it related to the corresponding "is revealed" in v. 18? Does
it mean that this revelation of the divine wrath itself also belongs to
the content of the gospel?[2] Apparently not; for how, then, does Paul
come to write as he does: "For in it the righteousness of God is revealed through faith for faith," a formulation that allows no supplementation—to say nothing of contrasting content. Moreover, the
closer definition of the revelation of wrath, "from heaven," stands in
explicit contrast to the righteousness of God that takes place in the
gospel, just as the double-edged arguments—the argument from the
promise of the scripture in v. 17 and the argument from natural
revelation in v. 18—correspond in contrasting fashion. Or should the
relation between the two revelations be understood to be that they
occur to different kinds of men, the godly and the ungodly? This
explanation would turn the text upside down, since God's righteousness is definitely imparted righteousness (3.24). Faith may never be
seen as the presupposed condition for the revelation of the "righteousness of God," in the way "ungodliness" and "wickedness" provide
the reason for the revelation of God's wrath. Paul shows this difference
by the change of prepositions "through faith"—"for faith"[3] in v. 17,
in contrast to "against" in v. 18. The purpose of the broad exposition
of 1.18–3.20 is just this: to show the lostness of the whole world in sin
and its subjection to the punishment (3.19f.) under the law from which
no one is excepted.

Usually, therefore, the relationship between the revelation of God's
wrath and the revelation of God's righteousness is understood in another way: either as juxtaposition or as succession. In the first case,
"is revealed" is given a timeless meaning. The final judgment could
not be intended, since according to ch. 2.5 this is explicitly still to be
expected; and the revelation of wrath as a constituent part of the
gospel itself is excluded for the reasons mentioned above. Thus the
present tense of the verb can have only the character of constant

duration and must mean that way of making known the divine judge's will which takes place constantly over the world and is to be seen repeatedly in the world itself. "The corruption of morals that reigns everywhere in the pre-Christian and non-Christian human world is as it were a language of facts in which God himself from heaven speaks just as clearly as in the gospel and discloses the truth that men, who outrageously suppress the true knowledge of God by religious error, are subject to God's wrath, which will erupt over them at the future last judgment in all its force" (Kühl). "By this (sc. 'is revealed . . . from heaven') the universality of this revelation of wrath is emphasized and characterized in the same way as an element of the world-directing activity of God" (B. Weiss). "It is his . . . disclosure of a wrath of God occurring now and then during the course of this world" (Zahn).[4] "No conscience that is not yet completely dulled can escape this testimony, and in the knowledge of the divine wrath, thus awakened, is achieved a clear perception of a just divine judgment that always has penetrated pagan hearts."[5] Correspondingly, reflections on the relationship between love and wrath in the concept of God are inserted here, as by B. Weiss on this passage and Th. Haering (*Der Römerbrief des Apostels Paulus*, 1926, p. 23).

A similarly widespread solution of the problem, that appears to do more justice to the salvation-historical thinking of Paul, is given by the statement: the revelation of the wrath of God characterizes the past epoch which God has now ended in Jesus Christ. "1.18–20 depicts the situation prior to the gospel" (Lietzmann); Paul shows here "how the whole of mankind without exception was subject to the wrath of God in the time prior to the gospel" (Jülicher). It is fully consistent with this that Lietzmann describes the argumentation of Paul in ch. 2 as hypothetical[6] and paraphrases 1.18: "(until now) namely (only) God's wrath from heaven is revealed . . ."[7] What is problematical in this understanding, apart from other objections, especially with respect to 2.5–12,[8] is the fact that Paul himself in 3.25 calls this alleged period of the revelation of wrath the time of God's "forbearance," which is ended in Jesus Christ.[9] The redemption in Jesus Christ (3.24), then, does *not* have the sense of differentiating the periods of salvation history into "wrath" and "forgiveness," but, on the contrary, places them in contrast to each other as the time of patience and the time of the "showing of his righteousness."[10]

How, then, is the relationship of the two revelations in vv. 17f. to be understood? We ask the question in order to answer it later.

II

Paul establishes the event of the revelation of God's wrath from heaven over all the "ungodliness" and "wickedness" of men with a reference to the revelation of God in creation (1.19–20). In the presentation of this natural revelation of God, Paul, as is known, shows himself to be influenced in such a striking way by Stoic terminology and apologetic trains of thought, such as are characteristic of Hellenistic Judaism (especially the Wisdom of Solomon and Philo), that one must ask the question about literary dependence.[11] The substantive connections are extensive. They concern the following essential propositions:

(a) The ingenious construction of the world gives cause for human viewers to ask about their Creator and to infer his divine greatness from the glory of his work. Though invisible to the senses, the deity is seen in his works by the "mind"[12] (cf. ch. 1.19f.).

(b) This knowledge of the Creator does not only represent a theoretical confirmation of the existence of a prime cause but is at the same time a comprehension (cf. v. 21, "knowing God"—v. 32, "knowing God's decree") of the law.[13]

(c) Therefore the honoring of God and an obedient life belong to the right knowledge of the Creator (cf. v. 21ff., 28).[14]

(d) The closing of oneself to the true knowledge of God leads to the abomination of idolatry and a brutal life (cf. v. 23ff.).[15]

These individual propositions have in common a characteristic context in the Hellenistic doctrine of God that one seeks for in vain in Paul. The "from below to above," ascending knowledge of God arrives at a deity that is nothing other than the life principle of the world itself. Whether he is the Creator of the temporal "world" or the Ruler of the eternal is therefore a question that can be left on one side (Cicero, *Tusc.* I, § § 68–70). What is decisive is that the world be understood as God's "holiest and most worthy temple," because the divine reason penetrates and fills everything with an "indwelling power of life and motion,"[16] as *logos* that governs everything and is the soul of the whole (Chrysippus, see Arnim, *Stoic. vet. frgm.* II, 1076). Thus the deity itself is the "common law,"[17] and the law is "the king of all divine and human things" (in Arnim III, 314). This identity of the deity itself with the world in its living order[18] is the reason for its namelessness or in some instances its many names: "For all are He and He is all. And for this cause hath He all names, in that they are one Father's. And for this cause hath He himself no name, in that He is Father of all" (*Corp. Herm.* V, § 10). So Seneca calls Jupiter "ruler and guardian of all, soul and spirit of the world, lord and fashioner of this work, for whom every name is fitting; if you wish to call it fate, you will not err . . . if you wish to call it providence, you will speak correctly . . . if you wish to call it nature, you will not err . . . if you wish to call it world, you will not make a mistake" (*nat. quaest.* II, 45).[19]

It is completely wrong to see in this Hellenistic concept of the world only a system of abstract principles and to understand the deity only as a principle of reason. This view of the world is determined much more by an ardent wonder, ascending even to ecstasy, about the living powers of the universe.[20] The deity is a living power that is therefore praised with ancient, holy attributes: "Greetings, most glorious of the immortals, of many names, almighty Zeus, ruler of nature, you who govern the universe according to law." Cleanthes' *Hymn to Zeus* begins in this way.[21] Thus even in the concept of world-law, as late as the Hellenistic period, the ancient power of the political understanding of existence, though freed from its concrete political associations, is never quite extinguished by a view of the world and God dominated by the ideas of individualism and cosmopolitanism. Even the "world" is considered under the concept of "city," and in the law that governs, binds, leads, rules the universe the idea of the political order of human existence lives on.[22]

The constant efforts of Philo to contest the identity of the Creator with the creation and to overcome pantheism in the development of the concept of God and the description of the genuine knowledge of God need not concern us here. They themselves live from the presuppositions of a Greek understanding of existence. As a result, his doctrine of the logos is a thoroughgoing dialectical ontology that moves between pantheism and dualism,[23] and the only manner of knowledge that contrasts with the "from below—upwards," ascending "knowledge," is the ecstatic vision.[24]

However, this still does not sufficiently describe the context of the propositions of Hellenistic theology which are important for the understanding of Rom. 1.19ff. It is disclosed only in the Stoic statement that man comes to himself in the knowledge of God and of the law: "whoever will not obey the law flees from himself and denies human nature" (Cicero, *de republ.* III, 33), for it is the essence of men, that "they do not linger away from and outside of the divine . . ., but come into existence in it, even more grow together with it and adhere to it in every way" (Dion of Prusa XII, 28).[25] "For we Thine off-spring are, and all created things that live and move on earth receive from Thee the image of the One" (Cleanthes' *Hymn to Zeus*, line 4f.). That means that man shares in the essence of deity. The microcosm of his life corresponds to the macrocosm of the universe. The same "law" governs their life: "God is whatever you see, whatever motion you make" (Lucan, *Phars.* IX, 580). Because the law of nature's life is the meaning of man's own life, he therefore fulfills it when he fits his life into the great harmony of the universe.[26]

As is well known, this philosophical understanding of the law exerted a decisive influence on the apologetic argumentation of the Hellenistic-Jewish writings that have as their theme the demonstration of the agreement of the Mosaic law with the law of reason (Aristeas, IV Macc., Sibyll., Philo) and led to the resulting theory of the dependence of Greek philosophy on Moses' giving of the law that extends into early Christian apologetics.[27]

The basic identity of the knowledge of God, the world and existence is grounded in this understanding of the Law. Philo himself reflected on this connection in the introduction to his interpretation of the Law (*de opif. mundi* § 3):[28] "His exordium, as I have said, is one that excites our admiration in the highest degree. It consists of an account of the creation of the world, implying that the world is in harmony with the Law, and the Law with the world, and that the man who observes the Law is constituted thereby a loyal citizen of the world, regulating his doings by the purpose and will of Nature, in accordance with which the entire world itself is administered."[29] Thus in him the Stoic "to live comformably to nature" finds its "goal" in the fellowship with God (cf. the interpretation of Dt. 5.31 in *quod deus sit immut.* § 23ff. and Dt. 4.6, 7 in *de migr. Abrah.* § 56). That is the "noblest harmony" (*quod deus sit immut.* § 25) that is accomplished in the "confession of deeds throughout life"; and it is fulfilled precisely when man, receiving the "completed world" as God's gift, and bringing a sacrifice of praise to God anew, honors the Creator: "The harmony and tunefulness in this case is mightily attested by the words which say that they have offered their gift to God, that is, that they have duly honored the Existent by clearly acknowledging that this universe is His gift. For it says in words most agreeable to the truth of things, 'what a man found, this he offered as a gift'" (*de ebr.* § 117f.). In this sense, which connects the Stoic "confession"[30] with the Old

Testament meaning of the term as the confession of grateful praise, the confessor is the symbol of the highest manner of attainable existence for the soul who leaves behind the representatives of the lower steps of knowledge that only lead to the consummation.[31] The knowledge of God, the world and human existence thus find their unity and lead man to a blissful, hidden life in laws of nature given by the providential deity: "He that has begun by learning these things with his understanding rather than with his hearing, and has stamped on his soul impressions of truths so marvellous and priceless, both that God is and is from eternity . . . will lead a life of bliss and blessedness, because he has a character moulded by the truths that piety and holiness enforce" (de opif. mundi § 172; cf. also § 171).[32]

It follows naturally from this self-contained view that idolatry and immoral life are the results of irrational and deficient knowledge of God. This favorite theme in the late Jewish literature also has its antecedent in the Hellenistic critique of religion.[33] Thus, the goal of philosophical reflection and religious teaching is to lead man out of the fog of this ignorance back into the right knowledge of the divine world and of himself. For futile and vain is the effort of fools "who do not want to hear and know of the all-governing law of God; senseless and inconstant do they chase here and there" (line 23ff.), pulled by their folly into agitated, pitiful fervor. So we read Cleanthes' *Hymn to Zeus,* which therefore ends with the prayer: "Therefore all-giving Zeus, clouded in darkness, powerful as lightning, save men from their miserable foolishness; banish them, O Father, from their souls and let them acquire reason, with which you rule all in justice, that we, so honored by you, return to you the honor, for there is nothing higher for mortals and for gods than, as is proper always, to praise the all-governing law" (line 32ff.).

It is known well enough how closely Rom. 1.18ff. touches especially the motifs and thought-pattern of the Wisdom of Solomon[34] (ch.12, 13), and that the parallels in question are to be found side by side with the Pauline ideas about the knowledge of God from his works that reveal him as Creator and Lord and about the responsibility of the Gentiles, the foolishness of their idolatry and the judgment of God on the Gentiles occurring in the idolatry itself.

III

Paul speaks the language of this Hellenistic-Jewish apologetics, yet it would be wrong to call Rom. 1.18–3.20 an apologetic excursus. The section is not an apology but an accusation. In this direction it differs terminologically and conceptually from the parallel literature. The missionary-apologetic sermon of Hellenistic and Jewish character aims at awakening the knowledge of God from a look at the world, for in this knowledge man finds his destiny. Therefore, it seeks to displace "ignorance" and to disclose to its hearers the nature and rule of the deity on the basis of man's concern and of what he basically already knows. Thus apologetic and pedagogical motifs are united in the development of that which is every man's overwhelming knowledge, and in an appeal to cease to obscure this knowledge from himself. So the thoroughgoing presupposition in the Gentile and Hellenistic doctrine of God is this, that the knowledge of God, because it stands in agreement with the reasonable understanding of the world open to every man, presents an open possibility from which no one is excluded.

Paul alters this idea completely, not by contesting the knowledge of God but by understanding it radically. He does not understand it as an open possibility closed to no one, but as the reality under which the whole world in fact stands. Not the "ignorance of God" but the knowledge of God is the sign of the ungodly world. They have the truth of God, albeit as those who "suppress the truth by wickedness" (v. 18); they know him, even if they have not proved this knowledge (1.28). But the presence of the revelation (1.19), the boundlessness of "knowing God" (v. 21) prevails and gives to the world its profile. The natural revelation of God is not finished with the sinful fall of man, so that it is now a futile remembrance, a fruitless conceptual possibility; but it is the present basis for the inexcusableness of man (v. 20). For the sake of the reality of this knowledge of God, man is in a lost, impossible situation.

Thus in detail, too, Paul's progression of thought runs very differently from the parallel texts under consideration. The question of how the knowledge of God occurs does not concern him further. In the philosophical-religious literature of the surrounding world it is a cardinal question and it is answered in long discussions in terms of the "analogy of being": "For from the greatness and beauty of created things comes a corresponding perception of their creator" (Wisdom 13.5). "If through delight in the beauty of these things men assumed them to be gods, let them know how much better than these is their Lord, for the author of beauty created them. And if men were amazed at their power and working, let them perceive how much more powerful is he who formed them" (Wisdom 13.3f.).[35]

Paul does not have this reflection about the connection between creation and creator that seeks to awake man's reason through comparisons, chains of reasoning, and paradoxical formulae. That creation is the relevation of the Creator is not based in the affirmation that the "world" itself[36] is God's "image," but in the fact that God has willed it so. The addition "because God has shown it to them" (v. 19), tautological from the standpoint of a Greek understanding of the world, is in no way superfluous for Paul. From the outset he points to the freedom and majesty of God. Thus a description of the nature of God, in which an ascending wisdom issues from a viewing of the world "by comparison" or "negation," is not to be found in Paul. What is revealed to man in creation is that God is the invisible, eternal, acting and demanding Creator.[37]

This knowledge of God is not reserved for the wise, but is open to all since the creation of the world. Because of it, men are guilty. Very characteristic is the uncertain fashion in which Wisdom 13.6f. decides the question whether the godless world can be said to be guilty. The mistake of the Gentiles, in so far as they have not fallen victim to a foolish idolatry, is basically nothing other than an error. Men with their knowledge were entirely on the right track, but, of course, they have not consistently and singularly pursued it to the end. In the reckoning a fatal error has crept in for them. They stopped too soon. Being close to the goal, they thought they were at the goal. Thus they have pinned the honor of the deity to the creature, and this, of course, is inexcusable in view of the wisdom with which they have investigated the world. Their wisdom should have made it possible to reach the Lord of the world. Paul, on the other hand, does not trouble to trace this failure in the course of knowledge that in itself is right, but then unfortunately at a certain place erringly leads to "ignorance," because he does not see the basis of godlessness in the error of a right knowledge of God but in an abysmal failure of man in view of the revelation of God that now, as ever, stands over him and judges him. This mistake marks mankind as a whole. Man has denied his obligation of obedience to God, not thanked him, not glorified him, and thus turned away from the ground of his existence. That is true precisely because of the unlimited validity of "knowing God" in view of the fact that men have the truth of God even in unrighteousness and in the form of the lie (vv. 18, 25).

Thus Paul frees the concepts and arguments that he takes from contemporary non-Christian philosophy and theology from the pre-suppositions of Greek thought, and the sense in which he uses them becomes entirely different.[38] The knowledge of God as question and accessible possibility does not concern him. What concerns him, rather, is the question whether this knowledge is personal (1.28), whether the truth of God remains truth and its power is acknowledged (1.18, 25). Thus what concerns him in Rom. 1.18ff. has nothing to do with the disclosure of the divine being, but with the uncovering of human existence. This existence is basically wrong because men have not thanked and praised God. Therefore, their hearts are subjected to futile ideas and the darkness of their senseless heart (1.21).

Once more the meaning of this judgment can be clarified through a comparison with the parallel texts. Paul's sentence, "knowing God . . . they became futile in their thinking," appears to be contradictory. How can Paul in the premise ascribe to men the knowledge of God and at the same time say that their thoughts are nothing and their wisdom foolishness (v. 22)? Can, then, the "thoughts" be something other than the development of the knowledge of God? And is it not therefore more appropriate to say with Wisdom (13.1): "For all men who were ignorant of God were foolish by nature"? However, Paul abides by the "knowledge of God" because it is not nullified even in the conceit and vanity of men and man has not ceased to be God's creature. Because man does not want to be God's creation, now therefore knowledge and thinking are sundered. Man should have offered himself in thanks and praise and devoted himself to the eternal power and deity of the Creator. But now his "thoughts," loosed from the foundation of an obedient, thankful, worshipping subjection, have become the means by which he seeks to become as powerful as God. He has exalted himself *above* God and begun to think *about* God. In this, the relationship between Creator and creature is inverted, and the vanity, darkness and foolishness of man is sealed.

Man's bungled possibility of praise and thankful devotion to the Creator should have been the deed through which he was basically to find the destiny of his creaturely existence. Here, too, Paul is clearly different from Philo. Like Paul, Philo, as the passages cited above show,[39] also discusses the connection between the knowledge of God and honoring of God. For Philo, however, praise is the last attainable step to which man can raise himself. Therefore, the "praising mode of life"[40] reaches its goal in ecstasy: "For indeed the very word denoting confession (of praise) vividly portrays the acknowledgment that takes a man out of himself and offers itself up to God" (*leg. alleg.* I, § 82). The confessor is "immaterial and incorporeal"; therefore in Ex. 28.17f. the color of the ruby is assigned to Judah, to the "praising mode of life" ("for he is permeated by fire in giving thanks to God, and is drunk with a sober drunkenness," *leg. alleg.* I, § 84). For Paul, "giving thanks" and "glorifying" has another meaning. It is not the "mind's" last possibility of completion in ecstatic ascent, but the acceptance of creaturely existence in obedient, thankful subjection under the Creator. It is the practical confirmation of the knowledge of God in the acknowledgment of the Creator that basically determines the total man.[41]

In the refusal of this obedience and in the foolishness of the autonomous, vain thinking released as a result, the religion of man takes shape. It is the formation of the anti-divine revolt of mankind.[42] To a great extent, the folly of this activity was already a matter of concern to the Hellenistic critique of religion. As is well known, its arguments about the origin of myth and the notion of gods move with a tenacious stereotype through the fields of Jewish and Christian apologetics like a shallow river.[43] Using common rationalistic or philosophical arguments, the criterion by which this critique of popular religion decides is entirely the principle of reason. Before it the gods of the people demonstrate themselves to be empty illusions.[44] In this it is very characteristic that Stoics, beginning with the same principle, found positive access to popular religions because the gods are nothing else than epiphenomena of the one divine nature.[45] Accordingly, there was a concern for a maintenance or restoration of national religion on political or pedagogical grounds. Here negative and positive attitudes toward religion stem from the same basis.

Certainly in Rom. 1.23 Paul also intends that every man is to be able to understand his words. The irrationality of pagan idolatry does not become less clear from what he says. And yet the execution of his judgment is completely different. He does not conduct the argument for the purpose of bringing man to reason, thereby to show him how he can find his way back to the true God about whom the "world," "mind" and "conscience" give information. For religion for Paul is not a foolish and miserable possibility for which man unknowingly decides, but a reality in which the natural man is grounded. It is not the manner in which his error appears but the result of his mistake. It had to happen this way.[46] Now because God was refused the "glory,"[47] religiosity becomes the determining factor of the worldview. "The turning away of the world from the revealed God to itself deepens to become the apotheosis of the world . . . the illusion of wisdom ends in the grotesqueness of barbaric and Hellenic idols."[48] This inversion of creation and Creator—the exaltation of the creation to deity and the degradation of the deity to the creation of man—is the lie in which men have inverted God's truth (v. 25). The anarchy of their moral life is also based on this. In their enthusiasm, the ungodly world becomes a horrid place of unbridled passions that upset all of God's order.[49]

This event is not a natural process of change in which God's truth and law are submerged; rather, this truth remains over the world, and for men their sin is not eased in that the knowledge of God is denied to them. "If the world no longer obeys God, it thus obeys itself as God. In this 'as God', it reveals its knowledge about the commandment" (Schlier). However, this persevering pointer to the unquenchable truth[50] is, as we saw, no offering of a saving anchor. For man, loosing himself from God, is subject to himself, and this godlessness and subjection is the situation in which God himself as judge holds him ("therefore God gave them up," v. 24, cf. vv. 26, 28). *Since God executes his judgment over men, the possibility of an autonomous life, chosen with a measure of freedom, is actually the constraint allotted to them by the brazen necessity of a powerless death.* Men are established in the vanity of their thoughts, the darkness of their foolish hearts, the inversion of their religion, the error of their passions.[51]

Therefore, this is precisely the reason for the question, what sense there is in speaking of the revelation of God in creation as still always occurring, of the revealed nature of his law,[52] of knowledge about the legitimacy of the judgment of death on sin (v. 32). The numerous parallels, stretching over the entire section of 1.18–32, themselves definitely show that Paul is of the opinion that everyone could understand this view, although no one is excepted from the affirmation that "their thoughts are vain, their senseless hearts are darkened." Is it not therefore justified to ascribe to Rom. 1.18ff. a pedagogical or propaedeutic purpose, and not to understand the expressions about the subjection of men literally, but only as a penetrating expression of the terror of a senseless, vain life, against which one must guard himself, or from which one should free himself?

To do so would be to misunderstand Paul's words completely. If

Paul speaks to man as he does in order that he may know about God's creative power, his law, the folly of idolatry, the sacrilege of a deification of the world, the error of the moral life and the legitimacy of the death sentence which comes as a consequence, he is saying that this knowledge does not represent a solution for him at all. Rather, it seals his lostness. Thus, the all-pervading intention of his statements and their difference from the parallel texts becomes fully clear. Therefore, Rom. 1.18ff. is not an apologetic and pedagogical discussion, because *the intention of the Apostle is not to infer God's being from the world, but to uncover the being of the world from God's revelation; not to prove the revelation of God before the judgment of the world, but to unveil the judgment of God over the world revealed in the law.*

IV

Without question Paul has the Gentiles in view in the first chapter, although he speaks about "man."[53] Correspondingly, he begins the section 2.1ff., directed to the Jews, with the address, "O man, whoever you are," which is at first still puzzling.[54] Thus right from the beginning he joins the two, not, of course, in a vague generality but in what they both are as those who stand responsibly before God. Therefore Paul does not seek a formula by which both sides could be understood, a characteristic feature which they both have in common, but he speaks to them about what they both are. So in ch. 1–3 he speaks *ad hominem* about the judgment of God and introduces it by the insight "For God shows no partiality" (2.11).

Now, of course, he can speak still more clearly and more sharply, for the knowledge about the responsibility of man before God's judgment, which in ch. 1 Paul has summoned from the natural consciousness of the Gentiles, is preserved for the Jews in definite and clear knowledge about God's judgment. So he closes the section about the Gentiles with a reference to the judgment ("Though they know God's decree that those who do such things deserve to die"), which every Jew as a knower of the divine law concedes to him (note the clarification of the expression of 1.32 in 2.2, "We know that the judgment of God rightly falls upon those who do such things"), and turns his knowledge of law and judgment against him. In this way he begins his call for repentance to the Jews (vv. 3ff.). Here it is important to see that initially Paul still has no interest in a dispute about the law, but that he presents to the Jews in sharp, simple

antitheses the same "either-or" in the relation between deed and
reprisal from the idea of judgment (vv. 6ff.) as he did from the
description of human sin to the Gentiles.[55] For the law of the Jews
and the law of the Gentiles is one, although it is manifested to them in
different ways[56]—not as a rational system of certain virtues but as the
norm of God's judgment before which Gentiles and Jews are neither
excused as ignorant nor privileged and protected as knowledgeable.
Thus, only after Paul has questioned the Jews to their face as those
who stand under the law before God's judgment does he examine the
law in terms of individual commandments (2.21ff.). Only after he has
compelled his opponent to look at "what is secret" (cf. also the connection between "He is a Jew who is one inwardly" in 29 and the
general "the secrets of men" in 16!) by the question about his standing
in God's judgment does he fully disarm him and take from him any
superiority as seen in human perspective ("to be better off," in 3.9).[57]
That by which God distinguishes the Jew ("advantage," 3.1)
changes nothing. The promises which are given to the "circumcised"
and to which God remains faithful seal, rather, the complete opposition of the "faithfulness of God" and the "faithlessness" of men
(3.3).

In the imaginary discussion of 3.1ff., the Apostle once more rejects
the speculation of the Jew about law and promise with repeated
reference to the judgment, and thus rejects the attempt of the Jew
to bypass his own situation as that of a sinner under God's law and
promise through theological reflection. The Jew argues: the meaning
of the law definitely must be a different one from that established by
Paul. It surely is impossible that the promises of God could exist in
opposition to the conduct of man and his truth live from our lies.
Otherwise as a necessary result one would have to establish the
principle: "Let us do evil that good may come" (3.8). Thus the law
must exhibit a correspondence with the promises, and since the
promises are given to us, our conduct must be judged in a different
way from that of Paul. Paul only puts the counter-question about the
judgment (3.6) and stops the discussion ("their condemnation is just"
in 3.8), since perhaps a studied counter-questioning would still not
silence it (Why am I still being condemned as a sinner? v. 7).

Both Gentiles and Jews under the law are subject to God's judgment (3.19), for they have made his revelation an occasion for a view
of the world and of God,[58] and have not perceived it obediently as
God's word directed to them. The Gentiles have done so in that they

denied God, conferred on creation the glory of God, and exchanged
the tie to the Creator with slavery to their own passions. The Jews
have done so in that they have converted the revelation of God given
to them into a proud privilege, that it should empower them to stand
before the world as the "blessed possessors" and to endure God's
judgment as those who could compare themselves advantageously
with the world. In teaching them to understand this situation from
what they both know,[59] Paul lets them hear the testimony of the law
that silences everyone and lets them recognize their own depravity
(3.19ff.). The "knowledge" by which Gentiles and Jews understand
themselves and which Paul does not dispute with them, but which he
brings under the law, no longer has the function of disclosing to man
the being of God, exalting him and making him happy, but that of
enclosing him in the lostness of his sin.[60]

Thus the section 1.18–3.20 is a large unit. The reality of their life is
disclosed to Gentiles and Jews from the perspective of their own
knowledge as lostness before God's judgment. If one notes how Paul
in the first part frees the natural understanding of God and the world
from its Greek presuppositions through specific Jewish terms and
thoughts, and again in the second part bursts the boundaries of the
Jewish understanding of law and judgment through the reference to
the law that the Gentiles know, a comprehensive characterization of
the entire section results: Paul forces the natural understanding of
God's revelation, the Gentile-religious understanding of the "world,"
into the clarity of the knowledge of the divine will given to the Jew.
In this way, he places the Gentiles under the reality of the eternal,
judging God. Similarly, he frees the Jewish understanding of God's
law from the enclosure of theological certainty and places it under the
simple, inescapable, unmistakable and natural testimony of conscience
that shuns all theological evasions, thereby placing it before the
abysmal reality of disobedient man seeking himself, subject to his
own pride and sin.

v

Rom. 1.18–3.20 is the penetrating accusation that "all are under sin"
(3.9, cf. 10ff.). Paul has aroused the understanding of this circum-
stance by turning the knowledge of God given to Gentiles and Jews
against them and intensifying it to a self-knowledge in view of God's
judgment. Thus he has made possible the insight that God has the
right to declare the sentence of judgment and has developed the

basis for what he proclaimed in the introduction to the entire section: "For the wrath of God is revealed from heaven . . . For what can be known about God is plain to them."[61] The existence of God's revelation over the world is the rightful basis for his being revealed in the wrath of judgment.

If now we ask again the question which was raised at the beginning, about the relationship between the revelation of God's wrath and the revelation of his righteousness, it appears to produce a dilemma for the understanding. Surely the "revelation" of God's righteousness in the gospel means that this now becomes an eschatological event. Its revelation is an event that changes the ages. Is the revelation of God's wrath in the same sense a present eschatological event that has not happened before? Apparently against this understanding is the fact that in Rom. 1–3 Paul has dealt with realities that always have given the lost world its profile and that God's punitive judgment on it is not happening now for the first time. On the one hand, the judgment of God is always occurring (1.24, 26, 28). On the other hand, it is as much as ever in the future (2.5ff.). Therefore, nowhere in ch. 1–3 do we find descriptions of sudden events of judgment now breaking in, as the apocalyptic writings like to depict them. Paul discloses no apocalyptic mysteries, but deals with a reality about which he can address Gentiles and Jews. But does that mean that God's wrath on Gentiles and Jews is recognizable only now? In that case, the same tenses in vv. 17 and 18 would certainly be understandable, but the sense of "to be revealed" would be different in each case. In the second instance it would have lost its character as event.

Thus it would seem that one must either give up the same meaning of "is revealed" in 1.17 and 18 in order to save the same meaning of the tenses—in v. 17 it would mean "come to completion," in v. 18 "become recognizable"—or one must surrender the same meaning of the tenses in order to validate the character of the revelation in both as event. That means that the righteousness of God becomes event "now," but that on the other hand the wrath of God occurs perpetually in the world. Neither possibility of understanding appears to me to do Paul justice. That he uses the eschatological terms "wrath of God" and "to be revealed" and ties 1.18 so closely to 1.17 apparently means that only now in the sign of the gospel is the lost world moved into the light of the "final event," to which the previous history was directed, in spite of God's (perpetually hidden) "forbearance" (3.26). The world can be addressed on the basis of the signs of its lostness and thereby also on the basis of the thrust that its history has received under the judging hand of God. But it must be told—precisely with the eschatological word of 1.18— that its imprisonment in sin must be so radically understood that the history of the world already lies, so to speak, in the glare of the fires of the last day. This is not to be developed from the presuppositions of its knowledge, however much, in the opinion of the Apostle, Gentiles and Jews could understand it.

By itself, in the light of the previous revelation of God in creation and law, the world cannot announce that its time has come. The possibility for this is disclosed only through the "now" that has dawned over the world in the revelation of God's "righteousness" in Jesus Christ.[62]

This "now" with which Paul repeatedly marks the antitheses of lostness and salvation[63] is the eschatological Now of salvation history, that puts an end to human history under the "law" (I Cor. 7.29; 10.11; Rom. 13.11 and others) and ushers in a new age. It is God's grace that he does not bring mankind to the law's end in any other way than in Jesus Christ, who bears the death and curse that comes to man as the "end of the law" (cf. Rom. 3.24f.; 5.6ff.; 10.4; I Cor.1.30; II Cor. 5.21; Gal. 3.13 and others). God lets it be said to the world first through the messengers of the new covenant that the law kills, because it is in the order of things that a cover lies over the "old covenant" which veils the fatal "glory" of God for man until it is removed in Christ (II Cor. 3.7–16). Therefore, Paul calls the time before the revelation of Christ the time of God's forbearance (Rom. 3.26).

Now, however, that the "righteousness" of God is revealed "apart from law" (Rom. 3.21), the cover is also removed from the law and the "law" as the power of death over sinful mankind is revealed. The prison that now is opened (Gal. 3.22f.) releases sinners subjected to death. God speaks the word of grace to them by presenting them with his "righteousness." That means at the same time that he does not let them die their own death but lets them die with Christ, dying to the law and the world in order to live for him (Gal. 3.19f.; Rom. 5.8ff.; 6.5ff. and others).

From this it is understandable how closely the expressions about the revelation of righteousness and of God's wrath belong together, and that the "for" in 1.18 is not a "simple transition particle"[64] but explicitly establishes what it said in 1.16f. about "salvation." Of course, it is correct that this "salvation" does not simply have the negative sense of rescue—in other words of just escaping—but at the same time the positive meaning of healing.[65] In spite of this the former meaning remains completely in force, that the "righteousness" given to believers preserves them before the "wrath" of God, a wrath now already revealed to the lost world. Rom. 5.9 says this explicitly in view of the last judgment of God: "Since, therefore, we are now justified by his blood, much more shall we be saved by him from the wrath."[66]

The revelation of this saving "righteousness" of God is an eschatological event that is accomplished in the "Now" of salvation history. To this same hour is bound the revelation of his wrath from heaven over all the unrighteousness of men. Because he lets his "righteousness" be made known, all the "wickedness" of men also comes to light.[67] In that he lets it be said to the world that in its sin it is subjected to the "wrath" of God, that there is no righteousness in it and that he alone is righteous in the dispute into which it entered with him (3.4), at the same time he lets the world be told that he has disclosed this "righteousness" of his to believers. Thus the revelation of redemption happens at the same time, too: "This was to show God's righteousness, because in his divine forbearance he had passed over former sins," and at the same time "it was to prove at the present time that he himself is righteous." The final sentence summarizes both: "that he himself is righteous and that he justifies him who has faith in Jesus" (Rom. 3.25f.).

NOTES

[1] The basic ideas of this essay were given in a lecture in a theological course in Posen in March 1935. The study appeared in *ZNW* 34 (1935), pp. 239–62. Here the exegesis of 1.17 and 18 is not insignificantly reworked and supplemented. From more recent literature I mention only M. Pohlenz, "Paulus und die Stoa," *ZNW* 42 (1949), pp. 69ff.

[2] Following earlier exegetes, thus again A. Pallis, *To the Romans* (1920), p. 40: "briefly expressed for 'for it is revealed in it (= the gospel) that there will wrath'."

[3] "The meaning of the passage appears, then, to be as follows: the righteousness of God is entirely from faith, yet growth does not make it more real but only gives it greater clarity." (Luther, *Römerbrief* II, ed. J. Ficker (1908), pp. 15.6ff. ET by Wilhelm Pauck in *Luther: Lectures on Romans* (Library of Christian Classics, Vol. XV) 1961, p. 19). Cf. also Bengel, *ad loc.*: "It speaks pure faith."

[4] "An expression of divine wrath takes place simultaneously and just as constantly" (p. 88). Zahn understands by this the "innumerable evil and pain" in world catastrophes and in the life of the individual, "wherein even the believer cannot recognize a proof of God's goodness as Creator."

[5] E. Weber, *Die Beziehungen von Röm. 1–3 zur Missionspraxis des Paulus;* Beitr. zur Förderung christliche Theologie IX, Heft 4, p. 38; cf. further A. Jülicher, in *Die Schriften des Neuen Testaments* II (1917³), *ad loc.*: "The revelation of wrath is not bound to a particular time."

[6] Cf. *An die Römer, HzNT* 8 (1933⁴), p. 40, and the argument of Schlatter with Ritschl about the same interpretation. A. Ritschl, *Die Christliche Lehre von der Rechtfertigung und Versöhnung* (1889³) II, p. 316, and A. Schlatter, *Der Glaube im NT* (1963⁵), pp. 325ff.

[7] Correspondingly Jülicher: "Indeed only God's wrath is unveiled . . .", where the inserted particle is apparently to express the general intelligibility of the assertion.

[8] Cf. K. Oltmanns, "Das Verhältnis von Röm 1.18–3.20 zu 3.21ff.," *Theol. Blätter* (1929), cols. 110ff.; this is also an excellent discussion of the history of the problem.

[9] Thus justifiably Schlier in *TWNT* I, p. 361, lines 20f., under *anoche* (ET, *TDNT* I, pp. 359f.).

[10] The term *dikaiosunē* ("righteousness") is used differently in vv. 25 and 26. It means primarily the covenant faithfulness of God, with which through the blood of Jesus he reconciles and restores the covenant, broken by the trespasses of past generations. Verse 26 first uses the term in the peculiar Pauline sense of the eschatological work of salvation that is no longer oriented to the idea of the covenant people. Thus justifiably E. Käsemann, *ZNW* (1950/1), pp. 150ff., to prove the thesis already supported and represented by R. Bultmann, *TNT*, p. 47 (ET, *NTT* I, pp. 46f.), with different terminological bases ("expiation" only here, "blood" always pointing back to phrases of the tradition), that Rom. 3.24f. is a proposition stemming from a Jewish-Christian tradition which Paul interprets in a new sense.

[11] Cf. the material and literature in Lietzmann, *op. cit.*, pp. 31ff.; a short survey of the various hypotheses in G. Kuhlmann, *Theologia naturalis bei Philon und bei Paulus* (Neutestamentliche Forschungen I, 7, 1930), p. 43, n. 1.

[12] The references are collected in such abundance that a few examples suffice: Pseudo-Aristotle, *de mundo*, ch. 6: ". . . the guide and father of all things, being invisible to all other reasoning . . . since having become invisible to every mortal he is perceived from their works." The proof follows in stereotyped fashion thus: "For none of the works of human art is self-made, and the highest art and knowledge is shown in this universe, so that surely it has been wrought by one of excellent knowledge and absolute perfection" (Philo, *de spec. legg.* I, § 35). For further material see among others E. Norden, *Agnostos Theos* (1913 = 1956⁴). pp. 24ff.; J. Kroll, *Die Lehren des Hermes Trismegistos* (1914), pp. 37ff.; H. Daxer, *Rom. 1.18–2.10 im Verhältnis zur spätjüdischen Lehrauffassung*, Rostock Dissertation (1914), pp. 37ff.; A. Fridrichsen, *ZNW* 17 (1916), pp. 161ff.; R. Bultmann, *ZNW* 29 (1930), pp. 172ff. and 188ff.; H. Lietzmann, *op. cit.*, pp. 31ff.; on Philo: G. Kuhlmann, *op. cit.*, pp. 17ff.

[13] "Others again who have had the strength through knowledge to envisage the Maker and Ruler of all have in common phrase advanced from down to up. Entering the world as into a well-ordered city . . ., struck with admiration and astonishment they arrived at a conception according with what they beheld, that surely all these beauties and this transcendent order has not come into being automatically but by the handiwork of an architect and world-maker; also that there must be a providence, for it is a law of nature that a maker should take care of what has been made. These, no doubt, are truly admirable persons and superior to the other classes. They have, as I said, advanced from down to up by a sort of heavenly ladder and by reason and reflection happily inferred the Creator from his works." (Philo, *de praem. et poen.* § 41–43n.). Cf. also *de opif. mundi* (see p. 53 above).

Therefore, physics culminates in the "word concerning gods . . . Therefore they tell the traditions of this in public celebration" (Chrysippus in Plutarch, *de Stoic. repugn.*, ch. 9, 1035 AB). Life according to the *nous*, that governs the phenomena of the *kosmos*, is the most perfect dedication: "Since life is a most perfect initiation in to these things and a ritual celebration of them, it should be full of tranquillity and joy" (Plutarch, *de tranq. animi* 20, 477 D).

[14] Xenophon, *Memorab.* IV, 13: ". . . you are content to praise and worship them because you see their works"; Marcus Aurelius, *pr. heaut.* XII, 28 (in Norden, *op. cit.*, pp. 28f., compared with Acts 14.23). "Therefore those who render worship for the sake of the gods set out three forms for us" (*Aetius Plac.* I, 6, *Stoic. vet. frgm.* II, 1009, edited by H. F. A. Arnim, 1964); Philo, see p. 53 above.

[15] Cf. Daxer, *op. cit.*, pp. 15ff.; Lietzmann, *op. cit.*, on 1.23ff.; Kuhlmann, *op. cit.*, pp. 27f., and see above, p. 57.

[16] Plutarch, *de tranq. animi* 20 (477 C D); cf. Norden, *op. cit.*, p. 22.

[17] Cf. the equation: "the common law = the right word, coming through all things = Zeus" (Diog. Laert. VII, 88; Arnim, *op. cit.*, I, 162).

[18] Early Christian apologetics plays off this idea against the discrepancy between gods and laws in Greek mythology. Cf. Aristides, *Apol.* XIII, 7. J. Geffcken, *Zwei griechische Apologeten* (1907), pp. 20f. and 80.

[19] The atheistic and pantheistic definitions of the term *kosmos*, therefore, are not differentiated substantively at all. Cf. Arius Didymus in Eusebius, *Praep. Evang.* XV, 15: "The whole ordered world . . . with all its parts they call god, and say that he is one alone, and finite, and living, and eternal, and god: . . . the name world . . . also means the system compounded of heaven, and the air, and earth, and sea, and the natures contained in them; and again the name world means the dwelling-place of gods and men" (Arnim, *op. cit.*, II, 528; ET by E. H. Gifford in *Eusebii Praep. Evang.*, Part III, 1903, p. 878). "In both instances the world is understood from itself as self-contained, self-powerful being. The deity is only the essence of the intellectuality of the world—but this in the sense of an impetus to itself—and thus becomes an exponent of its autonomy" (Kuhlmann, *op. cit.*, p. 30).

[20] Cf. the Fifth Hermetic Tract, "That the invisible god is displayed".

[21] Text in U. von Wilamowitz-Moellendorff, *Hellenist. Dichtung* II (1924), pp. 257ff.

[22] Cf. the passages in Arnim, *op. cit.* III, pp. 79ff. (esp. 327–39).

[23] Cf. on this G. Kuhlmann, *op. cit.*, pp. 9ff., and K. Staritz, *Augustins Schöpfungsglaube* (1931), pp. 23ff.

[24] Cf. Bultmann, "Untersuchungen zum Johannesevangelium," *ZNW* 29 (1930), pp. 181f., and G. Kuhlmann, *op. cit.*, pp. 20ff.

[25] Cited in Norden, *op. cit.*, pp. 18ff., in connection with Acts 17.27ff.

[26] Concerning man as microcosm, cf. Geffcken, *op. cit.*, on Aristides, *Apol.* VII, pp. 58f.

[27] Rabbinic Judaism was not able to make this universality of the law, which also was important to it, understandable from the subject itself. So men made use of legends and scribal theories to express the idea, which was also established in Rabbinism, that God had also given his law to the Gentiles and that they, too, had no excuse: through the theories about the six Adamitic and the seven Noahitic basic commandments and the legends about the four or seventy world languages in which the law was proclaimed on Sinai, or about the translation of the laws by Moses after receiving the tablets, which the Gentiles at once rejected. Cf. StrB III, pp. 36ff.

[28] For the connection of this interpretation of the work of creation to the biography of the patriarchs living before the giving of the Law and the exegesis of the

Law itself, cf. E. Schürer, *Geschichte des jüdischen Volkes im Zeitalter Jesu Christi* III (1909⁴), pp. 66off. (ET, *The Jewish People in the Time of Jesus Christ*, Second Division III, 1891, pp. 338ff.; the ET translates an earlier edition and thus does not follow exactly the 4th ed.).

²⁹ *Corp. Herm.* VIII also deals with this connection between God, the world and man.

³⁰ For the understanding of Stoic homology, cf. my essay, "*Homologia*, Zur Geschichte eines politischen Begriffes," *Hermes* 71 (1936), pp. 377ff.

³¹ Cf. *de ebr.* § 107f.; *leg. alleg.* I, § 80ff.–II, § 95; III, § 26.

³² The same sense of the honoring of the divine becomes clear in the characterization of the universe and of man in Dio Chrysost., *Or. I*, §42 (Arnim, *op. cit.* III, p. 82, No. 335): ". . . according to its common nature (sc. the totality's) and ours under one rule and ordered law and sharing its policy; which he who honours and protects also does nothing contrary to what is lawful and blessed and orderly, etc." Therefore *Corp. Herm.* V, § 10f., also ends the great view of the world with the hymn that includes the words: "For you are whatever I am, you are whatever I do, you are whatever I say. For you are all things and nothing else is what you are not."

³³ Cf. the abundant references in Daxer, *op. cit.*, pp. 17ff. Concerning the Hellenistic religious enlightenment, P. Wendland, *Die hellenistisch-römische Kultur* (1912²,³), pp. 106ff. and 140ff.

³⁴ Cf. Lietzmann, *op. cit.*, excursus on 1.25; Grafe, "Das Verhältnis der paulin. Schriften zur *Sapientia Salomonis*," *Theol. Abh. für Weizsäcker* (1892), pp. 253ff.; Norden, *op. cit.*, pp. 128ff. In opposition, Daxer, *op. cit.*, pp. 3ff.

³⁵ Similarly Pseudo-Aristotle, *de mundo*, ch. 6: "It is necessary to consider these things concerning God: strong power, decent beauty, immortal life, mightiest virtue, since having become invisible to every mortal nature he is perceived from their works."

³⁶ Cf. Kleinknecht, *TWNT* II, pp. 386ff. (ET, *TDNT* II, pp. 388ff.); esp. *Corp. Herm.* 8.2, 5.

³⁷ The numerous exegetical endeavours to find a series of characteristics that Paul could have summarized under "deity" (cf. Daxer, *op. cit.*, pp. 12ff.) do not therefore represent a Pauline concern.

³⁸ In this it becomes clear in detail that the section 1.18–32 shows not only the influences of Stoic philosophy (cf. the Hellenistic abstractions: "his invisible nature . . . clearly perceived, eternal power, deity, immortal, natural relations, mind, improper conduct," cf. also "do by nature what the law requires" in 2.14 and the list of vices in vv. 29ff. that show their Hellenistic origin; see Lietzmann, *op. cit.*, excursus on 1.31ff.) but also Old Testament terms and phrases: "wrath of God" (18), "senseless heart" (not "mind," v. 21), "the Creator" (not "artificer" as in Wisdom 13.1, or "maker" in 13.5 or similarly, v. 25); "ungodliness" and "wickedness" (18) perhaps are related to the two tablets of the Decalogue (thus Schlatter, *Gottes Gerechtigkeit*, 1935, p. 49); Jer. 2.5 is suggested in 1.21, Ps. 106 (105).20 in 1.23; v. 25 ends euphemistically with a Jewish doxology (cf. Lietzmann and StrB, *ad loc.*); also, the Greek concept of the "conscience" in 2.15 receives in Paul a non-Greek, eschatological function. On the term "conscience" cf. M. Kähler, *Das Gewissen* I (1878), pp. 216ff.; Norden, *op. cit.*, p. 136, n. 1; H. von Soden, "Sakrament und Ethik bei Paulus," now in *Urchristentum und Geschichte* I (1951), p. 242, n. 3.

³⁹ Cf. p. 53 above.

⁴⁰ Cf. *leg. alleg.* I, 82; II, 95; III, 26; *de plant.* 134ff.; *de mut. nom.* 136; *de congress. erud. grat.* 177; *de somn.* I, 37.

⁴¹ Cf. Bultmann, *TWNT* I, p. 705, lines 7ff., under *gignōskein* (ET, *TDNT* I, p. 705).

[42] "Does Paul think of religion as the deed of mankind that makes it guilty? Yes, for its religion is its fight against truth, its battle against God." Schlatter, *op. cit.*, p. 64.

[43] Cf. Geffcken, *op. cit.*, p. 6; Aristides, *Apol.*, ch. III (here the explicit citation of Rom. 1.25, of course with the un-Pauline introduction "not having known God . . ." line 4!); in addition, pp. 41ff., ch. XIII, and the commentary, pp. 76ff. Athenagoras, *Apol.* XVff., XXVI and p. 197; concerning euhemerism, pp. 317 and 322, footnotes (in addition, cf. Wisdom 14. 15ff.).

[44] Wisdom and foolishness are measured according to whether the knower has the right insight into the "reason" of all things. Thus Philo, *de ebr.*, §107ff.

[45] The passage cited above on p. 51 from Seneca, *quaest. nat.* II, 45, begins: "Nor yet did these ancient sages believe that the Jupiter we worship in the Capitol and the rest of the temples ever really hurled thunderbolts from his hand. They recognized the same Jupiter as we do, the guardian and ruler of the universe, etc." (ET by J. Clarke, *Physical Science*, London, 1910, p. 92). Cf. Wendland, *op. cit.*, pp. 110ff, 140ff., for further material.

[46] "Does he (sc. Paul) think of religion as its (sc. mankind's) punishment, as a bitter fate that they must suffer? Yes, for it forcefully enslaves peoples and immerses them in illusion" (Schlatter, *op. cit.*, p. 64). In addition H. Schlier, "Über die Erkenntnis Gottes bei den Heiden," *EvTh* (1935), pp. 22ff.

[47] Inappropriate though it is in 1.20 to reflect about the attributes of God that perhaps come into question, nevertheless it may be justified to include under the "glory of the immortal God" (v. 23) the designations of God which Paul takes from the testimony of creation (v. 20), and whose revelation is not removed even by the error of mankind. The antithesis "of the immortality of God" and the "mortality of man" is, indeed, directly connected to "his eternal power and deity" (20), just as "the glory" (23) is to "did glory (honor)" (21).

[48] Schlier, *op. cit.*, p. 22.

[49] Cf. my essay: *Gesetz und Schöpfung im Neuen Testament* (1934), pp. 17f., and esp. the interpretation of Schlier, *op. cit.*, pp. 23ff.

[50] Verse 28: "And since they did not see fit to acknowledge God." Verse 32: "Though they know God's decree."

[51] On the idea of the correspondence between sin and retribution, cf. E. Klostermann, *ZNW* 32 (1933), pp. 1ff.; J. Jeremias, *ZNW* 45 (1954), pp. 119ff.

[52] That God's Law is known to the Gentiles, indeed that there are Gentiles who naturally do the works of the law, Paul says explicitly in 2.14–16. The passage is not correctly understood if by a comparison with 1.18ff one gains the knowledge that Paul does not mean quite so absolutely and generally the lostness of which ch. 1 speaks; certainly he knows how to speak about Gentile morality in an entirely different fashion. There the interpretation is subjected to the misleading question of how far Paul has judged the moral circumstances of mankind, especially of the Gentile world, optimistically or pessimistically. The question to which 1.18ff and 2.14–16 are subjected in the same way is, however, only about the judgment of God. The assertions that the work commanded by the law is written in the heart for the Gentiles, and that they even do these works of the law, "serve an entirely different purpose: that works of the Law can be demanded also from the Gentiles, that the judgment according to works is always just" (Schlier, *op. cit.*, p. 13). To reflect further about the quality of their works on the basis of Rom. 1.18ff. (as Schlier does, pp. 15f.) is therefore not allowed. The intention of the passage is only to prove that God's law is known to the whole world and is concretely attested, and that therefore his judgment falls upon a responsible mankind. The conscience, according to 2.15f., has just this (non-Greek) eschatological function of confirming God's "law" by making it present in the light of his judgment. In his conscience

man experiences in his deeds that he is not finally disclosed to himself, that he "is not what he wants to be" (v. Soden); hence the discord of his thoughts, which means that he stands and falls according to the judgment of God. Cf. the excellent, short characterization of "conscience" in v. Soden, *op. cit.*, p. 242, n. 3. It should also be noted that these remarks of Paul on the attestation of the law in the conscience among the Gentiles are found in the section direction to the Jews; thus they demonstrate to them that God lets them experience their responsibility concretely, and they aim precisely at showing to them: "you do not have the works!" (K. Oltmanns, *op. cit.*, col. 113.)

[53] Schlier justifiably notes: "That has its basis in the fact that this expression about the knowledge of God of the Gentiles is an expression about the paganism of man generally. Paul naturally wrote these sentences in context with the Gentiles already in view, but initially he wrote them just to maintain that which they and all already are" (Schlier, *op. cit.*, p. 11).

[54] It should not be contested that in 2.1ff. the Apostle, in fact, has the Jews especially in mind; cf. Lietzmann, *ad loc.*

[55] Ch. 1.21ff. thus contains first of all the obvious correspondence between sin and damnation in the concrete life of the Gentiles, according to which the last judgment of God is accomplished; 2.9f. brings the positive supplementation in the description of this order of judgment. The connection of both sections, 1.18ff. and 2.1ff., is marked by the use of similar terms: "wrath," 1.18, 2.5, 8; "wickedness," 1.18, 2.8; "truth," 1.18, 2.8; "without excuse," 1.20, 2.1; "immortal"—"immortality," 1.23, 2.7; "is revealed"—"revelation," 1.18, 2.5; "law," 2.12ff.; cf. also "truth"—"lie," 1.25, and "truth"—"falsehood," 3.7.

[56] Cf. my essay, *Gesetz und Schöpfung*, pp. 15f.

[57] As it is celebrated, for instance, in Wisdom 15.1ff. (Lietzmann, *op. cit.*, p. 38); numerous further references in StrB III, pp. 126ff., 139ff.

[58] As we saw, the parallel texts compared above definitely aim just at this.

[59] Cf. further the identity or correspondence of the terms: "they knew God," 1.21 (also 28, 32); "claiming to be wise," 1.22; "they did not see fit," 1.28; "to acknowledge God," 1.28; "you know his will," 2.18; "you call yourself a Jew," 2.17; "you approve what is excellent," 2.18; "having in the law the embodiment of knowledge and truth," 2.20. In addition, see n. 55.

[60] The agreement between the description of the experience of the Gentile under the testimony of creation and that of the Jew under the law becomes particularly clear from ch. 7.9–25. Just as creation bears the divine revelation even beyond a godless humanity, so the law remains holy, righteous and good, even though it gives rise to sin (7.12f.). Just as the Gentile, striving for life in a divinely transfigured world, sinks into a chaos marked out by death precisely because he has not responded to the knowledge of God in creation with thankfulness and obedience, so, too, the Jew learns under the law the enigma of lost, unredeemed existence. The law does not bring him security of life; he seeks life and finds death; despite his zeal, death is all that he brings about (7.13, 15). This is what man experiences, precisely because it is still always true for him: "his invisible nature . . . is clearly perceived (present tense) in the things that have been made", 1.20; and: "I of myself serve the law of God with my mind," 7.25 (cf. 7.21f.). But the *nous* does not show him, in the only terms that would make sense on Greek presuppositions, his link with God; it shows him that precisely because he cannot get free of the law, he has separated himself from God. Paul says of the man who consciously assents to God's law: "Wretched man that I am! Who will deliver me from this body of death?" (7.24). Paul expresses this contradiction, this dichotomy in which man has his existence as one who is lost under the law, by constant use of the word "I" (7.20–23). The thought that "this knowledge and joy in the law

serves as a comforting substitute to Paul for his lack of good works" (against this, rightly, Schlatter, *Der Glaube im Neuen Testament*, p. 327) is inherent to that exegesis which does not understand Paul's remarks in the light of the antithesis between "life" and "death," i.e. in the light of the divine judgment, but interprets it psychologically, along the lines of the "Platonic" approach (W. Bousset, *Kyrios Christos*, 1921², p. 123). But cf. Bultmann, "Rom. 7 und die Anthropologie des Paulus," *Imago Dei (Festschrift für G. Krüger)*, 1932, pp. 53ff. (ET, "Romans 7 and the Anthropology of Paul," in *Existence and Faith*, Shorter Writings of Rudolf Bultmann, 1960, pp. 147ff.). (On Rom. 7, cf. the essay, "Sünde, Gesetz und Tod," *DEdG*, pp. 51ff.; ET in this volume, pp. 87ff.)

61 The basis is to be related in this way (with Zahn, B. Weiss, Kuhl and others against Lietzmann).

62 On the relationship of both revelations cf. also W. Elert, *Der christliche Glaube* (1940), pp. 170ff.; R. Bultmann, *TNT*, p. 271 (ET, *NTT* I, pp. 275f.); W. Michaelis, "*Orgē*" in *TWNT* V, pp. 432f. (ET, *TDNT* V, pp. 431ff.). The question remains undiscussed in H. Schulte, *Der Begriff der Offenbarung im Neuen Testament* (1949).

63 Cf. Rom. 3.21, 26; 5.9; 6.22; 8.1; II Cor. 5.16; 6.2, etc.

64 Thus Lietzmann, *ad loc.*

65 Cf. Wagner, "*sōzein* und seine Derivate im NT," *ZNW* 6 (1905), pp. 205ff.

66 The fact that here, as also in I Thess. 1.10; 5.9; Rom. 2.5, 8 (and in the numerous passages that refer to the last judgment still to be expected), Paul sees the revelation of God's wrath in the future, does not change the fact that the event proclaimed in 1.18 also has an eschatological meaning; any more than "righteousness" as the object of hope impairs the eschatological meaning of the revelation of God's "righteousness" occurring now. That the world even now stands in the last event is indeed the eschatological meaning of the early Christian proclamation. It would be well to raise the problem especially from I Thess. (vv. 9f.!). The most recent monograph is H. Braun, *Gerichtsgedanke und Rechtfertigungslehre bei Paulus*, Untersuchungen zum NT 19 (1930).

67 In view of the lively theological discussion about the question of the natural knowledge of God, this connection is especially to be noted. It follows that there is no sense in speaking of the natural revelation of God in creation without the creation being understood as a witness of God's law; i.e. without the call to obedience of the creature over against the Creator being heard in it; and there is no sense in speaking of this law of God without saying that man under the law is a sinner; further, it is senseless to speak of this sin without saying that man is subject to it, and thus has no possibility to loose himself from it; and finally, it is not evangelical preaching when one preaches this judgment of God without saying that this preaching only occurs and is entrusted to the servant of the gospel because the righteousness from faith is opened in the gospel. This chain of sentences is to show how dangerous a certain "systematic" procedure is, by which one breaks out of an indestructible connection of individual sentences and uses them as *dicta probantia* for a theory that has grown from very different roots.

Additional literature: Cf. the more recent commentaries on Romans by C. H. Dodd (1949), O. Michel (1957²), O. Kuss (1957), F. J. Leenhardt (1957), C. K. Barrett (1957). Also A. Feuillet, "La connaissance de Dieu par les hommes d'après Rom. 1.28," *Lumière et Vie* 14 (1954), pp. 207ff.; W. Eltester, "Schöpfungsoffenbarung und natürliche Theologie im frühen Christentum," *NTS* 3 (1956), pp. 93ff.; H. Hommel, *Schöpfer und Erhalter* (1956); on 2.14f., G. Bornkamm, "Gesetz und Natur," in *SzAuU*; and on the entire section, "Glaube und Vernunft bei Paulus" in the same volume; ET, "Faith and Reason in Paul," in this volume.

V

BAPTISM AND NEW LIFE IN PAUL[1]

Romans 6

THE QUESTION ABOUT the relationship between baptism and new life is raised by the peculiar and apparently contradictory joining of indicative and imperative words, which is characteristic of the apostolic proclamation. By this we mean the joining of such expressions as those which speak of the redemption that has happened to believers and the admonitions which then call for a resolute fight against sin and a laying hold of the new life. If believers are separated from sin (Rom. 6.2), how can they then be admonished to separate themselves from sin (Rom. 6.12f.)? If they have put on Christ Jesus in baptism (Gal. 3.27), what then can the imperative "Put on the Lord Jesus Christ!" (Rom. 13.14) mean? Compare also Col. 3.3ff.: If they have died with Christ in baptism, how can they then be summoned: "Put to death therefore what is earthly in you"?—Does not the indicative take away the impact of the imperative, and does not the imperative limit the certainty and validity of the indicative?

The question is raised with special urgency, first because Paul can give the same full content to both indicative and imperative: you have died—therefore put to death; you have put on Christ—therefore put him on; "if we live in the Spirit, let us also walk in the Spirit" (Gal. 5.25). The expression that describes the redemption that has occurred is thus not limited to a modest beginning that must then be supplemented through the activity of man. The summons does not admonish the believers as it were to the very last mopping-up operation. Rather, it has a comprehensive intention. Then again, the question becomes important in that both indicative and imperative are solidly related to each other. The indicative establishes the imperative, and the imperative follows from the indicative with an absolute unconditional necessity—a necessity that is determined by what has happened to us through God's activity. Thus it does not simply stem from the painful discrepancy between theory and practice, ideal and reality, as has repeatedly been thought.

If we want to put the point very briefly, it can be stated in this way: The question that concerns us is raised by the "therefore" in Rom. 6.12. What is the meaning of this "therefore," that we find emphasized in the same way in Col. 3.5: "Put to death therefore what is earthly in you!"

If we immediately bear in mind this connection of Pauline expressions, all attempts to understand the Pauline antinomies by characterizing one of the two expressions as a kind of inconsistency are immediately excluded.[2] This is true whether, with Weinel, one puts the entire weight on the indicative, "that alone really corresponds to the moral religion of redemption" (*Biblische Theologie*, 4th ed. 1928, p. 257), because "from the experienced grace of God man can do nothing other than the good" (2nd ed. 1913, p. 330)—in which case the imperative must appear as a relapse into legalism (3rd ed. 1921, p. 322)—or whether one acknowledges that the true grasp of reality belongs to the imperative and characterizes the indicative, the theory of sinlessness, as a "heaven-storming idealism" (H. J. Holtzmann, *Neutestamentliche Theologie* II, 2nd ed. 1911, p. 164), or regards it as a bold anticipation of a condition "that in contrast to tenacious reality can be translated only slowly into the concrete morality of individuals" (Lüdemann).[3] Both types of attempts at a psychological explanation, which we do not want to explore further here, fail to do justice to the very definite bracket that joins both expressions of Paul firmly together.

I

We shall try to gain an understanding of the question that concerns us by a look at Rom. 6.1–10.[4] Rom. 6.11–14 directly combines proclamation and summons, but 6.11 itself is simply a consequence. What is its basis?

The thesis that 6.1–10 is concerned with reads: we are freed from the power of sin. This proposition certainly does not cross Paul's lips so obviously and easily as our edifying language, in which one is not allowed to weigh every word that is spoken and must always tacitly allow for the pathos of religious exuberance. But Paul has to maintain this proposition against another thesis which, as it first appears, initially has more to support it in features of the "reality" of life because it grants this "reality" and makes it bearable with a theologically illuminating argument. The question of 6.1 is not so absurd as we perhaps think: "Are we to continue in sin that grace may abound?" It has the legitimacy of a formal logic to support it, and appears to be the only possible consequence for the life and conduct of the believer that issues from Paul's own thesis, formulated in 5.20: if it is true that grace demonstrates its actual power nowhere else than in the area of sin, have we then anything else to do than by constant sinning to offer the opportunity for grace (the much misused *pecca fortiter*, sin bravely!) to prove its greatness? Precisely in contrast with all perfectionism and moralism, should it not be our good "Pauline" right to actualize and make evident, so to say repeatedly in practice, the dialectical relation between sin and grace? It is difficult to decide whether this consequence could be held against Paul by Jewish or Judaistic opponents as an objection to the danger of his message or whether a very real, robust libertinism comes to the surface here. It is probably neither the one nor the other. Rather, the Apostle wants to clarify a possible consequence that still constantly pursues and threatens faith "like a dark shadow" (E. Ellwein) with regard to the sole effectiveness of grace, even if it is not always formulated so precisely and consciously. It is a satanic possibility (cf. 3.8), theologically masked, as the devil acquiesces in a theology that perverts the justification of the sinner into a justification of sin (II Cor. 11.14f.; cf. Matt. 4.1ff.). Hence there follows the passionate "never!" (v. 2.)

What this dialectical pseudo-theology will not admit and turns upside down is the simple fact that what the victory of grace over sin does is not to inaugurate a dialectically suspended condition but to establish a reality behind which we can no longer go. Therefore Paul does not argue: we have received through grace the vision of a new ideal of life; we stand under a new imperative (to speak of this imperative belongs in a completely different place!). The basis for the incompatibility of sin and grace and therefore of sin and Christian life is not initially a duty, but a fact; not a decision to which we are called, but a decision that has happened to us. We have died to sin (a dative of condition, not an instrumental dative); we have no more life that we could leave to it. Therefore it means no less than this: we have death behind us, at our back, no longer before us. Our own existence, which sin could still have at its disposal, is past.

In contrast to the "once and for all," by which that misleading and foolhardy question of v. 1 seeks to create a dialectic of sin and grace to last for ever, Paul erects the "once and for all" of the decision that has happened to us in the death and resurrection of Christ (6.10).

In v. 2 Paul demonstrates the validity of his proposition by recalling baptism. He already can presuppose its understanding in the congregation.[5] What has happened to us in baptism? Answer: We are transferred to Christ (in any case, the preposition "into" has this meaning), but this means that we are submerged in his death, taken in, so that now it also means that we have died (v. 2). Verse 4a conveys this without actually leading further to the still stronger expression: "We were buried therefore with him by baptism into death"[6] and thus radically surrendered to his death. The transfer to Christ ("into") therefore means being baptized into the fate of his death ("with"), and that means with the utmost reality. The sense is certainly not only that of a mystical imitation, and corresponds to Paul's failure to include any reflection about the symbolic character of the baptismal event.[7] Just as the "he was buried" in the kerygma (I Cor. 15.4) is a sealing of the real, corporeal death of Christ, so the "to be buried with him" is a seal of the believer's dying with him. "If we are baptized into his death, we also are dead and buried. We are already covered up . . . Where is the grave? Christ's death. That is sweet and lovely to hear, that Christ's death is my grave, in which I am buried" (Luther, W.A. 17, 338, 2ff.).

Verse 4b first leads further; the "so that" sentence[8] introduces the divine condition and demand under which we now stand. The verse no longer speaks only about Christ's death, but about his resurrection, and includes in this certainty the condition of our existence ("so that as Christ was raised from the dead by the glory of the father ["glory," the power of God's new world], we too might walk in newness of life").[9] If this expression of Paul's deals primarily with the reality and possibility of life, opened for us by God in the resurrection of Christ, its character as demand is clear. It is characteristic that Paul does not say: "so that . . . we might rise from the dead," but "we might walk." Therefore the future resurrection is already to become apparent in the conduct of the one freed from sin.[10]

For an understanding of what follows, which gives the explanation and basis for everything said up to this point, especially v. 4, the exact parallel character of the sentences in vv. 5–7 and 8–10 is to be noted:

vv. 5–7	vv. 8–10
Protasis: "For if we have been united with him in a death like his"	"But if we have died with Christ"
Apodosis: "we shall certainly be united with him in a resurrection like his."	"we believe that we shall also live with him."
Explanation and Consequence: "We know that our old self was crucified with him so that the sinful body might be destroyed, and we might no longer be enslaved to sin."	"We know that Christ being raised from the dead will never die again; death no longer has dominion over him."
Basis and Result (formulated as a sentence): "For he who has died is freed from sin."[11]	"The death he died he died to sin, once for all, but the life he lives he lives to God."

In this structuring of the sentences it already becomes clear that the baptismal event and the Christ-event are not only related to each other in terms of analogy, but are identical with each other. In the baptismal event the Christ-event is present. "His death is present" and incorporates into itself all "who are baptized through faith and the word of God" (Luther, W.A. 17, 338, 4f.). Paul can speak in this way of baptism, not because it possesses a magic power in itself, but because Christ's death and resurrection are not simply historical data but eschatological occurrences.[12] The death and resurrection of Christ concern the old aeon of sin and death as a whole. For Paul, all powers to which the Christ-event is directed bear the mark of a universal condition: sin, law, flesh, death, powers of the world (Gal. 4.3, 9; Col. 2.8ff., 20). Christ takes the encompassing might of this old aeon upon himself: he comes under the law (Gal. 4.4), bears the curse (Gal. 3.13), takes the curse and sin upon himself in the form of sinful flesh (Rom. 8.3), and dies on the cross erected by the rulers of the world (I Cor. 2.8). Thus he intercedes for sinners, was made sin for them (II Cor. 5.21), and opens access for them into the grace of God (Rom. 5.2). As the beloved, they are the victors over the powers of this aeon (Rom. 8.37ff.).

Thus the Christ-event, relating to and overcoming the world as a whole, is not simply a continuing occurrence for Paul. The past tenses in which he speaks of it clearly show that this event does not mean any timeless myth; it is singular, unrepeatable, even in the cult. The Christ of God is Jesus, who then and there died and was raised. And yet it is not an event that becomes past in the sense of other events, transcended by other occurrences, but an event that means "once and for all" and includes a "no longer" (Rom. 6.9). The effect which Christ's death has will not come to nought; the life directed toward God suffers no vacillation: "The death he died he died to sin, once for all, but the life he lives he lives to God" (Rom. 6.10).

Paul can use such comprehensive expressions (the end of the old, the beginning of the new aeon) about this singular event in the course of history, the death and resurrection of the historical Jesus, because this Jesus is the Christ of God. It is not by chance that he does not say here (as he does also for the most part elsewhere[13] where he speaks of the meaning of the cross and resurrection for salvation) "Jesus," nor even "Christ Jesus," but "Christ." That means that he designates him as God's eschatological bringer of salvation. The fact that Paul can occasionally use the name of Christ as a "proper name" has caused the widespread view that the title "Christ" has become almost meaningless for him and been replaced by the title "*Kyrios*" (Lord). However, this is quite incorrect. Both names usually serve as titles for him, and each has a thoroughly different function. He almost always uses "Christ"—apparently following the tradition—in kerygmatic phrases where it concerns the death and resurrection of Christ in their meaning for salvation; *Kyrios*, on the other hand, is the name used to make confessional response.[14]

Therefore Paul speaks of the Christ-event in order to unfold the baptismal event. For this reason, the parallel series of thoughts in 5–7 and 8–10 follow the sentences in 2–4 dealing with baptism. The manner of their parallelism must, of course, be noted: vv. 6f. speak of man and his end; vv. 9f. of Christ and his life. In this antithetical parallelism, which in no way abolishes the "with" that permeates the baptismal sentences and those that follow in vv. 5 and 8, a permanent difference between "us" and "Christ" becomes apparent. When speaking of this present existence, in looking at "us" Paul speaks of death; only in looking at Christ does he speak of death and life. This differentiation is of considerable importance for the Pauline under-standing of baptism. However, we can only take up the question after we have considered the exegetical difficulties of the much-disputed verse, 6.5. It is already clear here that the Christ-event is present in the baptismal event. The death which the baptized and Christ die is only one death, i.e. the death of Christ himself, and through baptism this death becomes the death of the believer. As a sacramental presentation of the Christ-event, baptism establishes the basis of Christian existence; in it the condition to which we are called is revealed and on it the certainty with which we await eternity is based.[15] Therefore, Paul does not say: as Christ died on the cross, so we die in baptism. Correspondingly, Colossians, which in this matter authentically interprets Rom. 6, does not say: Like Christ you were circumcised with a circumcision not done by men, but speaks of baptism as the "circumcision" of Christ (Col. 1.11) and describes the event occurring here as dying and rising with Christ. Of course, Col. 2.12 also speaks—unlike Rom. 6—of the latter as an event already completed in baptism. But otherwise it says in essence what Rom. 6.5 also says: "If we have been united with him in a death like his . . ."

But the understanding of this sentence has yet to be ascertained. The first problem that v. 5 presents includes the phrase "likeness of his death," the second the connection of "we have been united." Both questions are closely connected. On the first: "likeness" can mean as much as image, a copy of an original, an imitation of a model, but also simply "the same form,"[16] i.e. a designation of a form which is not only similar to the form of another but the same. Decisive here is the fact that "likeness" presents the essence of the image portrayed. From the passages where the term occurs in Paul himself (Rom. 1.23; 4.14; 8.3; Phil. 2.7), Rom. 8.3 and Phil. 2.7 are especially illuminating. They clearly show that "likeness" characterizes a *concretum*, not the abstract property of similarity or sameness.[17] Thus Rom. 8.3: Christ in the form marked by the flesh and sin.[18] It should surely not be overlooked that Paul does not say: "in the body of sinful flesh" here. "Likeness" expresses a relationship and connection, but at the same time maintains a difference between Christ and us. However, this difference should in no way suggest that the form of Christ is almost similar to ours. It is not the form which he bears that differentiates him from us, but the bearers who bear this same form who are to be differentiated (correspondingly Phil. 2.7; cf. also Hebr. 2.17). "The likeness of his death" thus characterizes the death of Christ. With him, that is, with Christ as the crucified, we are united. Correspondingly we shall be united with the form of his resurrection, that is, with him as the Resurrected One. (In the clause that follows, "and we shall be united with him in a resurrection like his" should be added.)

That means that on the second: "we have been united" is to be directly connected with "in the likeness of his death." The direction of the sentence demands it, as does the fact that all connections with

"with" ("buried with him," "crucified with him," "died with Christ," "live with him") concern the person of Christ. Therefore, the dative form of "likeness" is not an instrumental dative but an associative one; i.e. the term is not related to baptism as the image of his death and resurrection but directly to the person of Christ. This exegetical conclusion is important; it offers decisive support, *inter alia*, against the thoroughly un-Pauline "cognitive" meaning that Karl Barth imputes to baptism on the basis of a misunderstanding of our passage. So the term "likeness" has absolutely nothing to do with the sacrament, even though according to Paul the union with Christ naturally occurs in baptism.[19]

What has been said also answers the further disputed question touched on above, whether Paul already includes in the meaning of the baptismal event not only the share in the dying and crucifixion of the old self, but also the share in the resurrection. Col. 2.12 suggests an affirmative answer to this question; and Rom. 6.11 ("So you also must consider yourselves dead to sin and alive to God in Christ Jesus") shows clearly that life, too, is awarded to the believer on the basis of the resurrection of Christ. Furthermore, in 6.4 "in newness of life" does not mean the life of the Christian which has yet to be realized, but the life of Christ that already has become revealed and in which the believer is to walk. Does, then, the future tense in v. 5 ("we shall be") and v. 8 ("we shall live with him") have only a logical sense?[20] The answer must be: not at all. It is a genuine future. God has indeed opened for us the possibility of new life in baptism, or in the resurrection. He has done even more: he has opened the reality of "life," but this "life" is still hidden by lowliness and dying, a paradoxical reality, based entirely on faith (v. 8). Its revelation is the object of expectation. The parallel passage that stands closest to Rom. 6.5, 8, appears to me, therefore, to be Phil. 3.10, where Paul similarly—only without relationship to baptism, but in a general description of Christian existence—speaks of becoming like the death of Christ (the body of humiliation) and of the expected transformation into the body of the resurrection.[21]

The course of the entire section 6.1–11 clearly shows why Paul could reject so definitely the thesis formulated in 6.1. Because the "once for all" of Christ's death and life includes the "no longer" of the reign of death, it is true even for believers that with the single event of their baptism the once-for-allness of their liberation from the slavery of sin is sealed. It hardly needs to be said that the "so you also must consider . . ." is intended not in the sense of a mere comparison but as a conclusion ("therefore"). It does not have the sense of "as if," but opens the reality before them, made accessible in Christ to believers, from which in faith they may understand their existence and to which they may direct their life.

II

How do the admonitions of the second part (vv. 12–23) of ch. 6 relate to this baptismal doctrine of Paul in the first part? Initially, one may say this much: the admonitions based on baptism do not make the baptismal expressions conditional, but receive their power precisely from the unconditional validity of the latter. "Obedience is not that which establishes the effectiveness of baptism, but rather that which makes possible a richly fruitful reception" (Schlier).[22]

We still, however, have to ask the real question: what is the difference between the "effectiveness" of baptism and a "richly fruitful reception"? What does it mean that the new life—to use the traditional formulation—is gift and task? This certainly characterizes the question initially, but it does not answer it any more than does the well-known formula: "Become what you are."

1. In answering one would do well to remember a fact which can quickly be recognized, and needs to be referred to only with a few words—namely this: if it is true that we receive a sharing in the death and life of Christ through baptism, then an essential decision about the new being of the Christian has already been made. For the death and life of Christ are not in fact simply events that have occurred, which were as it were completed in Christ, phases and conditions of his career; rather, his dying and life represent a decision accomplished not only by him but through him, in him, the turning-point between sin and God, the old and new aeon. In the sacrifice of him, God acts to show his love to sinners (Rom. 5.8); in that he sacrifices himself, he himself acts, and his "life" now means, not that he exists somewhere as the risen and exalted one, but that he is now constantly at work: "what he lives, he lives to God." Now he is no longer held back by any power of sin, no longer marked by any limits of death; i.e. he surrounds his own with his love, directs and keeps them through his word; he has not only opened for them the access to the Father but holds it open: "through him we have peace with God" (Rom. 5.1), so that he constantly intercedes for his own (Rom. 8.34).

In that Christ takes his own into his death and his life, he thus places them together with him in this activity. He separates them from sin and gives to their life out of death a constant direction toward God. Already in Rom. 5.1ff. Paul has shown how the believers are now initially activated through justification and the pact of peace: the Spirit moves their hearts through the love of God, which is poured into our hearts (5.5). And then comes the praise of hope, indeed praise not only in the middle of trouble but even because of affliction. This new activity means "endurance"—"character"—"hope" (Rom. 5.4). "I press on to make it my own because Christ Jesus has made me his own!" (Phil. 3.12). "Dead to sin, alive to God" —that is no attained condition but the release of life, and now genuine activity for the first time. Paul makes this clear in Rom. 6.15ff. by describing liberation from sin not only as separation from its power but immediately as incorporation in a new relationship of obedience, as a service in the new being of the Spirit (7.6). The new conduct is thus already included with the new being; it is the release of a life open to God, now truly turned toward the future for the first time.

This still does not answer the question about the necessity of the imperative, but it prevents the formulation of the question from becoming a foolish distortion.

2. The necessity of admonition has its actual basis in the hiddenness of the new life that is given to us in baptism. The old aeon has turned, but in such fashion that a new world situation has not directly and openly begun. Paul cannot say that sin is dead or that death is dead. But he says that we have died to them. He cannot say that the "flesh" is done away; rather that we no longer live "in the flesh" (Rom. 7.5f), and that we are no longer forced to live "according to the flesh." Colossians, too, does not say that the powers are done away, but that they are disarmed, incorporated as the vanquished in the triumphal procession of Christ (Col. 2.15). As in a triumphal procession in which the subjugated follow behind the victor, all still are visible and must proclaim the greatness of the victory that has been achieved through the very might of their appearance. So the "rulers" and "powers" are still there, but for believers they no longer bear any weapons and thereby they glorify the victory of Christ. Finally, Paul does not say that the law is destroyed, but that we are free from it; no longer are we subjected to its rule, but grace rules over us (Rom. 6.14; 7.1ff.).

The hiddenness of the new aeon is evident in the very fact that the

powers are still visible and effectual. They seek to establish their rule
again. They can even do this with the hope of success, since believers
are still within reach, are still to be found in the old aeon. They still
bear the body, and this body is not just an outward shell of their
existence. It is themselves, whose new life has not yet appeared. The
body is still exposed to the "desires," to the autonomous excitements
of life, that constantly appear to make the fact of the death of the
baptized illusory. It is true that the body we bear is no longer a body
of sin, i.e. possessed by the power of sin. That body is destroyed in
baptism, our old man is crucified with it (Rom. 6.6). But it can still
be enticed. It is true that the body we bear is no longer a "body of
death," i.e. subject to the power of death, but it is nevertheless a
"mortal body" (6.12).[23]

Believers have the new life presented to them nowhere else than in
Christ: "hid in Christ with God" (Col. 3.3). "This life does not possess experience of itself but faith" (Luther). The baptized person is
nothing but one who believes and hopes. It is in this way that he has
justification and the new life presented to him in baptism. So, too, the
tension of his temporal existence is determined: "If we have died with
Christ, we believe that we shall also live with him" (Rom. 6.8). The
event from which we originate is baptism, i.e. death ("we have
died"); faith is ours in the present ("we believe"); life in the future
("we shall live with him"). In the faith that is based on what has
happened and that reaches toward what is coming, death and life
are together present. Of course, faith is not itself the basis. It is to be
noted that faith is hardly mentioned in connection with the baptismal
texts of Rom. 6 and Col. 2.[24] The basis is rather the resurrection of
Jesus Christ, in which the life of baptized persons is already a real,
though hidden, present (Rom. 6.9–11).

Because of the hiddenness of this new life, baptized persons are
reminded that what has happened to them in baptism will be spoken
to them repeatedly and that this "we know" (6.9, 6) will be explained
for them. For the baptismal event cannot be presupposed as a foregone conclusion which is effective naturally. Rather, baptism itself
must constantly become the object of proclamation. So it is in Paul.

Therefore, believers are also reminded constantly that the imperative is spoken anew to them and that they are called repeatedly
to the obedience into which they have been taken in baptism and
which they have accepted in baptism.

Thus the hiddenness of the new life is the basis for the necessity of the doctrine of baptism itself and the basis for the impact of the imperative.

3. What does Paul say about the course of the new life? The decisive point is evidently that in the admonitions he only repeats what has already happened in baptism itself. The admonitions do not lead beyond the circle of what has occurred in baptism. The content of the admonition is nothing other than dying-with-Christ (now become a whole life throughout), nothing other than living-in-Christ (now become *this* whole life throughout), nothing other than the putting on of the Lord Jesus.

So the imperative does not appeal to the good will; it does not mobilize the good powers that lie in man, but it gives and demands in one—it is *paraklēsis* as summoning comfort and as comforting summons.

(*a*) Thus the course of the new life cannot begin anywhere else than in the deed of Christ himself. It is characterized by a new beginning, a new situation, a new horizon. We are taken from sin's region of death. It is dethroned and banished. The imperative confronting the baptized therefore does not say: throw down sin from its throne, but: do not allow it on its throne any longer (Rom. 6.12), and he stands under the sure comfort: *ou kurieusei*, (sin) will have no dominion (v. 14). It is very characteristic that in Rom. 6.12 Paul does not immediately say: do not sin, let us not sin, but rather: therefore do not let sin reign! Yet again he speaks of it in personal terms, as a power; but here, no sooner has it been designated as a power than the stripping of its power becomes visible. That is the new horizon in which the new life of believers takes place.

(*b*) The new life of the baptized is characterized by a new urgency. Now the horizon of his own decisions is opened for the believer: he is placed in the battle between God and sin, between the old and the new aeon. And this decision occurs again and again quite concretely in his own decisions: in his body. Even more concretely, it occurs in his members (Rom. 6.12f.),[25] and thus in an obedience that has "hands and feet."

The admonition receives its urgency from this. For the deceitful way of sin is that it wants nothing more than the members and thereby leads to the false impression that we ourselves remain unmolested and that we have not succumbed to it in relinquishing our members to it completely. No longer does it make a frontal attack, but detours through the "desires" of the body.[26]

But the urgency of the imperative is even more appropriate because the decision has been made! We are freed from sin, we have become bond slaves of God (according to 6.17b "surrendered" to the baptismal confession)[27] and thus subjugated to the righteousness of God and to sanctification. What the believers have to do is very plainly and simply to "yield," to leave themselves and their members to God.

The decision is no longer open—an "either-or." Rather, what holds is "Once—Now," "Then—Now" (Rom. 6.19–22; 7.5f.; Col. 1 and 21f. *passim*). Therefore Paul speaks penetratingly and triumphantly. The "Once—Now" echoes the "much more" from Rom. 5.15ff. The belonging-to-Christ is incomparably greater than the belonging-to-Adam, the reign of grace is incomparably more glorious than the reign of sin, the law, death. Only humanly speaking can Paul compare service under sin and service of God (Rom. 6.19); for this is truly freedom itself.

(*c*) The new life that is presented to believers and on which they obediently lay hold occurs with new simplicity. Since through baptism they are set in the one decision of Christ between the power of sin and the power of God, between "flesh" and "spirit," their life is ordered in simplicity. No longer do the many "dogmas" of the old law and the various "elements" of the world bind them (Col. 2.8. 16ff., 21ff.), but they are bound by the liberating law of the life-creating Spirit in Christ Jesus (Rom. 8.2). They obey the law of love—that means they fulfill the law of Christ (Gal. 6.2). Being God's slave no longer begins with the sacrifice of the "members" of our body but with "yielding ourselves" (Rom. 6.13), and "yielding your members to God as instruments of righteousness" follows from this.

The simplicity of the new obedience is evident also in the fact that the demands are not for special accomplishments. Instead they very simply require what is good and pleasing to God (Rom. 12.2). The fruits of the Spirit are really nothing other than love, joy, peace, patience, kindness, etc. (Gal. 5.22ff.), but they receive their unity, their new condition, their basis for life in the fact that they are fruits of the Spirit. Thus the imperative that confronts faith is not arbitrary. Rather, it is: "If we live by the Spirit, let us also walk by the Spirit" (Gal. 5.25).

(*d*) The new life of Christians is determined by a new hope. It is the hope that our life, now still hidden with Christ in God, shall become revealed (Col. 3.3f.); that we, as those who have already died with

Christ (Rom. 6.5ff.), and already live to God in him (Rom. 6.11), shall live with him (Rom. 6.8), rule with him in life (Rom. 5.17), shall stand openly as righteous through the obedience of Christ (Rom. 5.19); and that we shall be united also with the Risen Lord (Rom. 6.5). This hope already permeates the Now of believers in which nothing other than struggle, suffering, temptation, running, fear and trembling are visible; in the middle of troubles, jubilant praise already awakens (Rom. 5.3f.). Already through patience, perseverance and hope one begins to cross the sure bridge that spans the abyss of "suffering" and "temptation" (I Cor. 10.12f.) and which is securely planted on the other shore where our life is hid. All the imperatives of Paul have their basis in what has happened to us through Christ in baptism—and all imperatives, which are to be obediently laid hold on here and now, can be summarized in the words: "seek the things that are above" (Col. 3.1).

In baptism everything is given to us for this and for the future life; nothing remains that we have to add to it. The obedience of believers cannot penetrate further than to what has happened to us at the beginning. It takes place in the constant "crawling-under-baptism" (Luther). In this sense one may formulate it pointedly: Baptism is the dedication of the new life, and the new life is the appropriation of baptism.

NOTES

[1] The essay is based on a lecture given in 1939 in Halle and Königsberg, Prussia, and published in *Theol. Blätter* 18 (1939), cols 233ff.

[2] On what follows, cf. R. Bultmann, "Das Problem der Ethik bei Paulus," *ZNW* 23 (1924), pp. 123ff.; H. Windisch, "Das Problem des paulinischen Imperativs," *ibid.*, pp. 265ff.

[3] Lüdemann, *Die Anthropologie des Paulus* (1872), p. 141.

[4] On Rom. 6 cf. K. Mittring, *Heilswirklichkeit bei Paulus* (1929); G. Matern, *Exegese von Röm. 6* (Konigsberg Dissertation, without year); W. T. Hahn, *Das Mitsterben und Mitauferstehen mit Christus bei Paulus* (1937); G. Bornkamm, "Die neutest. Lehre von der Taufe," *Theol. Blätter* 17 (1938), cols 42ff.; H. Schlier, "Die Taufe nach dem 6. Kapitel des Römerbriefes," *EvTh* (1938), pp. 335ff., now in *Zeit der Kirche* (1956), pp. 47ff.; on the exegesis of the Reformers, E. Ellwein, *Vom neuen Leben* (1932), pp. 74ff.; K. Barth, *Die Kirchliche Lehre von der Taufe* (1943) (ET, *The Teaching of the Church regarding Baptism*, 1948); on this: H. Schlier, "Zur kirchlichen Lehre von der Taufe," *TLZ* (1947), cols 321ff., now in *Die Zeit der Kirche* (1956), pp. 107ff.; O. Cullmann, *Die Tauflehre des Neuen Testaments* (1948) (ET, *Baptism in the New Testament*, 1956); E. Fuchs, *Die Freiheit des Glaubens* (1949), pp. 27ff.; P. Brunner, *Aus der Kraft des Werkes Christi. Zur Lehre von der*

Heiligen Taufe und vom Heiligen Paulus in Röm. 6 (1950); R. Schnackenburg, *Das Heilsgeschehen bei der Taufe nach dem Apostel Paulus* (Münchener Theol. Stud, 1, 1950); O. Kuss, "Zu Röm. 6.5a," *Theologie und Glaube* 41 (1951), pp. 430ff.; "Zur vorpaulinischen Tauflehre im NT," *ibid.,* pp. 289ff.; "Zur paulinischen und nachpaulinischen Tauflehre im NT," *Theologie und Glaube* 42 (1952), pp. 401ff.; "Zur Frage einer vorpaulinischen Todestaufe," *Münchener Theol. Zeitschrift* 4 (1953), pp. 1ff.; V. Warnach, "Taufe und Christusgeschehen," *Archiv für Liturgiewissenschaft* 3, 2 (1954), pp. 284ff.; F. Mussner, "Zusammenwachsen durch die Ähnlichkeit mit seinem Tode," *Trierer Theol. Zeitschrift* 63 (1954), pp. 257ff.; R. Schnackenburg, "Todes- und Lebensgemeinschaft mit Christus," *Münchener Theol. Zeitschrift* 6 (1955), pp. 32ff. Cf. also the more recent commentaries on Romans by C. H. Dodd (1949), O. Michel (1957²), O. Kuss (1957), F. J. Leenhardt (1957), C. K. Barrett (1957).

⁵ Rom. 6 in no way offers any specifically Pauline doctrine of baptism, but follows the understanding of baptism already disseminated in the Hellenistic congregations ("Do you not know?"). The interpretation of this baptismal doctrine, that clearly betrays its origin from the concepts of the mystery religions, is certainly Pauline.

⁶ The connection of "by baptism" with "into death" ("by the baptism of death") is to be preferred to that of "we were buried" and "into death."

⁷ So already Tertullian, *de bapt.* c. 3. Cf., for example, also Faber Stapulensis (cited in Ellwein, *op. cit.,* p. 76), for whom the threefold immersion designates the "three-day burial with Christ."

⁸ *Hina* ("so that") frequently after kerygmatic sentences, cf. Stauffer, *TWNT* III, pp. 324ff. (ET, *TDNT* III, pp. 323ff.).

⁹ "Of life" is an epexegetical genitive, so like "newness" it has a pregnant, eschatological meaning, cf. Rom. 7.6. Luther's translation does not express this clearly enough. Cf. Matern, *op. cit.,* p. 12; P. Brunner, *op. cit.,* p. 24.

¹⁰ Cf. R. Bultmann, *TNT,* p. 139 (ET, *NTT* I, pp. 140f.).

¹¹ Paul uses a Rabbinic sentence here, cf. K. G. Kuhn, *ZNW* 30 (1931), pp. 305ff.; Schrenk, *TWNT* II, p. 222 (ET, *TDNT* II, p. 218).

¹² "The death of Christ is the sacrament, baptism the sacramental confession of him, in which participation in him is gained: the incorporation into the body of Christ." H. von Soden, "Sakrament und Ethik bei Paulus," in *Urchristentum und Geschichte* I (1951), p. 271. Of course, the characterization of baptism as "sacramental confession" is contestable.

¹³ Cf. I Cor. 15.3ff.; Rom. 5.6ff.; 6.8f.; 7.4; 14.9, 15; 15.7, etc.

¹⁴ I cannot enter further into this question here. It needs more exact investigation. Naturally the rule referred to above is not without exceptions.

¹⁵ Note the corresponding connection of sentences: (*a*) "as"—"so" (vv. 4, 11), (*b*) "so that" . . . (vv. 4, 6), (*c*) "if" . . . (vv. 5, 8); they join the event that has happened to us, the condition established for us, and the certainty given to us.

¹⁶ Deut. 4.16; Ps. 106 (105).20; II Chron. 4.3; Isa. 40.18, etc. On the term *homoiōma* (likeness), cf. most recently J. Schneider, *TWNT* V, pp. 191ff. (ET, *TDNT* V, pp. 191ff.); P. Brunner, *op. cit.,* pp. 68ff.; O. Kuss, *op. cit.*

¹⁷ So yet again, Schnackenburg, *op. cit.,* p. 47.

¹⁸ The meaning "same form" applies to all five passages in Paul: Rom. 1.23 (rightly O. Kuss against the clarification of Brunner, who wants to differentiate *homoiōma* and *eikōn, op. cit.,* pp. 21f.); Rom. 8.3; Phil. 2.7; Rom. 6.5; but also Rom. 5.14, where it is related to the *"transgression"* of Adam. Here *homoiōma* means the same concrete form of sin (namely as trespass of a definite commandment).

¹⁹ That Paul does not designate baptism as "a death like his," as the traditional view of the passage regards it, becomes clear for the following reasons: (1) for an

instrumental understanding of the dative, the decisive *autō* in 6.5a must be added, which is not at all justified; (2) on the other hand, *homoiōma* must be added to "resurrection." But if *homoiōma* is also in this case to be the baptism that already has taken place, then the future tense would be unintelligible. The problem of this future cannot be excluded from the discussion of Rom. 6.5a (against Kuss, *op. cit.*). Rather, 6.5b clearly speaks against the interpretation of *homoiōma* in 6.5 as referring to baptism. The sacramental misunderstanding of the term *homoiōma* (to begin with, the concern here is only for the term!) is also found in P. Brunner: "The image of Christ's death, present in baptism, is the death of Christ by virtue of its eschatological saving power, that breaks the barriers of space and time and breaks through the material-historical objectivity. The death of Christ in the event of this breakthrough—that is the image of Christ's death given in baptism" (p. 24). Similarly, J. Schneider in *TWNT* V, p. 195: "This sacramentally present death of Christ and this sacramentally present resurrection are the *homoiōma* of his historical death and his historical resurrection" (cf. ET, *TDNT* V, p. 195). Cf. also O. Kuss: "*homoiōma* means picture, image, and designates 'being buried' in the baptismal occurrence . . . we have been and still are (v. 5a) most closely connected with the baptismal event and with the salvation becoming efficacious for us in it (that is, finally: with Christ)."

[20] So recently again P. Brunner, *op. cit.*, pp. 26, 74.

[21] Colossians recognizes this also (3.5). However, the differences in the baptismal expressions of Rom. 6 and Col. 2 are not to be harmonized.

[22] *EvTh* (1938), p. 346.

[23] On this important differentiation see E. Käsemann, *Leib und Leib Christi* (1933), p. 123, and H. Schlier, *Die Zeit der Kirche* (1956), p. 49.

[24] Only Rom. 6.8 and Col. 2.12; but cf. also Gal. 3.26f.

[25] Cf. Matt. 5.29f.

[26] Cf. H. Schlier, *op. cit.*, p. 51.

[27] On *tupos didachēs* ("standard of teaching"), cf. Schlier, *op. cit.*, p. 53. Verse 17b is, of course, to be excluded as a later gloss. Cf. R. Bultmann, "Glossen im Römerbrief," *TLZ*, 1947, col. 202. To the un-Pauline phrases cited by Bultmann is likewise to be reckoned the un-Pauline passive ("to which you were committed"), which does not allow itself to be explained from traditional Jewish terminology.

VI

SIN, LAW AND DEATH
An Exegetical Study of Romans 7[1]

HARDLY ANY EXEGETE today would still contest that Rom. 7.7–25 concerns man. However, opinions may still differ as to whether or not the passage is primarily a personal confession of the apostle, and whether the "man" about which it speaks is man lost under law or man under grace. Let us postpone these latter questions for now. For the orientation of the exegesis of Rom. 7, however, it may be important to note that the undisputed and indisputable conclusion with which we began is not a sufficient description of the specific issue developed here by Paul. It is significant for Paul's concern that the "man" about whom he is speaking is not an object which one can describe like other objects. He is no *species* among others. It is not by chance that Rom. 7 does not speak about "man"; rather, it refers to that man which can be spoken of only in the first person, more precisely, in the first person singular (not even in the first person plural!). It is in the nature of things that Paul can only say "I"—not "man"—nor even "we." An interpretation which overlooks this fact, however correct it might be in detail, would not do justice to the content if it tried to speak *about* it rather than *from* it. So exegesis here must to a large extent be simply a paraphrase, a descriptive translation.

I

First let us recall the context and theme of our chapter.[2] In ch. 5.1 to 7.6 Paul has shown that the revelation of the righteousness of God in Jesus Christ without the law, and thus justification through faith alone (ch. 1–4), is our salvation. It is the salvation of believers from death, under whose power all stand, who by virtue of their own sin share in Adam's sin and death. Through the obedience of Christ, the new Adam, they are subjected to the kingly rule of grace, i.e. eternal life is opened to them through the "righteousness" based on his obedience, on his act of right, and now allotted to them.

Secondly, this "salvation" means that we, as those baptized into Christ's death and dead to sin, are delivered from the tyrannical power of sin so that this no longer has any claim on us. Through Christ's death, which has become our death in baptism, believers are acquitted, released from sin, liberated for righteousness, i.e. called to give themselves to righteousness, to be God's own slaves, in order to receive from him eternal life in Christ as a gift of grace (ch. 6).

Thirdly, freed from the power of death and sin, we are free from the law. Here, as Paul develops his argument with the allegorical use of propositions from the marriage law, the law itself, so to speak, witnesses against itself. Thus, released from the prison that held us captive in the bonds of sin and death, we are placed in the new reality of the Spirit and are no longer to serve in the old reality of the letter, i.e. the law (7.1–6). There ("under the old written code") one has an autonomous, selfish life in the flesh in the passions of sin, whose harvest and fruit are reaped by death ("to bear fruit for death"). It is a life, driven by sin toward death, the life of the prisoner, who as it were can move only to and fro between the narrow walls of his cell.

With this the great themes of ch. 7.7ff. and ch. 8 have already been initiated. The "but now" of 7.6 is taken up again at the beginning of ch. 8. What "to serve in the new life of the Spirit" means is developed in ch. 8. On the other hand 7.7–25 describes what "to serve under the old written code" means. However, this theme is woven into another which has also arisen from 7.1–6. It is the question of the relationship between the law and sin. One cannot keep in mind clearly enough the fact that the thesis of 7.1–6 ("freed from the law") expresses something unheard of. How can Paul incorporate the law into the list of enslaving powers, sin and death? Should one not expect: freed from sin we are free *for* the law? Does Paul really want to affirm that the law belongs together with sin and death? And if he really means that—which he definitely does—can we avoid the blasphemous consequence that the law itself is sin (7.7)? Does not, then, the good, i.e. the law given for life, become a power of death (7.13)? In order to avoid this conclusion, in 7.7ff. Paul introduces an apology for the law, in which on the one hand he establishes with great emphasis the unassailable holiness of the law, but on the other hand makes evident how law and sin could enter into such a contradictory and, for man, fatal connection. One is as important to the Apostle as the other. On the one hand there is the distinction between law and sin. Here one could appropriately say that whoever makes the law itself sin simultaneously also makes sin a "law." That is, he makes it a fate unfolding in a consistent way, for which no one is any longer responsible. But at the same time, on the other hand, there is the strange connection into which the law and sin have entered with one another. Therefore 7.7–13 describes how law and sin have come to this connection, i.e. they deal with the predominance of sin over law, while 7.14–25 speaks of how this fatal connection of both operates in man, in other words, how man succumbs to it.

With this characterization of the context and theme of our passage we are already confronted by an important exegetical decision. This will be confirmed in what follows. It is that the section 7.7–25 describes the situation of the unredeemed, not of the believer, the situation of man under the law, his existence "in the flesh." Already in ch. 7.1–6, but especially in ch. 8.1–11 (v. 9), Paul explicitly sees this existence changed by a new being "in the Spirit" that is opened to man. Of course, the misery of the unredeemed man is described from the standpoint of the redeemed man. Only from this perspective is his existence in its radical lostness under law, sin and death properly recognized. This understanding, already demanded by the context, has been carefully established and developed at all points by W. G. Kummel,[3] and now only a few exegetes dispute it. Of course, by this we do not affirm what many exegetes imagine to follow from it; i.e. that Rom. 7.7–25 may not be used for the self-understanding of the Christian. It will later become clear that this is an incorrect conclusion.

II

As has already been said, the apology for the law (7.7–13) emphatically rejects the apparently inescapable, but quite false and blasphemous conclusion, that the law itself is sin and the power of death.[4] It must give another explanation of the close connection between law and sin. This explanation can only be a confession in which the history of man and my way into lostness and death is portrayed. "In me" (v. 8), law and sin have concluded their deadly alliance for me. The character of the Pauline propositions as confession does not take away the essential stringency from what he says about the law, sin and death. Therefore he does not replace the essential argument through an elaboration of accidental, individual experiences. Rather, it becomes clear in the confession that law, sin and death can be properly articulated only as a history that has happened to me. How, then, did that fatal connection of law and sin happen? Paul answers: the law uncovered sin. Without the law I would have made no acquaintance with it, would never have learned of it (in the sense of the practical occurrence).[5] In this way, at the same time it awakened sin—Paul immediately replaces and interprets the term "sin" through the concrete term "desire." Therefore vv. 7a and b are to be understood as being completely parallel. Desire is related to sin as is the commandment to the law. The special nuance in "desire" and "commandment" is merely the concrete form of their appearance. It is only because Paul comprehensively and at the same time concretely designates the nature of sin as "desire"[6] that he can summarize the content of the entire law with one word: You shall not covet![7]

This is far from supposing that the law had checked or even destroyed sin. Rather, in taking on sin it has made an ally of what really ought to be its deadly enemy. In other words, it has made a tool and weapon against me of the weapon which according to all expectation ought to be directed against it. This is expressed by the double expression "finding opportunity" (vv. 8 and 11).[8] Sin began its attack against me in the law, in the commandment. It has brought about every desire—simply meaning coveting—and in just this way it killed me by kindling my urge to live, my will to self-assertion, while it (sin) itself revived. Thus "desire" in every form is the "effect of sin." "What is meant is not only the entire range of what is enumerated in Dt. 5.21, but every action of the 'I' in which it loses its freedom because it is subjected to a propensity or impulse. This includes the desire for good (i.e. life, 7.24), the desire for evil and for good."[9] Even if Paul thinks here primarily of the effect of "desire" in the concrete transgression of the law, it is still characteristic that he mentions only "desire" as the mark of this revolt and not actual evil deeds. That is, he allows room here even more clearly than in what follows for the possibility that "desire" can express itself nomistically just as much as anti-nomistically, i.e. in the zeal for one's own righteousness (Rom. 10.3). In the kindling of desire, that is, of my urge for life, the fate of death is sealed for me. Paul describes the process with almost mythological pictures by speaking of sin and the

"I" as two subjects. As in a duel, only one can remain alive at the place of battle; the life or the survival of the one means the death of the other. The mythological way of speaking is deeply rooted in the matter itself, for the event that Paul has in mind transcends the area of my own decisions and experiences. It is primarily an event in which a decision happens to me, however much I share the guilt for it. For Paul this murderous clash between sin and the "I" is not a timeless dialectic of human existence but a temporal, historical event. It has become an event in the "coming" of the "commandment." Not that sin in general first originated there (Paul never reflects about that), but it has received its "power to live" and has begun to work in my confrontation with the law. For now, in its battle against me, it has been strengthened from a side one would never expect, from the law of God.[10] On the basis of the connection between the law and sin that has now occurred, I have become a child of death at sin's expense ("and I died"). This, therefore, is the paradoxical occurrence that has happened through the strange revival of sin. "The very commandment which promised life (to lead me to life) proved to be death to me" (v. 10).

The same sentence as in v. 8 is repeated by Paul once again in v. 11, but with a characteristic variation. If in the first we read: "seizing its chance" in the commandment, sin has produced in me every desire, in the second we read: using the opportunity offered to it in the commandment, it has deceived me and through the same (the commandment) killed me.[11] Without question, v. 21 comments on the earlier statement (v. 8).[12] It then means that in the desire which sin has produced in me I show that I am deceived and am a child of death. The statement (v. 8) about the conduct of the "I," its reaction to the "commandment," is now radically tranformed into a statement about the being of the "I" itself. The "I" has its essence in illusion and death. Here deception and death are not to be understood *per se* as destinies of man, but as the effects of the fact that God's commandment has come. Sin, awakened to life by the commandment, immediately made use of it.

What constitutes this deception and death? The deception of sin can only consist in the fact that it falsely promises life to me. This it cannot do by itself, but only with the help of the divine commandment. Deceptively it appropriates the call to life, which actually declares God's law: do that, and you shall live. What it quietly and deceptively conceals from me is simply this, that it has now usurped this call to live, and therefore the encounter with the divine commandment is no longer direct. Sin always stands in between and has fundamentally perverted my relationship to God's commandment. This perversion is both deception and death. For it suggests that now I may grasp at life, which because of sin is never any longer truly an open possibility for me. In that grasp at life as one who desires, the life to which God's commandment calls according to its original intention ("the commandment which promised life") is finally closed to me. If we have correctly described the Pauline statement in vv. 10f., then it is clear that in the realm of this statement, which uncovers the basis of my existence, the alternative has no meaning. This is the case whether I show desire in open rebellion against the commandment or am one who seeks to wrest his own righteousness, and thus life, from the law. At the same time it is clear that death, inflicted on me by sin, is not just a dying expected at the end of life, but is even now the mark of my life destroyed by the deceit of sin. "and I died—sin . . . killed (me)." The past tense of both verbs characterizes the reality from which I always proceed. With the double description of the effect of sin—it deceived and killed me— what Paul wants to say in vv. 14ff. about the estrangement of the "I" is already prepared for, but it would still be premature to speak of this estrangement in the interpretation of v. 11.[13]

In vv. 7–11 (especially 9–11), Paul has developed the history of the "I" from which it receives its essence. Which history is intended here? To what are "when" in v. 9 and the temporal expressions emphasized by the verbs in 9 to 11 related? This also means: Who is the "I" of these sentences and what is the commandment by whose arrival sin is revived and I am subjected to death? The questions have been extensively discussed. Here we can be brief. The biographical understanding of the verses, as though Paul were speaking of the stages of his life's path, is still not finished. The "once" is then "the innocent paradise of his childhood" (O. Holtzmann), from which he was torn away by the encounter with the law, i.e. in effect at the time when the Jewish boy (13 years) becomes a man, a *bar mizwa* (son of the law), and now must keep the entire law. From this time on the boy first becomes responsible, though he has had the evil inclination (*yēzer hā rā*) in him from birth. But now it comes down to a battle of good and evil inclinations against each other. Here we may ignore the more or less insipid references to the "unforgettable day of the fall into sin" (Diessmann) of the young Paul and the psychological and psychoanalytical observations that have joined themselves to this passage, for which, of course, the sexual sense of "you shall not covet" is always the starting-point.

The most important reasons against this biographical interpretation are:[14] (a) that according to Jewish teaching, childhood can hardly be described as a "time without the law";[15] (b) that Paul speaks differently of his pre-Christian, Jewish life: in a tone of pride, not of contrition. In Phil. 3.5ff. Paul does not describe some scruple of conscience, but what for him had been a "gain" and what he considered as loss and refuse only for the sake of Christ; (c) that the expressions "I was alive" and "I died," which still have a pregnant meaning even if not intended in the sense of physical life and death, would have to be weakened and made harmless as only a process of consciousness: "I was alive" = "untroubled life of a child;" "condition of relative innocence;" "I died" = "he feels himself deceived;" "it was for him as if. . .," etc. Exegetes then speak of the experience of despair, of the emergence of anxiety about death, etc.[16]

The interpretation (represented, for instance, by Chrysostom) that applies it to the Jewish people in general is also out of the question. Nothing here in the text points to this and it is already excluded by the following reference to the contradiction in man as the fruit of this history.

The "I" could more plausibly mean Adam as the representative of mankind. In fact, a series of individual features recalls the accounts of paradise and the fall into sin (life without sin in God's presence, the coming of the law, desire, deception, death). And yet this interpretation, too, is incorrect. It is hardly by chance that the name of Adam does not occur here, but that we have "I." Also, in fact, 7.8f. ("apart from the law sin lies dead") does not refer to the primeval condition but to the being of man in a world in which sin already has gained entry, even if it has not become active and actual ("dead" = without activity).

Thus the "I" of Rom. 7 can have only a general meaning.[17] It is man under the law and sin who expresses himself in this "I," in whose history, of course, the story of Adam is repeated in a peculiar way. The "commandment" that encounters man is no longer the commandment of paradise but the decalogue from which "you shall not covet" is also taken. But in the encounter with this Mosaic Law, which leads to "knowledge of sin" (Rom. 3.20) and to the reckoning of sin (Rom. 5.13), the offense of the "I" first becomes analogous to the transgression of Adam in its actual meaning.[18] The Adam of Rom. 5.12ff. speaks in the "I" of Rom. 7.7ff. If this reference of the "I" to Adamic man is correct, it must be noted that it is still not right to speak of man, mankind. Here a mythological or even "salvation-historical"[19] way of speaking is no longer in order, because the reality of one lost under law, sin and death can be referred to only as "my" reality. Only under law, sin and death does man really become an "I," and in such a way that he is forced back to the basic nature of human existence in general.[20]

With sin deceiving and killing me with the help of the commandment, the history of the "I" which establishes its essence is ended. But only its human aspect has become visible; what this history means first becomes apparent under the divine aspect. Therefore Paul begins again in v. 12, by looking at it, so to speak, from above, with the justification of the law: "Therefore the law is holy and the commandment holy, right and good."[21] Two things in particular should be noted in this formulation: first, the fact that Paul characterizes the sentence as the consequence of what already has been said ("so") i.e. therefore not as a concession or limitation. This is not at all a matter of course. Does not v. 10 ("this proved to be death") mean that at least now, where sin has proven its superiority over the commandment, it is no longer possible to speak the way Paul does in v. 12? Paul is interested in describing the holiness, righteousness and goodness of the law and the commandment as not being a past quality that it has lost under sin. The present character of the statement in v. 12 is the second thing that must be noted (cf. v. 14). Looking retrospectively at the alliance into which sin and the law have entered with each other, and thus at the history that has led me out of life into death, this means that already the work of sin in me (deception and death) was only possible because sin could use this weapon that stems from God. But looking forward to the end that God pursues in this history, it means at the same time that the law in its holiness, which is something past, must still serve a purpose that is directed against sin itself.

The misuse to which sin has put the law has not changed it in its substance. It is not the good (i.e. the commandment) that has become death for me, "but sin is to be seen as sin in that it worked death in me through the good" (v. 13). The defense of the law therefore clearly has as its goal to maintain sin and death as the conditions of my existence, and not to let it become a characteristic quality of the law in the sense of Marcionite mythology. Thus v. 13 has given clear interpretation to the still misleading sentence "this proved to be death" (v. 10). So it definitely is not true, as one could conclude from 7.10, that sin had as it were taken God's law from his hand, as a land conquered by the enemy in war becomes enemy territory. No: now, too, indeed now most of all, the law proclaims God's will. Precisely now, where sin appears to have conquered it, the law accomplishes the last thing that it is destined to proclaim. It brings sin to light in its radical sinfulness, overrunning all boundaries, exceeding all thinking, disabling all willing, "in order that sin become sinful beyond measure through the commandment" (v. 13). Thus God has only apparently given the law over to sin. In fact, it has remained his instrument. God demonstrates sin as the power of death through its deceptive service of the law. Sin only lives by killing me.

III

Up to v. 13 Paul has spoken in the past tense and by this shown that an irrevocable decision, from which I always proceed, has occurred here. Then he changes into the present tense, for now it concerns the result of this irrevocable history and thus how this fatal alliance between the law and sin works itself out in me. The connection between the two sections (7–13 and 14–25) cannot be overemphasized. It is disastrous to connect the discussion of the anthropological problem of ch. 7 essentially only to 7.14ff., as usually happens.[22] In fact, 7.7–13 more than any other passage has already given the decisive answer to the question, who am I? I am the one deceived and killed by sin, i.e. man who is hopelessly caught in the illusion of life and who has long since forfeited his life. I always begin my life under the law as a child of deception and death. From this beginning my existence receives the terrible contradictory character developed by vv. 14–25. In the course of my existence, bondage to deception and death is revealed to me not so much as a destiny determined by the beginning and origin but as a painful, enigmatic end that I do not understand. This is to say that the insight into the character of my failure to understand, its basis at the beginning in the history that binds me, and its resulting way of appearing in my present existence, transcends the circle of experience possible to me myself. The misery of man referred to by Rom. 7 is disclosed only from beyond myself, i.e. from faith. Of course, that does not mean that the contradiction is only the mark of the believer, but that what the contradiction of man under the law, sin and death means is disclosed only in faith.

This contradiction consists first in the radical split between the law, that is spiritual (i.e. originates and belongs to God's sphere), and myself, since I am fleshly and sold under sin (v. 14). But with this split the issue is still not exhaustively described. One could probably come to resign himself to the hopeless opposition between the holy God and unholy man, between the law that is spiritual and the "I" that is sold to sin. This opposition receives its deep mystery only in that it presents itself as a split in me and tears me apart. I experience it in the enigmatic contradiction between willing and doing. "I do not understand my own actions. For I do not do what I want, but I do the very thing I hate" (v. 15).

But what does this opposition between willing and doing mean? The traditional interpretation, also maintained by Althaus and Kümmel,[23] understands this opposition as one in man, who as subject desires to fulfill the holy and good will of God as it encounters him in the commandment, and yet constantly fails.[24] Bultmann has emphatically opposed this interpretation.[25] For Paul elsewhere this inner subjective, ethical conflict is not at all the typical experience of man under the law. As he can say in view of his Pharisaical past that he is blameless in the law (Phil. 3.6), so he reckons also that the heathen may do the works of the law (Rom. 2.14). The original sin of the Jew is rather that he misuses the law as a means to self-praise and understands it as a way of salvation. From the outset it is improbable that Paul would not have given place to this view in this central passage. And, in fact, Paul here intends nothing else. Decisive for understanding is the correct grasp of the term translated "wrought" or "work" or "do," that we already find in 7.8 and 7.13 and later in vv. 17, 18, 20. The term looks to the result of the doing and what issues from my doing, not to the doing itself. But the result of all my deeds is death, although I indeed want to live. Thus "life" is the "good" (vv. 18f.), death the "evil" (vv. 19, 21). That is what constitutes the enigmatic contradiction that tears me apart: all my "doing" is directed against its own intention. "The split in man does not therefore consist in his consciousness, which can accuse itself or be detached from itself, but in the fact that man does the opposite of what he wills, that is to say of what he really, fundamentally wills—but not of what he from time to time wills in actual practice."[26]

The correctness of Bultmann's explanation is supported, I think, precisely by vv. 7–13, which concluded that I am deceived by sin and have become a child of death. Even if here Paul may initially have thought of the transgression of God's commandment, as the allusion to the Paradise story shows, it is still a fact that he does not speak of "transgression" but of arousing "desire,"[27] and that at least in v. 11 he included lawless as well as law-abiding conduct as possibilities of "desire." But this means that the question debated by Althaus and Bultmann, whether what follows concerns sin in the sense of transgression or the self-justifying establishment of "one's own righteousness," is no longer a relevant alternative for Rom. 7. In any case, in my conduct contrary to the law I begin as one who covets, that is as one deceived by sin, grasping in one way or another for life falsely promised, but in fact falling prey to sin. The "it deceived me" is the basis of "I do not understand" (v. 15). Of course, I would not dispute that Paul sees this trans-subjective conflict, which goes beyond the consciousness of the unredeemed, as certainly occurring and evident also in failure to fulfill the concrete commandment. In fact he speaks here of the unredeemed man from a viewpoint not yet possible to such a one himself. Therefore he also makes radical the concrete experience of failure to fulfill the concrete commandment so that it becomes a general experience of perplexity that is first disclosed to faith.[28]

This experience means the disruption of my "I" before God, for I experience in it the enigmatic contradiction between my doing that is without my willing and my willing that is without my deed.[29] This contradiction shows that I am sold under sin. That means I, not only as the stage of this conflict, but I who am myself this contradiction. Thus I myself, as one longing for life, must simply confirm the law's goodness. I in the contradiction, I as the contradiction, am the proof of the ambiguity of myself and the integrity of the good law. Verses 15f. similarily clarify "being sold under sin" (v. 14), just as they confirm the spirituality and goodness of the law. So it is precisely between "law" and "sin" that the mystery of the "I" first becomes fully clear. Paul now describes the contradiction that constitutes my existence a third time. Now he makes the contradiction apparent not only as a split between the law and "I" (which could be accepted with resignation), not only as a split between willing and doing (which could remain on the plane of general moral experience), but as the split between sin and the self. With respect to the earlier ones, the radicality of the expression in vv. 17f. consists of his now no longer speaking of sin as a power that enslaves me (the picture of being sold!) but of sin as the inhabitant within me. Thus sin is taken from the outside into the "I." At the same time, the contradictory splitting of the "I" is actually clear for the first time. For I am nothing more than a dwelling and workshop for sin. It dwells and works in me. I am only its unwilling instrument. The fleshly being that completely constitutes my "I" puts an end to my "I." Therefore the "I" in its nothingness is defined, not limited, by the "that is, in my flesh" in v. 18. With this the contradictory being of the "I" has first become apparent in its complete "mysteriousness." This mysteriousness consists in my no longer being at home in myself. Rather, sin is at home in me and therefore I bear my own murderer (7.11 and 13) in me.[30]

The expressions by which Paul characterizes the contradiction as opposition between sin and "I" are, of course, capable of being misunderstood, as if the entrance of sin into the "I" were a fate that has tragically come over me. In that case one could no longer speak of guilt, and the "I" could produce its alibi in the "not-I." The misconception is not lessened, but in a certain sense promoted all the more in vv. 22ff. by the way Paul develops the split between "sin" and "flesh" on the one side and the "I" on the other through the antithesis "mind" (or "inmost self") and "flesh" (or "my members"). In this he utilizes gnostic and dualistic terminology that has repeatedly led to the wrong interpretation that Paul differentiated between a lower subject of the "flesh" and its members, forfeited to sin, and the higher self of man, turned toward God's law, which in v. 17 he calls "I" and later "mind" and "inmost self." However, this misconception is rejected by Paul himself in that already in v. 14 he has described the "I" without qualification as "sold under sin." He sees this fleshly man as determined by the conflict between willing and doing, and by what follows establishes precisely, without qualification, the comprehensive validity of the statement that nothing good dwells within me, that is in my "flesh." This places the willing of the good, but not its accomplishment, at the disposal of the "I" (vv. 18f.). Thus Paul does not leave open any possibility of retreat from the misery of actual self-existence into the higher possibilities of the "mind." Therefore the unity and identity of the subject are stressed most strongly both at the beginning (vv. 14f.) and at the end of the statements, starting with v. 21 (twice "for me"), especially in vv. 24f.: "Wretched man that I am. Who will deliver me . . . So then I of myself." Thus "mind" and "flesh" are functions of one and the same "I" that is sold under sin, has lost itself and in this failure of itself has its existence in the negation of itself. Yet even this failing, godless man does not escape from God. Even as a prisoner of sin he remains God's prisoner, who must almost joyously confirm God's right in his law. Paul describes this double "must"—the necessity that being sold to sin forces upon him and the necessity under which God's law places him, by means of the contradictory double law, which in its twofold relationship constitutes the radical lostness of man from which the plaintive cry arises (v. 24). Here also he apparently speaks in Platonic or Gnostic fashion in characterizing the body of death as a prison from which the "I" is to be liberated by a savior.

We already have indicated what differentiates the Pauline statement from Gnosticism. The difference is given in that the "mind" and "inmost self" cannot be differentiated from the "flesh" as a higher and real self, and therefore salvation is not offered to this inner man, his "mind," but to the entire "I" that is sold to sin. This is shown very instructively, for instance, by the comparison of 7.24 with the similarly sounding passage in *Corp. Herm.* 13.14, where the initiate says to the mystagogue: "Tell me, O father: This body . . . is it at any time dissolved?" And the counter-question reads: "Dost thou not know thou hast been born a God, Son of the One, even as I myself?" For Paul, the knowledge of his own condition, revealed to him through the law, first seals the misery of man in the body of this death. On the other hand, through knowledge the Gnostic inserts himself in the divine "nature" and is liberated from the world.

Positively and negatively the end of Rom. 7 already prepares for Rom. 8. It does so positively, by the remarkable direct thanksgiving, by which v. 25a answers the plaintive cry of v. 24. It does so negatively, by the equally direct sentence in v. 25b that occurs once again between 25a and the beginning of Rom. 8. There is some probability that 7.25b is an exegetical gloss[31] that summarizes 7.14–25. Certainly the verse adds nothing new. If we leave the phrase in the text, then it once more as it were pushes the bar in front of the hopelessly locked door and wards off the illusion that I have to say yes to God's law with reason, the inner man, that I want the good and that it is not I who does evil but sin, that this is something like a beginning that must be helped, a footbridge, even if a fragile one, but one which could become sturdy by the working of divine grace and lead to freedom.[32]

In fact, ch. 7 as a whole presses forward to the one word that actually occurs in 8.1: "condemnation".[33] That it should now be said that "There is therefore now no condemnation" is itself the wonder of the message of salvation. The "in Christ Jesus" puts an end to the "I of myself" (7.25). This new being is opened to the believer— Paul speaks with encouragement in 8.2!—in Christ Jesus, who has appeared right where the "I" was in its lostness, "in the likeness of sinful flesh." Now the same thing is said about him (or about the Spirit) that was previously said about sin ("to dwell" in 7.17f. and 8.9, "Christ in you" in 8.10). There he has done what the law in its impotence could not do. The law has not broken through the bastion of the "flesh" but only locked me in my fleshliness and made me a child of death. Bearing the form of my flesh, marked and distorted by sin, Christ has sentenced sin to death and destroyed sin in the flesh— so to speak on its own ground and soil—and opened life in the Spirit to the one liberated. Therefore it can now be affirmed: but you are no longer in the flesh but in the Spirit (8.9).

IV

The exegesis has shown that the old dispute about whether man in Rom. 7 is to be understood as man under the law or man under grace must be answered in the first sense. Not even high respect for the representatives of the other interpretation (from the anti-Pelagian Augustine through the Reformers to Kohlbrügge and some recent representatives) nor theological misgivings about representatives of the first interpretation (Pelagius, Humanism, Pietism) can change this conclusion, held today by most exegetes.[34] The context clearly demands an interpretation that refers to the unredeemed. So, too, there is not a word mentioned about the Spirit in Rom. 7. It is rather about the opposition between "mind" and "flesh" in which the "mind," impotent over against the "flesh," seals the disruption of man, his complete lostness. The passage often cited from Gal. 5.17, where Paul still reckons with a battle between "Spirit" and "flesh," even for the Christian, does not refute the interpretation of Rom. 7 as "man under law," but rather confirms it. For first, Gal. 5.17 does not, as does Rom. 7, speak of a hopeless battle, but of a battle that stands under the promise of victory (for here the "Spirit," not the "mind," contends against the "flesh"). And secondly, the "flesh" in Gal. 5.17 is the power that threatens the believer, but no longer the power to which he is sold and lost. Furthermore, it is not true to say that in Rom. 8 Paul still speaks of the longing and sighing of the believer for redemption. Again the difference is clear. In Rom. 7, the man who cries out is the man to whom the Spirit has not yet been given and who therefore remains imprisoned in the past of his "I." In Rom. 8, on the other hand, the one who sighs is the one endowed with the Spirit, who therefore in his longing and sighing looks to the future. As a down-payment of what is coming, the Spirit connects him to that future.

We cannot discuss further here the question, raised especially by Althaus and Bultmann, about the discrepancy between Paul and Luther resulting from this exegesis.[35] Nevertheless, it appears to me that the question is not yet sufficiently clarified about what the "backward look" of Rom. 7.7ff. to the unredeemed being of man means. Certainly one may not say that here one looks back from the secure shore of faith to the storm and the ghosts which have accompanied the believer on his journey to this shore. Evidently one cannot leave behind the experiences of Rom. 7 as a vanquished and surpassed level of development. Rather the past and lostness of the unredeemed remains in a very definite sense present even for the Christian, as one forgiven and conquered. Indeed, the past becomes transparent for him only in faith. He does not have the righteousness of faith in any other way than by offering the sacrifice of his own righteousness. He has acquittal, being "in Christ," only in the confession of his lostness under law, sin and death. It is not by chance that Rom. 8 is once again filled with statements about man who in himself is ruined (8.5ff.), just as on the other hand the *interpretatio Christiana* of the unredeemed in Rom. 7 goes far beyond what the unredeemed can understand of himself. Thus the self-understanding of the redeemed (Rom. 8) and the self-understanding of the sinner (Rom. 7) are most firmly linked to one another. Therefore the past remains the precipitous foundation of the new being in Christ. In precisely this way it is shown that the righteousness of the believer is the *aliena iustitia* of Christ and that man in looking to himself is lost.[36]

NOTES

[1] First published in *Jahrbuch der Theol. Schule Bethel* N.F. II (1950), pp. 26ff., under the title "Der Mensch im Leibe des Todes."

² Cf. R. Bultmann, "Römer 7 und die Anthropologie des Paulus" in *Imago Dei* (1932), pp. 57ff. (ET, *Existence and Faith*, Shorter Writings of R. Bultmann (1960), pp. 152ff.).

³ W. G. Kummel, *Römer 7 und die Bekehrung des Paulus* (1929).

⁴ Which G. Kuhlmann perverts to mean the contrary in *Theologia naturalis bei Philon und Paulus* (1930), pp. 92ff.

⁵ The two words *gnōnai* and *eidenai* (meaning "to know") in 7.7 have a practical, not a theoretical, sense. Cf. Bultmann, *TWNT* I, p. 703 (ET, *TDNT* I, p. 703) and *TNT*, p. 261 (ET, *NTT* I, pp. 264f.). E. Fuchs, *Die Freiheit des Glaubens* (1949), pp. 56f., seeks to differentiate between the sense of the two verbs and keep the meaning "establish" (of an object) especially for *eidenai*. But this meaning does not fit for 7.7 (*epithumia*, i.e. "what it is to covet"), and the passages cited by Fuchs show without exception that the two verbs are used without distinction by Paul. Cf. also 7.15 and 7.18.

⁶ With the exception of a few passages, where *epithumia* designates desire (Phil. **1.23**; I Thess. 2.17; cf. also *epithumein* in Gal. 5.17), *epithumia* has a pregnant, not a neutral, meaning. Against A. Schlatter, *Gottes Gerechtigkeit* (1935), p. 232; T. Schlatter, "Für Gott lebendig in Christi Kraft," *Jahrbuch der Theol. Schule Bethel* I (1930), pp. 139f.; P. Althaus, *Paulus and Luther über den Menschen* (1951²), p. 87.

⁷ With "you shall not covet," the content of the ninth and tenth commandments are summarized here as in Rom. 13.9, and with them in our passage the entire Decalogue (already pre-Pauline, cf. IV Macc. 2.6). Any limitation of the *epithumia* to the sexual desire is thus beside the point. In I Cor. 10.6, too, *epithumein* is simply a term for disobedience against God's commandment.

⁸ *aphormē* ("opportunity") designates, e.g., the favorable starting-point for a military operation. This use is instructive, even if Paul apparently uses the term without recalling such an idea.

⁹ Cf. E. Fuchs, *op. cit.*, p. 57.

¹⁰ As a flood throws the stones and beams of a torn-up dike against frail cottages and collapses them, sin and the law now cover me, so that it is not possible to hold them back, and drag me into death.

¹¹ Grammatically, "in the commandment" probably belongs to "finding opportunity."

¹² Not the reverse. In opposition to Fuchs, *op. cit.*, p. 60.

¹³ In opposition to Fuchs, p. 65.

¹⁴ More detail in Kümmel, *op. cit.*, and in his *Das Bild des Menschen im Neuen Testament* (1948), pp. 27ff. (ET, *Man in the New Testament*, 1963, pp. 48ff.).

¹⁵ "Apart from the law" concerns the absence of the law, not only the condition of ignorance.

¹⁶ Cf. O. Pfister, *Das Christentum und die Angst* (1944), pp. 187f.

¹⁷ "Within himself as it were he carries on a general process" (Ambrosiaster).

¹⁸ Cf. G. Schrenk, *TWNT* II (*entolē*), pp. 546f. (ET, *TDNT* II, pp. 550f.).

¹⁹ Against Stauffer, *TWNT* II, pp. 355ff. (ET, *TDNT* II, pp. 358ff.).

²⁰ E. Fuchs, *op. cit.*, pp. 60ff., thinks he is able to recognize behind 7.7–24 a model of Gnostic character used by Paul, and he reconstructs a two-verse song, in which the soul that stems from beyond laments its seduction by the *epithumia*, its sinking into death and into the prison of the body. Paul supposedly reshaped and added to this text and historicized the Gnostic myth in that he allegedly joined death with sin and sin with the law. However, I cannot really recognize the breaks and seams that Fuchs seeks to make visible by his analysis. I think rather that all expressions of the text are drawn from the theme "law and sin" and do not allow for the use of a Gnostic poem. For instance, the sentence that Fuchs attributes to the model, "nothing good dwells in me," appears to me to be completely un-

Gnostic. On the other hand, the thesis of G. Harder in *Paulus und das Gebet* (1936), pp. 31f., appears to me to be correct, namely that the question in 7.24 corresponds to the style of the prayerful sigh in the Psalms. Only this prayerful sigh is not to be characterized as Christian prayer, as Harder thinks, *op. cit.*, pp. 212f.

21 *men* in 7.12 corresponds to the *alla* in 7.13, which, of course, simultaneously and directly introduces the contrast to the preceding, negated question.

22 Cf. W. G. Kümmel, *op. cit.*, pp. 27ff. (ET, *op. cit.*, pp. 48ff.); P. Althaus, *op. cit.*, p. 31; R. Bultmann, "Christus des Gesetzes Ende," in *Glauben und Verstehen* II (1952), pp. 32ff. (ET, "Christ the End of the Law," in *Essays Philosophical and Theological*, 1955, pp. 36ff.).

23 Althaus, *op. cit.*, pp. 41ff.; Kümmel, *op. cit.*, p. 23 (ET, *op. cit.*, p. 43).

24 Ancient parallels in H. Lietzmann, *HzNT* 8 (1933[4]) on Rom. 7.15.

25 R. Bultmann, "Röm. 7 und die Anthropologie des Menschen," pp. 55ff. (ET, pp. 149ff., see n. 2).

26 Bultmann, "Christus des Gesetzes Ende," in *Glauben und Verstehen* II, p. 46 (ET, p. 52).

27 Fuchs, *op. cit.*, pp. 71f., has correctly taken up again the term *epithumia* in the interpretation of 7.15.

28 "The entire interpretation of the I is seen rather from the outside; thus it is a subsequent explanation of sinful existence," Fuchs, *op. cit.*, p. 72.

29 Entirely in the sense of Rom. 7, Hermann Melville describes the master-at-arms Claggart in his masterful story *Billy Budd*: "With no power to annul the elemental evil in him, though readily enough he could hide it; apprehending the good, but powerless to be it; a nature like Claggart's, surcharged with energy as such natures almost invariably are, what recourse is left to it but to recoil upon itself and, like the scorpion for which the Creator alone is responsible, act out to the end the part allotted it!" (ch. 12).

30 This conception of man is depicted in ghastly fashion in Shakespeare's *Richard III* (Act V, Scene 3): "What do I fear? Myself? There's none else by. Richard loves Richard; that is, I am I. Is there a murderer here? No—Yes, I am. Then fly. What, from myself?"

31 R. Bultmann, "Glossen im Römerbrief," *TLZ* (1947), cols 197ff.

32 So Althaus, *op. cit.*, p. 58: "There is a reality in man to which the Holy Spirit does not say no, but yes . . . What the 'inward man' (i.e. reason) begin, the Spirit takes up, continues, makes effective. . . ."

33 Bultmann, *op. cit.*, col. 199, takes 8.1 as well as 7.25b for an exegetical gloss (also Fuchs, *op. cit.*, p. 83). While the hypothesis is convincing to me for the first passage, for the second I think it improbable. Actually 8.2 would best be joined to 7.25a, and the sentence in 8.1 does stand in strong contrast to what precedes it. Above all, Bultmann can assert that "the sentence that there is no 'condemnation' for those who are in Christ Jesus" supposedly is not a very appropriate conclusion to what precedes it, since the longed-for salvation in 7.24 is not one from condemnation in judgment but from the "body of death." But it is just this further development that appears to me to be characteristic of Paul and to mark once again his opposition to Gnosticism. In fact, Rom. 8 indeed continues in the sense of the message of justification. Therefore, 8.1 appears to me to be understandable, not as a direct inference from 7.24 but as a new beginning that takes up again the "but now" of 7.6 with the emphatic "now" and thematically prepares for what follows. The "he condemned sin" in 8.3 corresponds to the "no condemnation."

34 A. Nygren, *Commentary on Romans*, (1949), recently again supports the interpretation of Rom. 7 as pointing to the Christian life.

35 On Althaus cf. the convincing remarks of R. Bultmann, "Christus des Gesetzes Ende," in *Glauben und Verstehen* II, pp. 43ff., 54ff. (ET, pp. 49ff., 60ff.).

[36] To say this is to say simultaneously why I cannot support as correct the thesis of Schlatter on Rom. 7, maintained earlier in *Jahrbuch der Theol. Schule Bethel* I, pp. 137f., and III, pp. 36ff.

Additional literature: Cf. the more recent commentaries on Romans by C. H. Dodd (1949), O. Michel (1957²), O. Kuss (1957), F. J. Leenhardt (1957), C. K. Barrett (1957). Also P. Althaus, "Zur Auslegung von Röm. 7.14ff." (against Nygren) in TLZ (1952), cols 475ff., and Nygren's answer, *ibid.*, 591ff. C. L. Mitton, "Rom. 7 reconsidered," *Expos. Times* 65 (1953f.), pp. 78ff., 99ff., 132ff.

VII

THE PRAISE OF GOD
Romans 11.33–36*

I

PAUL CONCLUDES THE large section in which he has dealt with the righteousness of God in Israel's destiny by ascribing praise to God (11.33–36). He formulates this in hymnically heightened sentences which correspond to the character of the doxology. That he uses a mosaic of scriptural passages in doing this does not detract from the unity of the hymn in the least. If one classifies this text as a "hymn," as is justifiably done,[1] this does not mean that the whole is therefore to be characterized as a consciously created piece of art. Its formulation is to be thought of as being more spontaneous. Nevertheless, the elements of hymnic style[2] are multiplied in it to such a degree (partly through the incorporation of Old Testament words in vv. 34ff., but also in vv. 33 and 36) that one can no longer speak justifiably only of exalted prose. Rather, one may accurately classify it as a hymn.

Here as well as elsewhere in the Old and New Testaments, the hymn is more than simply a favorite rhetorical device, or the expression of poetic rapture, or the language of an individualistic mood. Rather, its original context is that of worship, and it is an expression of homage and worshipful submission to the manifest and present majesty and power of God.

What moves Paul to these hymnic sentences in Rom. 11 becomes clear from the content of the entire section which they conclude. It is the fact that behind the dark, mysterious way of Israel which first awakened the lament of the Apostle, the goal of divine mercy has become apparent. The overwhelming power of God, the overwhelming power of his judgments, but most of all the overwhelming power

---

* Published as a sermon meditation in *Für Arbeit und Besinnung* 5 (1951), pp. 178ff., and in *Göttinger Predigtmeditationen* (1955/6), pp. 155ff.

of his mercy—each has its parallel in the rapture of the hymn. In the hymn nothing more is told, depicted, reported, nor is any detail reflectively laid out. Rather, the whole is embraced and raised to the height of an immortal present. As the praise of God's power the hymn expresses what transcends all thinking; it is the expression of awe.[3]

With E. Norden and G. Harder, the text of the hymn "with its parts and clauses" is best divided into nine lines:

33   O the depth of the riches and wisdom and knowledge of God!
      How unsearchable are his judgments
34   and how inscrutable his ways!
      For who has known the mind of the Lord,
      or who has been his counselor?
35   Or who has given a gift to him
      that he might be repaid?
36   For from him and through him and to him are all things.
      To him be glory for ever. Amen.

The text contains both Old Testament and Greek elements. To the former belong the citations from Isa. 40.13 and Job 41.2 (vv. 34f.) and the doxology (v. 36), but also the overtones of Prov. 8.18 (3.16) and Job 5.9; 9.10 (vv. 33a and b). These latter, even if they are not to be designated as free citations, still adequately show that the expressions of Paul are marked by the LXX.[4] Or to express it more exactly—this is important for the understanding of 11.34f.—they point back to late Jewish wisdom poetry. The verbal adjectives with alpha-privative construction stem originally from Greek theology. But as Harder has shown (*op. cit.*, pp. 51ff.), even before Paul they entered into Judaism's language of prayer and theology and are found frequently in early Christian hymns and prayers. The chosen phrase "depth of the riches"[5] in v. 33 probably also stems from the Greek and the "all" formula in v. 36 definitely does. Both have been transmitted to Paul through Hellenistic Judaism.

The hymn begins with a wondering exclamation about God's inexhaustibility and unfathomability, which are impenetrable by any human comprehension. Here Paul does not think speculatively in Greek fashion about the nature of God in general. Rather, he thinks historically about God's "judgments" and "ways."[6] They give meaning to the three terms "riches," "wisdom," and "knowledge."[7] "Riches," according to Rom. 9–11, probably means the riches of God in methods and ways of reaching his goal of salvation ("You have a way everywhere . . .''), and therefore at the same time the riches of God's mercy and patience (Rom. 10.12; Eph. 1.7; 3.8). "Wisdom" means the wisdom of God that once clothed creation (I Cor. 1.23) and is now embodied in Christ (I Cor. 1.30; Col. 2.3). "Knowledge of God" (subjective genitive, as can be seen from the fact that "of God" also belongs to the first two members), means God's recognition, i.e. his election (ch. 9 to 11; Eph. 1.4ff.).[8]

The judgments of God and the evidences of his grace are unsearchable and untraceable (33b). This does not, of course, mean that they are not accessible at all to human experience, but they are impenetrable in their depth. Man cannot pursue them and trace them back to their origin in God himself. This is why Paul speaks so little as one who has penetrated "behind" things. The more fully and clearly the large train of thought in ch. 9–11 discloses the judgments and ways of God, even up to the mystery (11.25ff.) of the final salvation of Israel, the more their depths become unfathomable.

All three questions that follow (vv. 34f.) demand the answer: No one! To understand this it seems important to me that they be joined to the three terms "riches," "wisdom," and "knowledge" in reverse order.

1. "Who has known the mind of the Lord?" (Isa. 40.13; cf. I Cor. 2.16.) Answer: No one who surveys the knowledge of God, i.e. the mystery of his gracious election. "O the depths of the knowledge of God."

2. "Who has been his counselor?" (Isa. 40.13.) "Have you heard God's secret counsel and laid hold of wisdom?" (Job 15.8.) "Do you think that you know what God knows and do you want to embrace it as perfectly as the Almighty?" (Job 11.7.) "But who has stood in the counsel of the Lord, who has seen and heard his word?" (Jer. 23.18.) Who therefore has played the role to which God has called "wisdom," to be his "counselor"? (Wisdom 8.9)—"O the riches of wisdom."

3. "Who has given a gift to him,"[9] so that God would now be obliged to return thanks for what he had received? Who therefore may say of himself that he had helped God to his "riches" and would now be justified, as it were, to sue for the fullness of the divine gifts?— "O the depth of the riches"—A clear climax of absurd assumptions!

After this threefold rejection of human presumption, Paul closes with an all-inclusive sentence (v. 36). The "him," emphasized three times ("from him" —"through him"—"to him") corresponds to "of

God" in v. 33. E. Norden has shown that the "all" formula (v. 36) has a Stoic origin.[10] The most striking parallel is in Marcus Aurelius (*Soliloquies* IV, 23), already noted by Wettstein, but properly observed again only by Norden: "All that is harmonious to you, O world, is also harmonious to me. Nothing comes to me too early or too late if it appears timely to you. All that your courses of years bring is fruit to me, O nature: 'all things from you,' 'all things in you,' 'all things to you.'" For the Stoics, "nature" is identical with God. The "all" formula related to it here is also found frequently elsewhere as a kind of Stoic confession of faith.[11]

Paul's change of this Stoic formula has been justifiably noted on several occasions. Paul's application of it to the history of God's judgment and grace (cf. v. 36 with 32) transcends the Stoic thought of immanence. If for the Stoics it concerns what emanates from God, enters into his being and is one with him, for Paul it is characteristic that there is no corresponding member to the "all things in you" in the "all" formula of Marcus Aurelius, cited above. Because of this the formula has lost its pantheistic meaning. It praises the work of the Creator, the Lord and Perfecter of history. The doxology that ends the hymn applies to him.

II

This text presents considerable difficulties to the preacher. They lie first in the text itself. Can one preach about a hymn of praise? May one transform it into instruction and encouragement? Is not the peculiarity of its ideas the fact that they are raised in thanksgiving? Can it therefore yield another application of the text than concurrence in the praise? Moreover, this praise closes a very definite train of thought embraced by ch. 9–11. Should we therefore take our text as the occasion to preach about the miracle and mystery of the church composed of Jews and Gentiles (Israel's call and fall, the meaning of her stubbornness for the Gentiles and finally Israel's eventual reacceptance)? But how shall we escape the danger of wanting to say the impossible in a single sermon and offering food that is much too solid and too demanding to a congregation that needs milk?

According to the lectionary, the sermon on this text is supposed to proclaim the mystery of the Trinity! But what clues does the text offer for this? The dogma and celebration of the Trinity are only of a later date. The festival of the Trinity has existed only since the Middle

Ages. Originally the Sunday after Pentecost ended the festival of
Pentecost. Our Epistle reading was appointed as a lectionary text for
that Sunday with this in mind and, in fact, suits it excellently. To the
theme "Trinity" it yields nothing, at least *expressis verbis*. We must
therefore guard against exegetical affectation and certainly may not
divide the three terms riches, wisdom and knowledge of God among
the three persons of the Trinity. Each of the terms speaks about God,
the Creator, the Redeemer and the Perfecter. As has been done
since the time of the ancient church, it is better to understand the last
verse with its tripartite statement as a pointer to the Trinity: "from
him" as a pointer to the Father and Creator, "through him" as a
pointer to the Son and Redeemer and "to him" to the Spirit and
Perfecter. But exegetically that is not really justified either, because
at least to the Apostle Paul this trinitarian differentiation is foreign.
Only I Cor. 8.6 would justify the differentiation of Father and Son.
But how little Paul actually differentiates is shown in that at one
point he relates the "through him" to Christ the Lord, at another it
speaks of God. Furthermore, "to him" is also related to God regard-
less of the fact that it can be related to the Son in Col. 1.16. Therefore,
there is nothing to support a trinitarian pattern here. But perhaps
this is itself an important hint that we as preachers of the New
Testament should not aspire to a *theologia gloriae* that attempts to
penetrate speculatively the inner mysteries of the Trinity. Rather, ours
is to witness to the revelation of the one God as Creator, Redeemer
and Perfecter, his threefold work towards us, the church and the
"universe." The mystery of the Trinity will disclose itself to us in this
way and only in this way. What the church has expressed in its
doctrine will help us to comprehend the unity of what we confess in
the three articles of faith. We dissolve this unity all too easily and
understand the revelation, as it were, as three acts that follow one
another in history and thereby change it into a mythical drama. This
is then presented, secularized where possible, simply as the historical
development of religious ideas. But the doctrine of the Trinity has
the result of freeing our thinking from such captivity and making
present for us the activity of God as his victory over the fatal powers
of time and history. We (and that means at the same time the church
and the world) are embraced by him, no longer given to a vain and
aimless running nor delivered to the nothingness of death. God the
Creator, God the Redeemer, God the Perfecter—this has the sense of
the event of revelation that is proclaimed by the message of the

Incarnation, Crucifixion, Resurrection, Exaltation of Christ and the sending of the Spirit through him to the glory of the Father. The sermon on Trinity Sunday has to unify and to confirm with praise this kerygma of the great festivals of the church year. In this it also has an essential and definite function for all further proclamation of the church year. It keeps us from preaching during that part of the church year "without festivals" about the words, deeds and stories of Jesus, while forgetting that Jesus Christ himself is the end of history and that he himself is the history, the deed, the Word of God, in which God as Creator, Reconciler and Perfecter is the One near to redeem us.

This mystery of the triune God in his creating, redeeming and perfecting work transcends our thinking and understanding. It does not allow itself to be comprehended in a "getting behind," but is grasped and praised in adoration. "Such high meaning the creature does not attain; you adore and follow in its train!"

NOTES

[1] Cf. G. Harder, *Paulus und das Gebet* (1936), pp. 51ff., and E. Norden, *Agnostos Theos* (1913 = 1956⁴), pp. 240ff.

[2] The double exclamation in v. 33; the three connected questions with parallel members in v. 34f.; the omnipotence-formula and the doxology in v. 36.

[3] Cf. Calvin on Rom. 11.33: "After having spoken out of the Word and Spirit of the Lord, and overcome at last by the sublimity of so great a mystery, Paul can do nothing but wonder and exclaim that the riches of the wisdom of God are too deep for our reason to be able to penetrate them. If, therefore, we enter at any time on a discourse concerning the eternal counsels of God, we must always restrain both our language and manner of thinking, so that when we have spoken soberly and within the limits of the Word of God, our argument may finally end in an expression of astonishment" (translation from the Latin by Ross MacKenzie, Calvin's Commentaries, *The Epistles of Paul the Apostle to the Romans and to the Thessalonians*, 1961, p. 259).

[4] Cf. on 11.33, Sir. 16.20 ("Who will ponder his ways?") and 1.3; see Harder, *op. cit.*, p. 53.

[5] Cf. Norden, *op. cit.*, p. 243, n. 3.

[6] Prior illustrations of the superiority and unsearchableness of God in the Old Testament and Judaism are: Isa. 40.12ff.; 55.8f.; Prov. 30.1ff.; Job 28.23ff.; Bar. 3.29ff.; Sir. 42.18ff.; Wisdom 9.13ff. Cf. StrB III (1926), *ad loc.*

[7] Luther's translation subordinates the two following terms to the term "riches"; in the text they are coordinated.

[8] Cf. Bultmann, *TWNT* I, p. 706 (ET, *TDNT* I, p. 706).

[9] On the text-form of Job 41.2 that deviates from the LXX, cf. H. Lietzmann, *HzNT* 8 (1933⁴), *ad loc.*

[10] *Op. cit.*, pp. 240ff. For similar formulae in late Judaism, cf. Harder, *op. cit.*,

p. 54, footnotes. Parallels from Hellenistic mysticism in R. Reitzenstein, *Poimandres* (1904), p. 39.

[11] Cf. Norden and Lietzmann, *ad loc.*

Additional literature: Cf. the more recent commentaries on Romans by C. H. Dodd (1949), O. Michel (2nd ed. 1957), O. Kuss (1957), F. J. Leenhardt (1957), C. K. Barrett (1957).

VIII

ON UNDERSTANDING THE CHRIST-HYMN
Philippians 2.6–11

I

LUTHER'S PENETRATING BUT excessively free paraphrase of Phil. 2.5: "Each is to be disposed as Jesus Christ also was," easily points interpretation in a wrong direction, for it makes the appeal to an ethical disposition the main thing and understands Jesus Christ as its example. Similarly, many of the older commentaries see this as the aim of the text, as does most preaching and teaching. Now certainly there is no doubt that our passage stands in the context of an admonition to humility (2.3) and begins with a powerful imperative. However, the question about the manner and meaning of the context is decisive, for the admonition and what is said here about Christ are interrelated. In no way is this context only one of example and moral imitation. Rather it is, as so often in Paul, a *foundational* context that can only be paraphrased by a "because," not by a "how." That already applies to v. 5: "have this mind" does not refer to a "disposition" oriented toward the ideal of a virtue. Rather, it means a "directing oneself toward," a "self-orientation" toward a given and fulfilled reality that is determined and opened "in Christ Jesus" ("which is also in Christ Jesus"). With concerted power our text directs all the thinking of believers to this. Consequently, what follows speaks in such all-encompassing fashion that to begin with there is not a single phrase about believers and the conduct of their life. There is no imperative, only the indicative that describes the way and story of Christ—a way which begins in heaven and a story which ends in heaven, that bursts all bounds of earth and yet precisely in so doing opens the horizon by which alone there can be a real life in faith.

II

Phil. 2.6–11, as E. Lohmeyer first recognized,[1] is a Christ-hymn, formed long before Paul and here appropriated by him. This understanding has rightly prevailed, even if the opinions of scholars do not agree on its origin, stanza-division and liturgical usage. The numerous motifs and phrases not to be found elsewhere in Paul[1a] point to an earlier origin. They point to the hymnic-liturgical character of the content, that reaches far beyond its context, as well as to formal characteristics. Among the latter are the relative clause, frequently used in the insertion of hymnic fragments (cf., e.g., Col. 1.15; I Tim. 3.16), the numerous participles and parallelisms, and the compressed and concisely formulated individual lines (*stichoi*).[2] The decisive caesura lies, as can immediately be seen, in the strongly marked new insertion and the change of subject between vv. 8 and 9. But a sub-division can also be seen ("who . . ., but . . . ., and . . . —therefore . . ., but . . ., and . . .") between the two parts. As is shown by the repetition of the last word from the preceding phrase (death) and by the typical Pauline term "cross," only the short phrase in v. 8, "death of a cross," may be an explanatory addition from Paul's hand (Lohmeyer).[3]

III

The first half of our hymn describes Christ's way from the most exalted heights into the lowest depths. He begins with the giving up of his divinity and is fulfilled in his becoming man and in his being man in humblest form, even unto death. "To be equal with God" and "to be equal with man," God's "form" and the "form" of a servant, stand in strict antithesis to each other. But each expression must be most closely considered here. About whom does v. 6 speak? According to the opinion advocated by most exegetes, in which we also concur, it speaks about Christ *before* his Incarnation, i.e. about the Pre-existent One. This exegesis is only possible if by contrast "he emptied himself" in v. 7 and the entire second stanza of the hymn paraphrase the *becoming* man, and the third stanza with its leading verb, "he humbled himself," first tells the story of the obedience of the Earthly One.[4]

But what do the individual phrases of the first verse of our hymn mean? Lohmeyer and others, most recently O. Cullmann, already understand it in the context of the biblical story of creation. Christ is depicted here (so Cullmann) as the pre-existent heavenly man (Son of Man), who, as the contrasting type to Adam, did not succumb to the temptation of *"Eritis sicut deus"* (you will be like God), but kept the image of God pure. The expression, "form" (v. 7), is alleged to be simply an interchangable term for "image" and to be understood in the sense of the Hebrew *d*ᵉ*muth* (or *zelem*) of Gen. 1.26. Thus the ancient christological title "Son of Man" (in the sense of Primal Man!) is supposed to appear here in Paul, albeit connected to the other christological title "Servant of God" from Isa. 53 ("taking the form of a servant"). The old controversy whether one should understand the peculiar phrase "he did not count it a thing to be grasped" in the sense of *res rapta* (as a treasure which one possesses) or of *res rapienda* (as a treasure which one would like to possess) is supposed to be answered in the latter sense.[5] Thus the hymn as a whole is thought to center upon ancient biblical ideas, and the three titles: Christ as the Son of Man (God's image), the Servant of God, and the Lord.

However, this explanation hardly does justice to the text. The identification of Son of Man and Primal Man is itself more than problematic (nowhere in Paul does the Pre-existent One also represent the heavenly man; rather, in Rom. 5.12ff. and I Cor. 15.45ff., Christ is the *second* Adam). And where is the idea of a temptation of the Pre-existent One in the sense of Gen. 3.5 even intimated? The two parallel phrases in v. 6 ("he was in the form of God" and "to be equal with God"), as well as what follows, "he emptied himself," show that the Pre-existent One *was* equal with God and gave up this divine mode of existence. The fathers were justified when they spoke of a *"res rapta."* In addition, however, it is to be noted immediately that this seldom-used expression is *not* to be understood verbatim at all, but as an original, now colorless manner of speaking, stemming from ordinary language ("to exploit something for oneself"). Although the idea of the obedience of Christ as the second Adam in Rom. 5.12–21 is employed as the antithesis to the disobedience of the first Adam, it has nothing to do with a contrasting relation to creation and fall in Phil. 2. The connection with Isa. 53 fares no better. For there the Servant of God in his nature and work is differentiated precisely from men, even if he suffers their punishment vicariously. Here, however, the text simply does not allow the paraphrase: "He took the form *of* (God's) servant." Rather, his servant-form (note the lack of the article!) places him in solidarity with men, as the additional phrases most decidedly show. Jeremias[6] has not made the connection with Isa. 53 more believable by his thesis that "he emptied himself," a really strange expression without parallels in Greek, is a verbatim translation of the Hebrew text of Isa. 53.12: "he poured out his life in death." Thus it allegedly does not point to the Incarnation but to the death of God's servant. Simply from a linguistic point of view, one must object that the Hebrew "*lammaweth,*" as well as the object "*naphsho,*" should not have been left untranslated. Moreover, only the last line of the first stanza in our text speaks of death; it does not previously occur in v. 7a.

Thus the general Old Testament idea of man in the image of God is no more to be found in Phil. 2 than is the special concept of God's servant from Isa. 53. The first impairs the simple peculiarity of which the hymn speaks, and the second makes unrecognizable the radical solidarity with men into which Christ enters through his Incarnation: he appears in the "same form" as they (cf. Rom. 8.3), and in his conduct and behavior shows himself as one of them. All that differentiates him from men is that according to his primary nature he "originally" is not like them, but like God. What applies only to him applies to no other man: his Incarnation hides an incomparable divine mystery, as the Christmas message and Christmas hymns of the church justifiably express in close connection with Phil. 2.

A special explanation is, however, demanded by the phrase: "he took the form of a servant." Indeed, the term "form" that also appears again here, and that previously in v. 6 designated not only the outward form and shape in contrast to his nature but his nature itself, also shows that the "form of a servant" is not a role that he plays, but the very nature that he assumes. But then it is surprising that humanity and servanthood here are identified so directly. Old Testament references for this identification are lacking, nor does Judaism know it. Yet E. Käsemann has justifiably referred to a particular Hellenistic view of the world and concept of man reflected by our text. Here the existence of the unredeemed man is, in fact, simply understood as "bondage," that is, as captivity and slavery under the reign of cosmic powers, of "elements of the world." Paul himself shows (especially in Gal. 4.1–5, 8f.) how strongly this idea, developed primarily in Gnosticism, also influenced the Christology and soteriology of early Christianity. But the phrase "bondage to decay" in Rom. 8.21, where the creation, too, is subjected for the sake of man, shows it just as much. The description of world powers and the service of the law in Col. 2.20ff. and Heb. 2.15 is similar. Heb. 2.14f. explicitly describes the self-humiliation of Christ as the assuming of flesh and blood and the fate of death for the redemption of those "who through fear of death were subject to lifelong bondage," just as Gal. 4.3f. calls the Incarnation of the Son of God a "being-placed-under-the-law" for the liberation of men enslaved by the world powers. Viewed from this perspective, the identification of servanthood and humanity in Phil. 2 also becomes understandable. Therefore one may not with E. Schweizer include in the phrase "form of a servant" the remembrance of the image of the suffering righteous one, expressed so extensively in the Psalms and late Jewish texts. One may not do so for the simple reason that the obedience-motif with its own new emphasis is inserted for the first time several sentences later, and the expression "taking the form of a servant" is initially attached wholly and exclusively to the Incarnation of the Pre-existent One. Thus it belongs to his taking of human "nature," though it still contains no expression about the manner of his humanity. Only by this explanation do the three steps of Christ's way described by the hymn come to full expression in their dramatic and paradoxical coordination: equal-to-God, Servant, Lord.

The most significant part of the text is, however, the statement about the *obedience* of Christ even unto death. For a moment one must imagine that this last phrase is missing. Immediately everything that has been said would become a mythical drama that would give classic expression to the basic ideas of the Gnostic redemption and redeemer myth of the descent of the messenger of light into the world and earth's sphere of fallen man. Then, in the Gnostic myth, there follows the return of the redeemer with the redeemed souls into the realm of light. That myth has no place for the obedience in humiliation and the bodily dying—death on a cross—meant in Phil. 2. For our hymn, however, the actual Christ-event is fulfilled only here. Indeed, the obedience of Jesus supports the entire hymn to such an extent, that the Pre-existent One's renunciation of his equality with God and his way into the form of a servant of men receive their actual meaning from that perspective. Likewise, his subsequent exaltation as Lord is founded only in his obedience even to death.

IV

The second half of our hymn (vv. 9–11) praises the exaltation of the humiliated and obedient One as Lord over all dominions and powers. Here God is the one who acts. He makes the story of Jesus, which for the eyes of men ends in the depths, destitute of all divine splendor,

into an "Epiphany of the Obedient One" (Käsemann). It is an
event in which God himself has given the answer to that story of
humiliation. Again it is instructive to compare our text with another
shaping of the myth. In the late Jewish "wisdom" teaching we find
the idea that the divine "wisdom" is sent to the earth but, scorned by
men, returns to heaven and there again finds a dwelling.[7] Thus God
withdraws it to punish the evil world. Phil. 2.6–11, on the contrary,
speaks of an action of God in Christ and thereby simultaneously on
the world and its powers. It happens in the cosmic-eschatological
event of Christ's enthronement. According to ancient ceremonial,
used in our passage and in similar christological texts (esp. I Tim.
3.16; Heb. 1.3ff. and others), its features are the installation of the
ruler in his place, the conferring of a new name as proclamation of
his worthiness before the world, and the acclamation of the subjugated powers of the world, who with praise must confess the new Lord
over the universe. We meet all three motifs again in our text. One
must give the expression "highly exalted" (v. 9) a heightened meaning beyond the bare simple form (although the Hellenistic language
terminology, tending toward plerophories, does not absolutely
demand this understanding). The translation advocated by Cullmann
is hardly relevant: "he has done *more* than exalt him."[8] Certainly it is
correct that the verse does not speak of a mere return of Christ into
the godlike position of the Pre-existent One. Rather, it gives him a
new position. This new dimension embraces "the name that is above
every name," which God has conferred on him. It is expressed in
v. 11: the name of Kyrios (Lord). It does not need to be said that
"name" here is more than a personal name and mark of differentiation. The "name" indicates "honor and essence, and at the
same time radiates essentiality and makes it manifest" (Käsemann).[9]
Thus the conferring of the name means the conferring of kingly
right and does so as proclamation, as divine manifestation to the
world. The "more" awarded to the Exalted One is thus certainly
not an increase in the fullness of power which the One equal to God
did not possess before, but rather the manifestation of the honor of
the One hidden before and with it the now public and rightful
subjugation of the world as a whole (Käsemann). At the name
Kyrios conferred on Jesus, all beings in heaven, on earth and under
the earth must bow their knees, and every tongue confess him:
Kyrios Jesus Christ. One cannot emphasize too much—Lohmeyer
has shown this with great force—that this event of enthronement

concerns the world and not only or primarily the congregation. Thus "Kyrios" does not mean Jesus' honored position in cultic worship in Christianity (so Bousset), but the cosmic ruler (Lohmeyer). It is God's own "name" that he has received in his exaltation, the name which God imparts to no one else (in the LXX, the rendering of the tetragrammaton). Has God thus transferred his own exalted name to the exalted Christ and forgone his own lordship? In a certain sense that is, in fact, the case, paradoxical though it may sound. Kyrios in the early Christian message is indeed Jesus' exalted name; God bears the name of Father. And yet it is immediately clear that this does not represent the surrender of, but the proof of, God's divinity. Henceforth the exalted Christ represents God's rule over against the world. God deals with the world, as long as it stands (I Cor. 15.28), only through him and in him, and thus gains the name of the Father in this conferring of his own name of Kyrios on Christ. Therefore, nothing would be so contrary to the sense of our text as the idea that God had, as it were, retreated from the world. Entirely the opposite: The Lordship of Christ means the complete and full turning of God to the world. The exaltation of the humiliated One is God's victory over the world. Therefore, the confession of it reads: "To the glory of God the Father."[10]

V

Our text presents theological reflection and proclamation with great difficulties from the very start by the fullness and breadth of its expressions. Is it properly a Christmas and Epiphany text or a Passion, Easter and Ascension text? Added to this is the fact that to a great extent it employs mythical concepts in the framework of a world-view that is no longer immediately ours. Anyone who thinks through the text with theological conscientiousness cannot help thinking how strange its expressions are for us, although it is familiar to us from the dogmatic and liturgical tradition of the church and is of unique value and worth. The story which it proclaims is by no means immediately recognizable as one that concerns us and expresses our own story.

That does not mean, however, that we need discuss the problem of "demythologizing" in all its breadth. The question that concerns us can be put in a more natural and limited fashion. It presents itself very simply and unavoidably by the manner and way in which our text speaks. It proclaims, so to say, in concise objectivity a story spanning heaven and earth, God and world, a self-contained event that one could call a kind of divine drama, highly paradoxical in its events and filled with tension in its plot. Though these "poetic" categories, which we use here, may excite contradiction, they are, in fact, suitable to our hymn's manner of speaking, but at the same time they show the more clearly the dangers and detours which threaten the proclamation, precisely when it wants to remain as close as possible to the text and seeks to call attention to nothing other than it. For it should be clear by now that the sermon never can be a hymn and does not have to recite a drama. If it is formed according to the laws of the hymn and speaks in its manner, it will necessarily become a kind of hierophantic speech, a *hieros logos* (sacred word), as the mystery religions know it, and a myth, as Gnosticism knows it. Thus, in no case does the sermon have to tell and to proclaim something like a sacred history of the gods. In other words, the deepest danger which threatens a sermon based on our text is that of "mythologizing". It is, I think, far more threatening and real than the alleged menace of "demythologizing," because such a mythologizing sermon may indeed give the impression of biblical and theological correctness.[11] Thus we would do well to make clear to ourselves the essential differences between hymn and confession on the one hand and proclamation and instruction on the other. In the New Testament the *former* speak exclusively of Christ (cf. in addition to Phil. 2 esp. I Tim. 3.16; Col. 1.15ff., and the hymns of Revelation), and with such an "objectivity" that the man for whom salvation occurs is not really touched directly. But the latter is the very feature that belongs inalienably to the sermon. A proclamation which does not speak simultaneously to the story of man and his life with himself is no proclamation, even if it contains the most incontestable biblical and dogmatic expressions. Applied to Phil. 2.6–11 and put pointedly, that means: the sermon *may* in a certain sense *not* follow the text and not simply agree in the manner of its expression. It must break the form of this hymn and deliver anew the story proclaimed in it in such a way that it still becomes perceivable now as the story that concerns us, opening and redeeming and freeing us.

But at this very point the dimension which the Christ-hymn opens, initially so strange and "mythical", becomes extremely significant. For the event spoken of here bursts the dimension in which all our experience and our thinking in the world and time and history move. Whether we are bewitched or sobered by it, this dimension always circumscribes the area of our captivity. But the message of our text breaks it and opens God's heaven, of course in such a way that it proclaims a very strange event: for the eyes of men there is no "epiphany" of the divine, no opened heaven, nothing of God's glory and majesty, but the story of a renunciation, the surrender of all divinity. One still understands how everything that faith confesses here also helps unbelief in its triumph, whether expressed as the mockers beneath the cross and Jews and Greeks over against the word of the cross or—as usual today—spoken in silence. In fact, it says, there is only a man like other men, bound to his time, a sacrifice to the times, impressive or even exemplary in the manner in which fate is endured even in failure. The answer of ancient Greek wisdom to the question of what is the strongest: "Necessity, it alone is unalterable!" has remained until today the secret or the open answer of unbelief even in view of the story of Jesus Christ. But God says no to this answer and pierces the dark foreground, the ghastly confining scenery of the prison in which even this story of Jesus Christ ends for our eyes. The boundaries of the world have fallen. The beginning and end of the divine will have been revealed. That has happened in this story. In the One who emptied himself, the One who became like us, One humiliated in obedience unto death, God himself has appeared and has not perished but has become the Victor. He has transformed the humiliation of Jesus Christ into exaltation. Henceforth faith perceives what no eye has seen and no ear heard and what has penetrated no human heart, the praise which the world with all its powers must already offer to him: Kyrios Jesus Christ. Does Christianity know what it does when it calls him the "Lord"? Does it really hear this confession out of the wild, confused choir of the powers of the world? And does it not fall into a distorted illusion when it imagines that it hears this? The answer can only read: It *is* a miserable, now only "illusionary" question, coming far too late, unless God has acknowledged this humiliated One and One obedient unto death and proclaimed his yes to him in the "Name above all names" of the world! Redemption now simply means "change of ruler" (Käsemann), liberation from the tyrannies of the powers of the world. But still more: it means liberation to obey him who himself was obedient and thus has become Lord and Victor. Here the language of myth is at an end. Myth, too, promises liberation and victory over the world, but never in any way other than that man himself, led to apotheosis, is deified—an illusion which actually only seals his captivity and slavery with finality. But God meets the man who wants to be as God by wanting to be nothing other than a man. The Lordship of this One is freedom. But this means at the same time that humiliation and obedience are now henceforth the kingly way of faith, the seal of the liberated, the pledge of coming redemption. Therefore, the congregation already now joins in the hidden praise of the world and makes it manifest—vicariously for the world for whom the truth of God is not yet open: "Jesus Christ is Lord—to the glory of God the Father."

NOTES

[1] *Kyrios Jesus*, Heidelberger Sitzungsberichte (1927/28), No. 4; republished *Kyrios Jesus, Eine Untersuchung zu Phil 2, 5–11* (1961).

[1a] "Form of God," "equality with God," "servant," "empty," "exalt," "bestow"; the threefold division into heavenly, earthly, and subterraneous; the lack of the resurrection and the saving significance of his death, which otherwise are expressed frequently in a "for the sake of" statement. Cf. E. Schweizer, *Erniedrigung und Erhöhung bei Jesus und seinen Nachfolgern* (1955), p. 52, n. 224 (ET completely revised), *Lordship and Discipleship*, 1960, p. 61, n. 1).

[2] Lohmeyer's division into six stanzas, each with three lines, has not remained unchallenged. Cf. J. Jeremias, "Zur Gedankenführung in den Paulinischen Briefen" (*Studia Paulina in honorem Johannis de Zwaan*, 1953, pp. 146ff., esp. pp. 152ff.).

[3] E. Käsemann's "Kritische Analyse von Phil. 2.5–11" (*ZTK* 47, 1950, pp. 313–60, now also in his *Exegetische Versuche und Besinnungen* I, 1960, pp. 51–95) offers a comprehensive critique of the older and newer interpretations of our text and is to be regarded as the best theological exegesis, to my thinking, even when contrasted with the works of J. Héring, "Kyrios Anthropos" (*Revue de Histoire et de Philosophie Religieuses*, 1936, pp. 196ff.), and L. Cerfaux, "L'hymne au Christ-Serviteur de Dieu" (*Miscellanea Historica in hon. A. de Meyer*, 1946, 1, pp. 117ff.), and the newest contribution in E. Schweizer's book, *op. cit.*, pp. 51ff., 66ff., 134ff., etc. (ET, cf. pp. 61ff., 66ff.); O. Michel, "Zur Exegese von Phil. 2.5–11," in *Theologie als Glaubenswagnis, Festschrift für K. Heim* (1954), pp. 79ff., and O. Cullmann, *Die Christologie des Neuen Testaments* (1958²), pp. 76ff., 178ff., 223ff., etc. (ET, *The Christology of the New Testament*, 1959, pp. 76ff., 174ff., 217ff.). Cf. also D. Georgi, "Der vorpaulinische Hymnus Phil 2.6–11" in *Zeit und Geschichte, Dankesgabe an Rudolf Bultmann* (1964), pp. 263–93.

[4] Even in the ancient church, there was another explanation alongside this, which relates all expressions of vv. 6 and 7 to the historical Jesus and challenges the idea of pre-existence in this and other Pauline passages, in more recent times advocated especially by F. Loofs in his last great essay, "Das altkirchliche Zeugnis gegen die herrschende Auffassung der Kenosisstelle" (*Theologische Studien und Kritiken*, 1927, pp. 1–102). Yet it fails especially in the expression "emptied himself." Loofs paraphrases: "Christ, the historical Lord, emptied himself of the fulness of the Spirit, of the 'fulness of divinity', which 'bodily' dwelt in him (Col. 1.19; 2.9), i.e. he acted as if he did not have this peculiarity" (p. 94). One sees

immediately how here the sense of the text is missed. For where is there in this or any other passage the expression that Christ emptied himself of the fulness of the Spirit? Loofs himself correspondingly must weaken "emptied" to an "as if."

5 Cullmann, *op. cit.*, p. 182 (ET, p. 178).

6 Cf. J. Jeremias, *op. cit.*, p. 154; also his article *"pais theou"* in *TWNT* V, pp. 708f. (ET, *TDNT* V, pp. 711f.).

7 For example, Eth. Enoch 42.1–3; Prov. 1.23–27.

8 *Op. cit.*, p. 184 (ET, p. 180).

9 *Op. cit.*, p. 347.

10 I see no reason to hold with E. Schweizer, *op. cit.*, p. 52, n. 224, and J. Jeremias, *op. cit.*, pp. 153f., that the phrase "to the glory of God the Father" is a Pauline addition.

11 What is said is certainly true not only for our text!

IX

LORD'S SUPPER AND CHURCH IN PAUL[1]

IN HIS LETTERS, Paul speaks of the Lord's Supper in only two passages. Both are in I Corinthians, each in its own context, and yet in content both are related closely to each other. Their inner, essential homogeneity will concern us in what follows. But first let us present the different contexts of both passages.

I. THE CONTEXT

(a) Ch. 10.1–22 occurs in connection with the question of eating meat offered to idols. Paul handles this special and seemingly peripheral Corinthian problem with the greatest care and, as it appears, with detailed breadth. For the most essential questions of Christian faith and life generally are tied into this problem: What do faith and knowledge of God mean? What does Christian freedom mean? What are the rights of the man who is freed from paganism and superstition? How may and should he show his freedom, and where does it have its limits? And finally, with everything in the passage aimed at this: What does responsibility for the brethren mean and demand? This is initially the context of I Cor. 10.1–13. There, using the example of the fathers in the wilderness, Paul most pungently demonstrates to the Corinthians that the greatest sacramental gifts of salvation mean no guarantee against judgment and rejection. Indeed, a congregation so richly blessed, if it falls prey again to idol-worship and unbelief, will taste the judgment of God that much the more terribly. Then, with a new idea in ch. 10.14–22, Paul positively develops the incompatibility of a participation in the Lord's Supper and in the sacrificial idol feasts, basing it on the nature and meaning of the Lord's Supper.[2]

The entire section, ch. 10.1–22, seems to be an intrusion into I Corinthians and has been the cause of comprehensive literary hypotheses.[3] Some ask how the rigorous prohibition of participation in the sacrificial idol feasts in ch. 10.1–22 can be harmonized with the apparently much more generous and unprejudiced position of ch. 8 and 10.23ff. In both of these sections Paul apparently still represents the position of the "strong" in fundamentals, although here also he aims at one thing: Think what consequences your free, careless behavior will have on the weak conscience of your brother who is not yet really free. He will do the same as you and thereby inwardly accept it and perish. Chapter 10.1–22 is different. There Paul, understandably, from his Jewish presuppositions, still has a place for the fear of demons that has not yet been fully overcome. This really ought to be renounced, provided that his own word applies: "Hence, as to the eating of food offered to idols, we know that an idol has no real existence, and that there is no God but one" (ch.8.4).

With others, J. Weiss tried to solve this question by regarding the section I Cor. 10.1–22 as the letter referred to in I Cor. 5.9, written prior to our I Corinthians as the very first of the letters in which Paul bluntly forbids intercourse with the ungodly. In fact, both Corinthian letters again and again raise the question of their literary integrity. II Corinthians in particular justifies the thesis that the "letters" are more a collection from the correspondence of the Apostle with the congregation than complete documents in themselves. Another question is whether regarding I Cor. 10.1–22 as the very first letter and excluding this section from ch. 8f. and 10.23–33 is convincing. The question is important here in so far as it contains the exegetical question of how Paul's arguments in I Cor. 10.1–22 are intended. Are they really, as J. Weiss thinks, the expression of that "fear of demons"[4] whose correlate is by comparison an all too definite magical-sacramental understanding of the Lord's Supper? I hold with H. von Soden, who has dealt carefully and discerningly with the question of the literary and theological unity of I Cor. 8–10,[5] that the argument of I Cor. 10.1–22 is not incompatible with that of ch. 8 and 10.23ff. Even if it opens a completely new aspect, it may fit consistently and necessarily into the other sections (see Excursus I below). Paraphrasing, one could reproduce the connection and difference between the one and the other series of thoughts in this way: in fact there are "actually" no idols and thus in this regard even the eating of meat offered to idols is not a question of ultimate meaning. However, the question about the salvation or damnation of the brother is a question of life and death. This is the scope of the first argument. In principle it allows that the "strong" are right. But

Paul is not satisfied with that, and in ch. 10.1–22 now turns to the allegedly unendangered strong, who actually are right, and shows what threatens even them. For—as one could not put the emphasis— these demonic *non-entities* are *demonic* non-entities; they have it *in* themselves. Anyone who meddles with them does not simply remain unmolested; he is torn away from fellowship with the Lord. Paul thus moves the whole question out of the sphere of a general theoretical discussion, on which the opponents base their free position, into the sphere of existence, to speak in modern terms. There it belongs; there the decision truly lies. His judgment about the demons "in them- selves" in ch. 10.1–22 is not different from that in ch. 8. He explicitly takes up again what he said there: "What do I imply, then? That food offered to idols is anything, or that an idol is anything? No, I imply that what pagans sacrifice they offer to demons and not to God. (Therefore it follows that:) I do not want you to be partners with demons. You cannot drink the cup of the Lord and the cup of demons. You cannot partake in the table of the Lord and the table of demons. Shall we provoke the Lord to jealousy? Are we stronger than he?" (I Cor. 10.19–22.) In other words: If the Lord has shown his power to free us from captivity to the demons, then may we dare put our freedom to the test so that we return to that fellowship? An absurd possibility!

In any case, attributing I Cor. 10.1–22 to the letter referred to in I Cor. 5.9 would hardly solve the alleged contradiction, as von Soden rightly notes. It still remains in the statements of two letters written one right after the other.[6] Indeed, one may maintain further that I Cor. 5.9 also contradicts the thesis. For Paul here corrects the misunderstanding of the radical separation from the godless de- manded by him, as if in his instruction to the Corinthians he had for- bidden every association with the world when actually he had intended and demanded separation from the godless and idol- worshipping brethren of the congregation. If I Cor. 10.1–22 had in fact stood in the warning-letter of I Cor. 5.9, then the Corinthians would not have misunderstood the Apostle, but would have under- stood him correctly. In that case, Paul would now be making a retreat and correcting himself, a correction which without justifica- tion he completely covers over through the reproach that the Corin- thians had twisted his word.

(*b*) In the section I Cor. 11.17–34 the Lord's Supper itself is the theme. From 11.2 to the end of ch. 14 Paul treats questions which the

Corinthians themselves have put to him. Here especially he deals with the question of the work of the Spirit in the life of the congregation generally and in the gathering for worship. Our section has to do specifically with the abuses in the Lord's Supper which had been reported to him. What had happened to cause the Apostle to intervene so vigorously? In the gathering of the congregation a system of cliques, a splitting of the congregation, had come to light, and it was not the kind of split that is unavoidable and even has its secret meaning *sub specie aeterni* because it announces the final separation of those who are of proven faith and those who are not (11.19). Nor was it the mischief of factions with their battle-slogans referred to in chs. 1–3. Nothing in our context indicates that the question of teaching and separation according to party leaders plays a part here, and that in one place those of Paul, in another those of Cephas, and in third and fourth place those of Apollos and Christ had sought their position.[7] Yet it was a division which placed in question the celebration of the Lord's Supper generally: "When you meet together, it is not the Lord's Supper that you eat. For in eating, each one goes ahead with his own meal, and one is hungry and another is drunk" (11.20f.). Thus the proper sharing of the gifts left everything to be desired. Certain ones feast, and the others starve and are forced to feel their poverty painfully and shamedly. In this way the congregation, which should be a congregation of brothers precisely in their gathering for worship, presents a shameless picture of social cleavage. If we add further to the picture from the warning at the end: "So then, my brethren, when you come together to eat, wait for one another" (v. 33), then it becomes clear that among the less well-off and lovelessly neglected are especially the humbler people, who cannot so easily leave their work when evening comes. This means, of course, especially slaves, who are not masters of their time and come too late, without the well-off having regard for them.

But from the text we can gather still more about the degeneration of the Corinthian celebration. This concerns the understanding of the Lord's Supper in Corinth generally and at the same time the very different understanding of the sacrament by Paul. What have the Corinthians made of the Lord's Supper? According to the usual view, the Corinthians have "abolished the idea of receiving the body of Christ: for them the blessed bread was no longer 'body' and they ate it as ordinary food" (H. Lietzmann).[8] But that meant, according to Lietzmann, that they had changed from the Hellenistic-Pauline type of the celebration of the sacrament to an older type, which originally was at home in Jerusalem and totally unrelated to Jesus' last supper and the redemptive meaning of his death. Rather, it was celebrated as the continuation of the table fellowship with the earthly Jesus, now, of course, with rejoicing over his resurrection and with the expectation of his coming.[9] But does anything point to such a process? Is it historically imaginable in a congregation founded and cared for by Paul? We must consider what that means. It means the deliberate abandonment of the words of institution and the intrinsic sacramental character of the celebration, and the transition to a type of celebration for which we can still find evidence in this form only in the Palestinian Church of the early period. One may well say: If that had happened in Corinth, Paul no longer could have called their celebration the "Lord's Supper" at all. Furthermore, the remembrance of the words of institution in I Cor. 11.23–25 would be unintelligible. For here, as in I Cor. 15.3ff., Paul does not present the "tradition" to the congregation as something which has generally been forgotten there, but as something very well known to them, as something given to him and to them as authoritative, but from which very different consequences result for the Apostle, as for the congregation. Therefore ch. 11.20ff. does not say: "When you now assemble, do not hold the Lord's Supper any more at all." It says, rather: "Through your conduct in the meal before it, the celebration of the Lord's Supper is placed in question and becomes an impossibility." In particular, the picture evoked by the thesis of the abandonment of the celebration of the sacrament in Corinth and the substitution of the Corinthian congregation's unsacramental celebration of joy does not fit at all with the picture that I Cor. 10 presents.[10] For there the Corinthians appear, as we saw, as very crude sacramentalists, to whom Paul in vv. 1ff. (vigorously) must indicate that the possession of the sacrament in no way guarantees eternal salvation.[11] The continuation in ch. 10.14–22 confirms this. There Paul clarifies for the Corinthians what *koinonia*, participation in the body and blood of Christ, means from their own familiar experience of their pagan past and their pagan environment. Again, he does not do this to say something new to them, but plainly to convince and win them over by something long familiar.

What does all this imply for ch. 11.17ff. and the abuses that have gained ground in Corinth? Evidently this, that the Corinthians have probably held fast to a highly sacramental celebration of the meal.

They celebrated it, as is also known elsewhere from early Christian literature, in the context of a regular meal in which they ate together what each contributed according to his means. In the course of this common meal, probably right at the end of the gathering, they then held—of course, as the high point—the actual sacramental act, in which the words of institution were certainly spoken and the believers received communion in Christ's body and blood as they ate the broken bread and drank the blessed cup. We also find the same order of meal and sacramental celebration in the synoptic gospels. They insert the words of institution into a meal already in progress as a final act and thereby clearly set it off from the whole. Thus Mark 14.22 reads: "And as they were eating, he took bread, and blessed, and broke it, and gave it to them, and said . . ." Then the hymn of praise follows and the celebration is over. The Didache also supports this movement of events. Ch. 9 first has table prayers over cup and bread, followed in ch. 10 by a prayer of thanks "after hunger is satisfied." Only then does the sacred act come, not described further but introduced through the formula in ch. 10.6: "Whoever is holy, come; whoever is not, repent; *Maranatha* (Our Lord, come). Amen."

Now, I think, the events in Corinth also become clear. The Corinthians have not done away with the sacramental Lord's Supper at all. On the contrary, they so completely regarded this as the main thing that the preceding meal became a thing which one could shape according to his own likes and for his own enjoyment. Therefore they had few scruples about the injury of the poor and the latecomers. No one was excluded from the high and holy sacrament. There even the poor of the congregation got their due. But up to this point they could confidently spend the time eating and drinking in table fellowship with family, friends and peers. Everyone can imagine the very understandable reasons which may have played a role there: the very human tendency to a sociability among one's own; antipathy for the embarrassment that comes when rich and poor, free and slave, sit bodily at one table—real table fellowship is something quite different from charity at a distance; the worry that the "atmosphere" for receiving the sacrament may be spoiled by such an embarrassing rubbing of elbows with the poor. All that had led to the "taking beforehand"[12] of their own meal.

We see that in Corinth the connection of what is later called the Agape (common meal) with the actual eucharistic action is still taken for granted, even if the increasingly high sacramental evaluation of the Eucharist had led to a devaluation of the Agape and to a mockery of this word. For Paul also, the connection of Agape and Eucharist is taken for granted. For this very reason Paul is so vigorously concerned to impress on the Corinthians that one cannot hold a high and holy celebration of the sacrament at the end when one has previously violated brotherly duty so scandalously. Of course, he also indicates something of the problems of connecting a meal and an act of worship. He explicitly emphasizes that the gatherings of the congregation are not simply to satisfy hunger. Hence his instruction in v. 22 (and later in v. 34): Do that at home! But this admonition initially says no more than this: Feed the growling stomach what it needs at home, that such painful things as have happened in your midst are not repeated. Paul in no way had in mind a fundamental and definitive separation of the common meal and the sacramental celebration, as it had been carried out from the beginning of the second century. Rather, for Paul meal and celebration still belong so closely together that he can maintain that the bad state of affairs in the common meal make the entire Lord's Supper illusory. His endeavor is therefore directed towards moving the Corinthians to different behavior in the meal. On the other hand, he does not hold that it is necessary to give the sacramental celebration another liturgical order.

According to all this, in contrast with the way this matter usually is presented, one could say that it is the meal in Corinth that has been profaned, not the sacramental act. Of course, without the Corinthians necessarily being conscious of it, in the mind of the Apostle the sacrament is thereby endangered, even though "liturgically" they may have observed it with utter correctness.

It is at once clear that the elucidation of this inquiry about the manner and theological background of the grievances in the Lord's Supper at Corinth is of considerable importance for understanding what was in dispute between the congregation and the Apostle, and thus for the understanding of his peculiar concern. But the actual question is presented only by the Lord's Supper text itself in I Cor. 11.23–25, which has so far not been discussed in more detail.

The meaning of the citation of this Lord's Supper "tradition" in this place is not immediately clear. J. Weiss speaks in his commentary of a loose connection, and notes in his *Earliest Christianity* II (pp. 848f.): "The full development of ideas in I Cor. 11.20–34, considered in relation to its context, is dominated by two different tendencies: vv. 20–22, 33–34 by the social, and vv. 23–32 by the sacramental, so that the critics seeking for interpolations might hit on the idea of rejecting the latter group of verses (23–32). And in fact it is not entirely manifest how far the appeal to the Lord's sayings and the exposition of the significance of the celebration are to serve the purpose of combating Corinthian immorality." Therefore Weiss is rightly concerned to read between the lines here and to make the connection between the two sections precise. Of course, he obstructs correct understanding through the thesis, mentioned earlier, that the Corinthians had made the sacramental celebration into an "ordinary meal." We must attempt to come to a different explanation here. But that can only succeed when we have answered the question about the peculiarity and meaning of the "tradition" in Cor. 11.23–25. We turn now to this, keeping in mind the question indicated of the concrete meaning of the words of institution in the context of ch. 11, in order to answer it later.

11. THE TRADITION OF THE WORDS OF INSTITUTION
I Corinthians 11.23–25

(a) On the term "paradosis" (tradition)

Paul inserts the words of institution as "tradition" which he himself has received from the Lord and transmitted to the congregation (v. 23a). What does *paradosis* mean here? It is certain that Paul appeals to a formula given to him previously, which is also familiar to the congregation and which he himself imparted to it. But where did he get it? The addition "from the Lord," especially if (with H. Lietzmann) we understand it to be antithetical to human tradition in the sense of Gal. 1.12f., appears to indicate the meaning: "I have received it directly from the Lord." That is, it is something like the revelation which he received as his gospel or together with his gospel on the way to Damascus. This understanding is frequent and has been advanced by well-known exegetes.[13] However, as one valid criticism has rightly shown, the terms "to receive from", "to deliver" have a clear significance. They correspond exactly to the Rabbinic academic expressions *qibbel min* ("to receive from") and *masar le* ("to deliver to"). With most modern exegetes—G. Kittel, A. Schlatter, J. Jeremias, R. Bultmann, E. Käsemann, W. G. Kümmel and others— *paradosis* is therefore certainly to be understood as the tradition passed on in the congregation, inconceivable without a chain of tradition in which Paul also includes himself as a member. If we ask when and where Paul received this tradition, we must certainly think of the time of his stay in Antioch, before he began his mission. The formulae in I Cor. 11 and 15 which he learned there may therefore have been known at the beginning of the forties in the Antioch congregation. But, in that case, what does "from the Lord" mean? According to J. Jeremias[14] the expression says nothing more "than that the chain of tradition goes back without interruption to the words of Jesus himself." But what does that mean? To the historical Jesus, who spoke these words then and there and who is designated in this phrase as the chronological beginning and the first member of the chain of tradition? However, even the preposition *apo* (not *para*) speaks against this. In no way does this immediately designate the direct predecessors in the chain of tradition. On this W. G. Kümmel[15] bases the conjecture that by it Paul perhaps wanted to designate the "Lord" not as guarantor but as originator. Certainly, but one may make this still more pointed. Evidently Paul means by "the Lord" not only the historical but also the exalted Lord, who obviously is none other than the one then and there given up to death, the historical Jesus, but now the Exalted One and one day the Coming One. Does this not mean the surrender of the assertion accepted here, that Paul refers to a tradition passed on in the congregation from member to member and not to a revelation of the exalted Lord given especially to him? By no means. Rather, one must say that the alternative: either a tradition mediated through men, going back to the historical Jesus, or a revelation through the Exalted One; is a false one. Both belong together: the mediated word is the word of the Living One. This seems to me to be exceedingly important for the understanding of our passage, as well as for the traditions of the Lord's words in the congregation that confront us elsewhere. One could formulate it pointedly in this way: The tradition not only passes on the Lord's word from the past—naturally it does that; but as this tradition it *is* his word. He himself meets us in this word and only this gives to the tradition its quality of revelation. For this very reason Paul thanks God in I Thess. 2.13: ". . . that when you received the word of God which you heard from us, you accepted it not as the word of men but as what it really is, the word of God, which is at work in you believers."[16]

The Lord's Supper formula cited by Paul apparently extends

from v. 23b to v. 25. Verse 26 is a Pauline explanation ("for"). Clearly the "as often as" again takes up the preceding sentence here. The last phrase ("until he comes") will be a remembrance of the eschatological word which originally stood in the Last Supper tradition. However, Paul himself no longer knew it as such an element of the formula.

(b) The date

"The Lord Jesus on the night when he was betrayed . . ." The night of Jesus' arrest is certainly intended. Whatever may have been known to Paul and the congregation of the events of the night that stand behind this formula, we do not know: the betrayal of Judas? More exact details of the arrest? The trials and the denial of Peter? These are idle questions and largely must be answered negatively, especially since we otherwise learn exceedingly little in Paul about the life of Jesus. Nothing allows us to interpret the verses as a citation extracted from the larger whole of a passion tradition. They are an entity in themselves and a piece of liturgical tradition. It is enough to know that this night of Jesus' betrayal before his death is remembered, an unmistakable indication that the Lord's Supper is not to be understood as a cultic celebration with a timeless myth after the manner of the mystery religions. It is anchored in a definite history and one ordained by God. For Paul uses "to deliver" and particularly the passive in reference to Jesus in the sense of God's history of salvation, who gave up his Son for us all (Rom. 8.32; cf. 4.25), or also of Jesus, the Son of God, who gave himself up (Gal. 2.20). Thus it was not as an expression of a police measure or a villainous deed of men.

Here we would point only to a peculiarity. The short phrase "on the night . . ." does not speak of the night of the Passover and certainly does not seek to characterize the Last Supper of Jesus as a Passover meal. As is well known, the question of whether Jesus' Last Supper is to be understood as a Passover meal plays a big role in scholarly discussion. J. Jeremias especially has concerned himself with proving this. To my thinking his expositions are not really convincing and indicate only the fact, challenged by no one, that the Synoptic writers have placed the Last Supper of Jesus within the framework of a Passover meal. However, this historical question can remain entirely out of consideration, as another fact appears to me unchallengeable and clear, that the accounts of the institution themselves contain hardly any relation to the Passover at all. What is

inalienably constitutive for every Passover meal down to the present
—the eating of the Passover lamb, the unleavened bread and bitter
herbs—does not play the slightest role in the words of institution,
and the words belonging to the Lord's Supper are not at all like a
Passover haggada in which the elements of the meal were explained.
On the contrary, the constitutive actions and words of the institution of the Lord's Supper allow themselves to be accommodated
in a Passover liturgy only with great effort and conjectures leading
into the hypothetical—not to say the improbable. The decisive
obstacle always remains, that in the Lord's Supper there are no
words of explanation for the lamb, unleavened bread and herbs;
and the Lord's Supper is constituted through a completely different
kind of bread-word and a cup-word that has no analogy at all in the
Jewish celebration, for a cup-blessing is still no "word of explanation."

What has just been said applies to the words of institution in all
four settings—Mark, Matthew, Luke and Paul. But for Paul more
can be said: the lack of any connection between the Lord's Supper
statements and the Passover, thoroughly surprising for us, is the more
striking since Paul knows very well the idea that Christ is our
Passover (I Cor. 5.7), also found elsewhere in the New Testament
(I Pet. 1.18f.; John 1.29 (?)). Even the Johannine chronology of the
day of Jesus' death clearly betrays a relation to the Passover, according to which Jesus already dies on the evening of the slaughtering
of the Passover lambs. But Paul mentions the thought—and that is
decisive here—without connecting it to the Lord's Supper. I Cor.
10.1ff. is also especially instructive. There Paul explicitly speaks of the
sacrament in the context of a scriptural proof—and thus one would
like to say that it is very near to the Passover story. But it is not
Passover and Exodus to which he refers; rather, the water-giving
Rock in the desert and the manna are the typological motifs which he
employs to explain the "food" and "spiritual drink," the heavenly
food of the Lord's Supper.[17] The result is therefore clear. Where the
Passover lamb is referred to, nowhere is the Lord's Supper referred
to, and *vice versa*. Where the Lord's Supper is referred to, the relation
to the Passover is missing. The result of this consideration is that the
accounts of the institution themselves do not receive their meaning
from the Passover at all, nor are they to be interpreted in the light of
the Passover. Therefore the interpretation recently put forward by
G. Walther and J. Jeremias is excluded, namely that the central
thought of the Lord's Supper is Jesus as the Passover lamb of the new

covenant.[18] Important though the Passover-motif may otherwise be in the christological ideas of early Christianity, for the words of institution it contributes nothing.

(c) *The words of institution in Paul in their relation to the synoptic texts*

As has already been indicated, the three synoptic writers, like Paul, arrange Jesus' act and word in an historical context. However, they do not lift the text of the words of institution out of a context.[19] Thus it may not be understood as a fragment from a chronological account, which only subsequently became a liturgical text. Rather, it is a liturgical text from the outset and behind each form is as it were a celebrating congregation for whom it is intended. That the words of institution are liturgical material need not be elaborately shown: everything is concentrated on the sacred action and the words that accompany it; all historicizing portrayal of a unique and unrepeatable situation is missing; nothing is revealed about the persons gathered for that celebration. In Paul, the festive language and parallelism in the words spoken over bread and cup betray their liturgical character even in the introductory words. Furthermore, the modifications of the text show that this liturgical style and character become stronger in the individual transmitters of the text. This is especially true of Matthew, who adds the word "eat!" to the Markan "Take!" and also renders the descriptive expression in the action with the cup: "And he took a cup, and when he had given thanks he gave it to them, and they all drank of it," imperatively: "Drink of it, all of you!" The addition "for the forgiveness of sins" in Matthew is theological interpretation, but also a liturgical formula.

A perhaps not unimportant note on the changing of the Markan "and they all drank of it" into a liturgical-imperative formulation (Matthew) might be added here. It concerns a peculiarity of the Markan text. It is striking here that Mark lets the cup-word follow the drinking of the wine, while in Matthew it follows the imperative "drink of it." The Markan text, which reports the completion of the drinking before the cup-word, is interesting in that it shows how little the evangelist knows the notion of a word of transformation. For it is impossible that such a word could be spoken after the content of the cup had already been drunk. Naturally that does not mean that Matthew, as he changed the "they drank" into "drink," was guided by the intention of giving to the cup-word the character of a trans-

forming word. Rather, one must say that this thought is still completely unknown to the evangelists, just as it is to Paul (and John 6).
This is an assertion which may not be entirely without meaning for
interconfessional theological dialogue.

Mark and Matthew apparently stand closest to each other. Both
have bread-action and bread-word, cup-action and cup-word, both
also have in common the eschatological word that follows, except
that the formulation in Matthew again is richer. That Mark is the
older throughout is clear in every respect.

Here we can forgo an extended discussion of the complicated text
of Luke, even the history of which is not clear. As is well known, the
text in its present form is strangely overloaded, because initially it
offers two quite independent eschatologically governed sayings about
eating the Passover and drinking the cup, which, however, in no
way have an explanatory character. But then it moves on into a text-
form of the words of institution that is closely related to Paul (I Cor.
11). Thus four actions and words result: a Passover word, an initial
cup-word and then once more a bread- and cup-word. There is a
variant of this text represented especially by the Western text, which
strangely stops after the bread-word: "This is my body." Many
scholars believed that this shorter text was to be appealed to as the
oldest text of Luke. Now, however, and I think with good reason,
most have been convinced by the view that the longer text is the older.
But this is apparently the product of a harmonizing of the Markan
tradition and a text-form closely related to I Cor. 11. For us, who
have Paul's text in mind, the only important thing is that Luke is not
directly dependent on Paul, but on a text-type represented in a somewhat older form, already more liturgically stylized by Paul. This is
shown especially by the additional "Do this in remembrance of
me,"[20] that stands only by the bread-word in Luke, but by both words
in Paul.

Thus Mark (14.22–25) and Paul (I Cor. 11.23–25) remain as the
two oldest text-forms. The agreement of the two texts is extensive.
Their very early date is undoubted and probably their home is in the
Palestinian-Syrian area of the church. Agreements and differences
are clear:

1. Bread-word:

Paul	*Mark*
This is my body which is for you; Do this in remembrance of me.	This is my body.

2. Cup-word:

Paul	*Mark*
This cup is the new covenant in my blood; Do this, as often as you drink it, in remembrance of me.	This is my blood of the covenant which is poured out for many.

J. Jeremias in particular has supported a very early date of the Markan text.[20a] The most important of his arguments are: Paul's text shows a large number of variations which in part aim at a strong Hellenizing and an avoidance of Semitisms (a), and in part betrays a tendency toward a stronger liturgical stylization (b). On (a): "which is for you" is already difficult in Greek, but it is impossible to translate back into Aramaic at all. On the other hand, Mark offers an abundance of Semitisms, only a few of which are to be found in Paul.[21] Of course, even Mark is not free of Hellenisms. For the phrase "my blood of the covenant" is likewise difficult in Greek, but again impossible in Aramaic.[22] On (b): liturgical-type phrases in Paul's text are: the additional "which is for you," which perhaps stands in the bread-word here to provide a better parallelism. The short phrase designates the offered gift and underlines the word's character as gift. Then the doubly indicated command to repeat the action belongs to the liturgical style of Paul's text. Paul's text also, as Jeremias thinks, shows a greater degree of theological reflection. This explains the additional "new covenant," which points to the promise of the new covenant in Jer. 31 (38).31ff. However, one also must acknowledge a degree of theological reflection in the Markan text; the only difference is that he does not make the cup-word allude to Jer. 31 (38) but to Ex. 24.8, the word about the blood of the covenant at the enactment of the Sinai covenant.

In spite of the unchallengeably correct arguments which Jeremias has presented in great number, we may not simply determine the order of age as first Mark, then Paul. Rather, we must identify the earlier and the later elements of the tradition in both, and this means —as is of special importance for all that follows—in Paul, too. Indeed, as far as the total character of the type of tradition is concerned, I regard him as the older in spite of his stronger Hellenizing and liturgizing.[23] The main reason is that "after supper"[24] is retained only in Paul (except for Luke). This means that the bread-word and cup-word are separated by the entire meal.

This fact has considerable consequences. The first thing to understand from it is the choice of the term "body". This represents an entity in itself and may not be bound together with "blood" as a pair of terms. The biblical pair of terms is "flesh" and "blood," nothing else. Since the time of John 6.51ff. and Ignatius[25] this, too, has had its established place, at least in one stream of the Lord's Supper tradition. But we may not immediately substitute the meaning of "flesh" for the term "body."[26] Secondly, the often-perceived "incongruence" of both words and the fact that "body" is matched with "new covenant" (not "blood") in Paul becomes tolerable only in the separation of bread-word and cup-word through the meal that lies between them. Exegesis must corroborate what that means. We only seek to prepare for it through these discussions of the historical traditions.

The result of this consideration of the historical traditions is this: both texts (Mark and Paul) generally represent a very similar tradition of the words of institution and yet are two types which differ in the extent of their Semitisms and Hellenisms and the degree of their liturgical stylizing. Both offer earlier and later material. In contrast with Paul, Mark, in spite of his Semitisms, shows himself to be the later in that he no longer includes "after supper". Only thus do the bread- and cup-action and bread- and cup-word become closely related and actions and expressions which are parts of a whole. Applied to the event and execution of the celebration, that means that here the same order of the actions is to be found as we already earlier identified in Corinth. That is, the sacramental celebration in which bread and cup were offered directly after each other, of course with the recitation of the words of institution, occurred at the end of the common meal.

Now we must certainly conclude that this order of the actions in the entire celebration—(1) meal, (2) sacrament—was also familiar to Paul himself. In the celebration familiar to him, therefore, it may be that the eating and drinking of the sacramental food belonged to one action. In other words, I think that the "after supper," preserved in his formula, is also for him only an ancient liturgical formula. For nothing in I Cor. 11 indicates that he seeks to move the Corinthians to an order of the entire celebration in which they would have begun with the first act of the sacramental event, that is, the giving of the bread and the bread-word, then have eaten together, and at the end have taken the cup.[27] Paul does not give instructions about an agenda that concerns the placing of the bread-action at the beginning of the entire meal; rather, he criticizes the conduct of the Corinthians in the Agape-meal that precedes the sacrament, which so disgracefully had lost its meaning. The "after supper" of his formula still retains a good, though altered, meaning in the form of the celebration which meanwhile has become the custom, a custom we infer from the practice of the Corinthians, as well as from Mark and Matthew, and which was not actually attacked even by Paul. It is now related to the whole of the preceding meal and the sacramental action celebrated at the end of it, and no longer to the common meal that originally followed the bread-action and bread-word.

Therefore, for Paul no emphasis is put on the liturgical rite. It does, however, seem to me to be extremely important that the text-form retained precisely and only in Paul with what seem at first to be trivial peculiarities, and, especially with the "after supper" retained only here, is the basis for the specifically Pauline understanding of the Lord's Supper. Thus it is also the basis for the particular and penetrating relation that exists for Paul between the Lord's Supper and the church.

III. THE MEANING OF THE WORDS OF INSTITUTION

Usually we are accustomed to designate the words of institution as "words of explanation." Yet we should be conscious of the problems attached to this expression. It may have become current because of a questionable effect of the interpretation of the Lord's Supper as a Passover meal that we already have rejected. Of course, there are "words of explanation" there, in the form of the haggada with which the head of the family answers the question of his son at every Passover celebration even today: "What differentiates this night from all other nights?"[28] A "word of explanation" is the same kind of word as that spoken about the unleavened bread. For example: "See, that is the bread of distress which our fathers who left Egypt have eaten"[29] (here the explanation varies: it is in remembrance either of the distress of the fathers in Egypt or of the haste of their departure). But here—in the Lord's Supper—nothing is explained in any real sense, i.e. as in the Passover the special nature of the food standing on the table is explained by the events and the circumstances of the people at that time in the past: rather, what is offered here is designated by direct description.

Thus the text does not give us the right to speak of a metaphor or parable which implies that "I must die,"[30] so that the breaking of the bread could be explained as the "breaking" of his body and the pouring of the wine contained in the cup as the streaming of his blood.[31] Rather, the words of the Lord are clearly not attached to the bread-breaking and wine-pouring, but to the gift itself, and in themselves contain nothing of that explanatory character which goes to make up metaphors and parables. "The similarity between the two is therefore not (or not only) a connection through analogy . . ., but a connection through identity" (E. Lohmeyer).[32] Only for this reason can Paul say in I Cor. 10.16: "The cup of blessing which we bless, is it not a participation in the body of Christ?"[33] This passage is the only authentic commentary in the New Testament itself on the words of institution. It does not only express the conception of Paul himself. He can also presuppose that the Corinthians have the same view, as v. 15 shows: "I speak as to sensible men; judge for yourselves what I say." But even more: because all forms of the words of institution—in Paul and the synoptic writers—agree in *this* formulation (this . . . is), there is not the slightest reason to give another meaning to the synoptic texts.[34] The idea expressed in the "this . . . is" therefore clearly points to a sacramental communion. To that extent the dogmatic term "real presence," however much it may need further clarification, is thoroughly appropriate to the subject. Thus those celebrating the Lord's Supper receive a share in the shed blood of Christ as they drink of the cup. But that means that they share in his death, for "blood" is never anywhere thought of as a mysterious, material substance.[35] And they receive a share in the body of Christ given in death as they eat of the bread. Here it also needs to be reiterated that "body" is not thought of as substance but means the corporeal person.[36] We may assume with certainty that Paul understood the Lord's Supper tradition of I Cor. 11.23ff., which he himself had received, in the sense of the "participation"-concept of I Cor. 10.16 and that he never passed it on with any other meaning.

Thus far there are no differences between Paul and the synoptic writers. These become apparent only in other parts of his formula. They appear, first, in the position of the "for you" which—as mentioned—stands in Paul without further addition in the bread-word, and in Mark/Matthew in extended form in the cup-word. Further, in the interpretative phrases, the cup and blood of Christ occur in differing connections to Old Testament passages. While the synoptic phrase "this is my blood of the covenant" typologically relates

Jesus' death to the sacrifice in the Sinai covenant (Ex. 24.8), the Pauline formula explains it as the fulfillment of the promised *new* covenant of Jer. 31 (38).31ff. Of course, it must be added that this occurs without giving up the connection to the Sinai covenant; for only from that, not from Jer. 31.31ff., does the phrase "in my blood" receive its meaning.

Finally, the double "command to repeat" (vv. 24f.) belongs to the peculiarities of Paul's formula. It would be difficult to see it as belonging to the oldest text; rather, it is evidently an addition, and a mark of an increasing liturgical stylization, since it still is easier to explain its addition than its omission.[37] However, the question is not so important, for in any case the words of institution in Mark/Matthew are also a piece of liturgy and thus intended for repetition.[38] More important is the question about the sense of the phrase "Do this in remembrance of me." As is shown by the "for" in v. 26 and the explicit reference to the two acts of eating and drinking, to which the "command to repeat" was added, Paul himself explains it by the phrase: "For as often as you eat this bread and drink the cup, you proclaim the Lord's death until he comes." The "remembrance" and the death of the Lord are thus placed in the closest relation to each other. This alone justifies the much-advocated thesis that the phrase "in remembrance of me" is chosen in dependence on the corresponding formula in Hellenistic memorial meals of the dead.[39] These parallels in fact come considerably closer to the phrase in the Pauline Lord's Supper than the large number of parallels advocated in similar fashion from Old Testament-Jewish tradition, especially those which relate to the Passover, but also to other festivals and which paraphrase their meaning as "memorial celebrations" (*l^ezikkārōn*)[40]; for in these the relationship to the death of a definite person is missing. However, in spite of all the terminological assonances, the analogy of those memorial meals of the dead does not extend far. That is to say, that in them a dead person is remembered, but not at all in the sense of religious worship,[41] and the meal celebrations are merely a pious meeting. But here in Paul the concern is for a definite sacramental act, the eating of *this* bread and the drinking of *this* cup,[42] which are qualified in a definite sense by the Lord's bestowing word and which give to the celebrants a share in the saving significance of his death. Thus the formulae from the memorial meals of the dead are appropriated merely because they contribute the motif of the death of this person to the meaning of the celebration. They are not able to conceal its actual sacramental meaning. But it is just this sacramental meaning which is definitive and decisive for the Lord's Supper. Characteristically, therefore, the "remembrance"-formula of Paul is not used for the meal as a whole, but for the two acts of eating and drinking in particular.

The explanation which Paul adds in v. 26 is important not only because it underscores the context of the "remembrance" occurring in the process of the eating and drinking with the death of the Lord, but also because it clearly gives the phrase "in remembrance of me" the sense of the proclamation of the saving significance of this death and the proclamation of the crucified Lord who is present in the cultic worship of the congregation. The fact that "you proclaim" in v. 26 must certainly be understood indicatively, not imperatively ("for"!), has led numerous exegetes astray into understanding the action as such as "proclamation." Yet Schniewind especially has justifiably raised an objection to this and emphasized the unrelinquishable *word*-character in "to proclaim."[43] Only because the word that rings out in the celebration of the meal is so decisive can it be said of the celebration as a whole: "For as often as you eat this bread and drink this cup, you proclaim the Lord's death until he comes." The sentence shows that the "remembrance" of the Lord also happens in word and is not only a case of the believers recalling one who died long ago. Liturgically, "remembrance" is probably to be understood as the giving of thanks, spoken over bread and cup.[44] It has the character of a confession of praise, directed to God, to whose revelation it responds, but simultaneously directed to the world, to whom the saving death of Christ and his present rule is solemnly announced.[45] Both, the direction to God and that to the world, belong inseparably to the nature of the early Christian confession. This becomes clear precisely in the explanation of the phrase "in remembrance of me" by "you proclaim the Lord's death." It is also supported by the language of the Psalms, which use "confession" and "to make remembrance," "to remember" and "to confess" or "to proclaim" as synonyms.[46]

The emphasis on the death of Christ,[47] already present in the phrase "in remembrance of me" (vv. 24f.) and completely present in v. 26, and the emphasis on the temporal limits for the celebration of the Lord's Supper ("until he comes") that echoes in the Maranatha-call of the Lord's Supper liturgy of the earliest congregation, without question contains a sharp contrast to the understanding of the Lord'

Supper in the Corinthian congregation. This will be discussed later. Here initially the words of institution of the Pauline formula are to concern us more closely once more.

We have already seen that only in Paul's formula and in the Lucan text, which is dependent on the same tradition, are the words "after supper" retained. They refer back, we said, to an old practice of the celebration, probably no longer demanded by Paul himself, in which bread- and cup-action, bread- and cup-word, were separated by the common meal. On account of this the bread-word and cup-word became relatively independent and self-contained expressions. They have retained precisely this sense in Paul, quite independently of the question whether the practice was still exercised or not. That applies to the bread-word as well as to the cup-word. If we begin with the latter, what is surprising about it, as we remember, is that in contrast to Mark/Matthew, the gift offered in the cup is not called the blood of Christ but "the new covenant" that is enacted by the atoning sacrifice of Christ. The difference between the texts in Paul ("the new covenant in my blood") and Mark ("my blood of the covenant") does not consist only in their different relation to the Old Testament (Jer. 31 (38) in the former, Ex. 24 in the later), but also in the different place of the terms "covenant" and "blood" in the sentence as a whole. While in Mark/Matthew "the covenant" is placed as an adjoining designation of "my blood," in Paul "in my blood" is an adjoining addition to "the (new) covenant." This is by no means only an insignificant variation in formulation.[48] Rather, the Pauline formula contains the problem of the "incongruence" of bread-word and cup-word, a weakening of whose theological significance is not allowed.[49] This "incongruence" is constituted by the fact that two apparently totally dissimilar terms, by no means simply a familiar pair of terms, are paralleled with each other: "body" and "covenant" (not "blood"!). W. Marxsen calls them two "in no way corresponding terms"[50] and thinks that on the basis of the first member ("body") a change in emphasis and position in the cup-word had necessarily to be undertaken for the purpose of parallelism. But is this correct? The answer will have to be that, in fact, it is easy to explain how the Markan form of the cup-word could grow out of the Pauline. But—and this must be emphatically added—that applies only to one understanding of the sacrament, one that is not simply to be accepted as Paul's. The change of "the (new) covenant in my blood" to "my blood of the covenant" only became necessary through a thinking

which understood the body and blood of Christ as the two constituents
of Christ given up in death. From then on, the interest adheres
consistently to the two elements representing the body and blood of
Christ. But it is very questionable whether this interest in the elements
which, as we know, plays such an exceedingly important role in the
history of the Lord's Supper problem, is present in Paul. This
emerges directly from the peculiarity of his text, that the words of
institution in which the bread-word and cup-word still were separated
by the meal itself ("after supper"). The Pauline formula makes
possible and indeed demands the making of each action of the meal—
bread-action and cup-action—into a self-contained entity and not
only a partial expression. The cup-word is, in fact, such a complete
expression: "This cup is the new covenant in my blood." New covenant means the new, eschatological order of salvation. In substance, this means the reign of the exalted Christ, established in his
death.

But the same also applies to the bread-word. I Cor. 10.16f. shows
that. Here it is clear that for Paul, the "bread"/"body"-word of
11.24, and only this, provides the basis for the formulation of the
ecclesiological sentence in 10.17. The strange sequence in I Cor.
10.16 (first the cup, then the bread) should not lead us wrongly to
assume a separate early Christian rite with a changed order. Here it
is to be understood by reference to the Jewish order of benedictions,
which we know, for example, from the Passover-*kiddush*, to which the
formulation "the cup which we bless" (*kōš šel bᵉrākā*) also refers.[51]
The explanation of this is simply that Paul can deduce the thought
about the congregation as the body of Christ, expressed in v. 17, only
from the participation in the body of Christ that the broken bread
mediates to us. If we want to understand this conclusion, we must
note here the extent to which the bread-word of the Pauline formula
of institution is already presupposed, precisely in its peculiarity. It
contains, as we saw, the addition "which is for you." Wherever Paul
relates the preposition "for" to Christ, it expresses on the one hand
the idea of atonement: Christ for us; that means given in death *for
our good* (I Cor. 15.3; Rom. 5.6, 8, *passim*), and on the other the idea
of substitution: Christ died *in our place* (Gal. 3.13; II Cor. 5.21,
passim).[52] Neither is to be sharply separated from the other and the
two can, as II Cor. 5.14f. especially shows, pass over into each other.
But in any case it is clear that from the death of Christ for us (or in
our place) directly follows the new situation of salvation, the new

existence of the believers and with it also the new task of their life. Now the life of the believers is a life *for him*. This result, expressed or unexpressed, is, one may appropriately say, always included in the "for"-formula: "one has died for all (substitutionary); therefore all have died. And he died for all (for their good), that those who live might live no longer for themselves but for him who for their sake died and was raised" (II Cor. 5.14f.). Therefore, the death of Christ for all includes directly as a result the life of the believers for him, not only as a moral duty of gratitude but as a reality in the history of salvation, given with the event of salvation itself.

For this very reason, I Cor. 10.17 also can conclude: "Because there is one loaf, we who are many are one body." For the body of Christ, which we receive in the bread, implies for Paul directly the "body of Christ" in which we are bound together in the sacrament. In it we receive the body of Christ and, by receiving it, are and show ourselves to be the body of Christ.

Therefore, the specifically Pauline[53] ecclesiological idea of the "body", expressed in v. 17, is also characterized by an equally real intention in "we are," as the "he is" of the formula of institution itself clearly was interpreted in the sense of a reality by the terms "participation" and "to partake." Thus there is no room for an explanatory interpretation by which the ecclesiological idea of the "body" would receive the character of a parable. From the beginning of v. 17 ("because there is one loaf") we are not to imply the abstract idea of unity, make the sentence into a metaphor,[54] and take away from the bread spoken of here the quality that it received through the "participation in the body of Christ" which has just been expressed (v. 16). An appropriate paraphrase might therefore be: For the body of Christ offered to us in this bread and given up for us is one, and just for this reason we, the many, are one body, namely the body of Christ.[55]

Thus the really Pauline turn of thought lies in the progress from v. 16 to v. 17. We may not simply equate the concept of the "body of Christ" in v. 16 with that in v. 17.[56] That would necessarily mean that even the gift offered in the bread is not the body of Christ sacrificed for us, but the spiritual body of Christ, the *corpus mysticum* of the congregation. But that it is impossible for the bread-word in the formula of institution in 11.24 and in spite of everything else is excluded there by the additional "for"-phrase, which here, as always, expresses the meaning of the death of Christ. But it is similarly excluded in 10.16, as the pair of terms "blood/body," taken up here from the tradition of the congregation, already show.[57] So the body of Christ, in which we receive a share through the bread, is his body, given for us in death.[58] The alternative of the body of the cross or the spiritual body is an entirely false one. For there is a sacramental communion with the body of Christ given in death only because the Crucified is at the same time the Exalted One and shows himself actively in the sacrament.[59]

In the sacrament the believers are received into the realm of Christ's reign. Paul does not hesitate to illustrate this with the picture of an apostate Israel[60] offering sacrifices to idols, with which he refers to the pagans and their sacrificial feasts (10.18–22). In so doing, he asserts a corresponding reality for the relation to the Lord established in the sacrament, something familiar and understandable to the Corinthians from their own past and from what was for them still a tempting, pagan environment. Here it is valid to note what the analogy of the table fellowship with demons means and what it does not. It illustrates the lapse of the table partners under the lordship of demons, not materialistic enjoyment in the food of the idols or demons[61] who entered by the food into those who ate it. Correspondingly, this applies also to the Lord's Supper. Here, too, the idea is not one of materialistic, natural or even supernatural participation in a mysterious substance, as if for Paul the problem of transubstantiation or consubstantiation, very familiar to us from the history of doctrine, could appear. "Participation in the blood" and "participation in the body" mean to share in the death of Christ and thus in Christ himself, the Lord present in the sacrament who died for us and offers himself to us in the bread and cup. Therefore, the limits of the Pauline expression need to be well observed. It is worth noting that Paul does not speak of eating the body and drinking the blood of Christ. Indeed, his formula does not express the simple equation of cup (content) and blood. Nor does the typological picture (10.1ff.) say: Christ *is* the miraculous drink which Israel was given to drink; he is rather the rock from which the water springs. So here, too, he does not change himself into a sacramental substance but is the *giver* of the spiritual drink and spiritual food. Further, 10.16 speaks about the *breaking* of the bread and the *blessing* of the cup as sacramental acts, not about eating and drinking. To this E. Schweizer[62] justifiably has pointed recently, and it needs to be noted, though consequences may not be drawn from it that place in question the whole sacramental sense of the eating and drinking. Therefore, because it obliterates the peculiarity of the sacrament, I regard Schweizer's formulation (in support of K. Barth) as quite unjustified: "Therefore, certainly the Lord's Supper is only our attestation of the event on Golgotha."[63] Thus, if we want to render Paul correctly, we shall have to hold very exactly a middle way between a spiritual interpretation of the Lord's Supper which makes it "only" (!) an attestation of the Golgotha event and thereby does not really let the real presence of Christ in the Lord's Supper—at least in this formulation—come into its own, and a sacramentalism which pushes the question of the elements into the foreground in an un-Pauline manner and does not do justice to the limits of what he says.

Our concern is not to extract a meaningless compromise formula that combines what is contradictory into a "synthesis," nor with maintaining elbow-room in which no real decisions ever happen. Rather, it has to do precisely with an advance to the real decisions in understanding the sacrament. Here, it is obvious that the texts of Paul may not be forced imperceptibly into the questions that have subjected us to a long, meaningful, as well as agonizing, history of the Lord's Supper problem. And yet it is valid to recognize that the actual questions over which the church and theology have struggled down to the present in looking for an understanding of the Lord's Supper are to an amazing degree already at stake between Paul and his opponents in Corinth. Therefore, now we must present the picture of this struggle once again.

IV. LORD'S SUPPER AND CHURCH

It is clear that according to I Cor. 10.16 there is still no dispute between Paul and his Corinthian opponents in the understanding of the Lord's Supper as a real "participation" in Christ's body and blood and thereby in Christ, who died for us and is present in the Lord's Supper. Here the Apostle can appeal to their understanding and speak in the language of a tradition not first coined by him. The uncanny thing is, however, that people can have such an understanding of sacramental communion and still basically miss the sense of the Supper and of the presence of the Lord in the sacrament. The actual decision about the right understanding of the Lord's Supper comes only beyond this consensus and first brings the test as to how far the agreement was genuine or only supposed.

We saw at the beginning that the Corinthians in no way wanted
to abolish the sacrament, as is generally maintained, nor had they
made the Lord's Supper into an "ordinary meal." Entirely the
opposite; they have shown themselves to us as robust sacramentalists.
This is the only thing that makes sense of the warning of the Apostle
against a security that relies on the possession of the sacrament
(10.1ff.), and his appeal to what they know from their pagan past and
environment. Even the grievances portrayed in ch. 11 actually become understandable only in light of the crude sacramentalism of the
Corinthians. Everything suggests that in Corinth all the importance
was attached to the sacramental act at the end of the celebration of
worship, and precisely for this reason the common meal was made a
matter of indifference. The alteration in liturgical practice which
moved the bread- and cup-action together, and thus necessarily
allowed the question of the elements to move improperly into the
foreground, could easily have misled them here. Therefore, Paul does
not again seek to familiarize the Corinthians with and to impress
upon them the idea of sacramental communion. This idea was all too
familiar to them. Indeed, they overemphasized it and made it the
one real thing about the Lord's Supper. It was just because of this
that Paul had so vigorously to oppose the absolutizing of the sacramental communion which had gained ground in Corinth, and thereby
to oppose a conception which perverted the sacrament into a magic-
working "medicine of immortality."

Paul conducts the battle by reminding the congregation of the
well-known formula of their own liturgy. Not only the Lord's Supper
tradition belongs to this. The verses that follow may also be formulated in closest dependence on parts of the introit liturgy to the early
Christian eucharistic celebration that we can reconstruct with some
certainty. They contain the invitation to the believers to "come" and
the exclusion of the unbelievers, and at the same time, explicitly or
implicitly, they include an admonition to self-examination and a
warning not to become guilty of Christ's death. Did. 10.6 preserves
such a formula: "If anyone is holy; let him come. If anyone is not,
let him repent. Our Lord, come. Amen." We find a similar one in
Paul at the end of I Corinthians (16.22): "If anyone has no love for
the Lord, let him be accursed. Our Lord, come." It may be left undecided whether we have to do here with a characteristic and usual
formula or with a shortened, free formulation of the Apostle in
dependence on such a formula, which one still can supplement with-

out difficulty by something like "If anyone love the Lord, let him come," to keep an exact parallel to Did. 10.6. For both, the frequent sacramental stylization in liturgical texts is characteristic. At any rate, the unquestionable relation of Did. 10.6 to the Eucharist is given in I Cor. 16.20 through the summons to the holy kiss, which belongs to the ritual of the Eucharist since the earliest period and on through the centuries.[64] A trace of this formula is also recognizable in Rev. 22.14f.: here the beatitude and the sharp rejection of the ungodly ("murderers, sorcerers," etc.) correspond to the invitation and anathema of Did. 10.6.[65] That this conclusion of Revelation is formulated in close dependence on the Lord's Supper liturgy is shown especially by the summons to prayer, Maranatha ("Amen, Come Lord Jesus," v. 20), occurring here in Greek translation, and by the invitation: "And let him who is thirsty come, let him who desires take the water of life without price" (v. 17), which still reflects the liturgy of the congregation.[66]

I Cor. 11.27f. also contains elements of style characteristic of sacral law[67] and constituents of such a formula. First it has a general warning against unworthy eating and drinking (v. 27)[68] and a summons to self-examination (v. 28). Paul only makes relevant application of this in v. 29, but it is still in closest proximity to the liturgical formula known to the Corinthians.[69] The peculiarity in the progress of the Pauline sentences, however, is that Paul here uses the well-known formula *against* the Corinthians themselves, as an admonition not only to call others to self-examination but to examine themselves. Verse 29 says what "unworthy" reception, i.e. reception inappropriate to the sacrament and leading to judgment is: "For any one who eats and drinks without discerning the body eats and drinks judgment upon himself."[70] Generally this "discerning the body" is understood in the sense of a differentiation between sacramental and ordinary food. However, after all that has been said earlier, we must ask whether this does justice to the scope of Paul's statement. We already saw that from their standpoint the Corinthians have not regarded themselves as guilty of a profaning of the sacrament; rather, they have taken it as a certain, mysterious means of salvation. But for Paul, the "bread/body" word of the formula of institution (11.24) already has another sense. The conclusion drawn directly from *his* Lord's Supper text showed that the "body of Christ" received in the sacrament becomes the "mystical body of Christ" of the congregation (10.16f.). It follows from this that in a corresponding formula "discerning the body" may have had something of the sense of a differentiation between sacramental and ordinary food as the Corinthians used and understood it. But Paul gives it another sense on the basis of the bread-word of the words of institution—and again only from this (as I Cor. 10.16f.). To discern the body, to esteem Christ's body in its peculiarity, means to understand that the body of Christ given for us and received in the sacrament unites[71] the recipients in the "body" of the congregation and makes them responsible for one another in love. "If one member suffers, all suffer together; if one member is honored, all rejoice together. Now you are the body of Christ and individually members of it" (12.26f.). If this is correct, it indicates that v. 29 is directed against a "profaning" of the "body of Christ" precisely under the mask of an increasing sacralization of the eucharistic food.

Even in I Cor. 10, this has the highest importance for Paul; for there the discussion of the Lord's Supper occurs, certainly not by chance, in relation to the question of responsibility for the brethren (10.23ff. follows 10.14ff.!). I Cor. 11 is no different. Here the concern is not just with "ethical" questions, which according to the understanding of sacramental "participation" may indeed occur in connection with "dogmatics", but still do not touch them at the core. On the contrary, here everything is at stake. Therefore, the last sentences of the chapter follow here, further illustrating the terrible possibilities of eating and drinking unto judgment. Without doubt they express the idea of *manducatio impiorum* (unworthy eating), a matter of dispute between the Lutheran and Reformed doctrines of the sacrament. Yet we should not overlook the strange irony in the history of this doctrine. While it stands as an index of a crude sacramentalism in the modern period, Paul uses the idea precisely to counter such a sacramentalism represented in Corinth.

To understand the sentences in detail one must note the following:

1. The concern in the general context is the members of the congregation. The question of communicating pagans, which is as abstract as it is absurd, remains completely beyond consideration.

2. Just as clear, of course, is the fact that according to Paul the effect of the gift received in the sacrament, but not the gift as such, is dependent on the faith of the recipients. Neither in Paul nor in the synoptic writers does the concept of faith ever appear in the context of the Lord's Supper texts at all. In any case, the efficacious gift is the sacrament, and even the unbeliever does not receive nothing. Here

Paul says about the sacrament what he says about the proclamation in II Cor. 2.16: "to one a fragrance from death to death, to the other a fragrance from life to life."

3. The difficult sentence in 11.30 about the weak, sick and dead is certainly meant by Paul as a general indication that the destructive powers of the old aeon—sickness and death—are still active among the Corinthians. Indeed, it indicates even more: that they are sent to them from the Lord to execute his judgment on their guilt. But never does he let this peripheral concern become inverted so that it suggests that the correct taking of the sacrament protects one from sickness and death. That would have meant, conversely, a direct judgment on the sick and dead who are mentioned, namely that they are dead because of their unworthy taking of the sacrament. However, the unworthy evidently remained very much alive physically. These somewhat grotesque considerations are only to clarify in what direction the thought of 11.30, already succinct enough, may not be developed.

4. Finally, the sentence in vv. 31f., which centers entirely upon the thought of judgment, contains also a clear defense against such a crude interpretation. "But if we had examined ourselves, we would not have been judged. But if we are judged by the Lord, then we are disciplined in order that we be not condemned with the world." Thus the believers are not immune against sickness and death, but are excluded from God's judgment in the sense of condemnation, and the troubles which come upon them have only the character of a gracious discipline that redeems them from the world and excludes them from the final damnation.[72]

The entire section 11.27–32 is permeated by the thought of judgment.[73] Thus it directs us back once more to the question about the eschatological meaning of the Lord's Supper. All the accounts of the Lord's Supper preserved for us refer to it, even if in very different ways. The comparison of the synoptic texts with the Pauline tradition has already shown that. While the eschatological viewpoint in Mark/Matthew occurs at the end and is limited to the cup-word, it occurs in Luke with a double application (to eating and drinking) before the words of institution. In Paul, on the contrary, it no longer belongs to the "tradition" itself at all, but is only preserved in the instruction that follows in the form of "until he comes," which, as we saw, may be a reshaping of the call "Maranatha." Thus the eschatological word necessarily shows an independent tradition as against the words of institution. That says nothing against its very early use. On the contrary, the fact that this word is only with difficulty inserted into a liturgical formula supports its early character. This means that in Paul it no longer appears except in the "framework," and in later liturgical texts (Justin, Hippolytus, Canons of the church, etc.) not at all.

Yet without question the saying in the synoptic texts is of the highest importance for the early Christian understanding of the Lord's Supper. For with this word the meal is moved to the limits of the *eschaton* and Jesus' death and farewell are designated as the inauguration of the "kingdom" that is breaking in. The word separates Jesus from his disciples ("I shall not drink again of the fruit of the vine . . ."), but binds him to his disciples in a new way, now in the "participation" of the sacrament and at the same time in the form of the promise of a new fellowship in the kingdom of God. The meal, as it continues to be celebrated here on earth, thus becomes a foretaste of the coming eternal fellowship with him.[74]

This eschatological motif of the celebration apparently had an exceedingly strong impact on the early Christian congregation, but it was also given a perilous degree of emphasis. From this perspective it can be understood that after Easter the early congregational celebration of the meal could have taken place in a quite unsacramental way exclusively in the consciousness of eschatological expectation and fulfillment. It is also understandable from this that in Corinth, now of course in a Hellenistic spirit, the Eucharist could have occurred as a sacramental celebration in which the communicants received the spiritual food and the spiritual drink as the medicine of immortality. It is not difficult to imagine how for the Corinthians this understanding of the sacrament could have grown directly from their pagan experience of the mystery religions in relation to their Gnostic experience of the spirit, and that now the Lord present in the sacrament was nothing more than a cultic god after the manner of other divinities. Indeed, we can also understand how easily these ideas could have been attached to the saying about the new, eschatological order of salvation, which indeed stood in *their* Lord's Supper "tradition," namely the one transmitted to them by Paul.[75]

Only with this background does the sentence of Paul receive its full importance: "For as often as you eat this bread and drink the cup, you proclaim the Lord's *death until* he come." In contrast to the enthusiasts' understanding of a Spirit-Christ, the phrase about his *death* now has an exceedingly pointed effect. It shows the limits of a fanatical transcending of the boundaries of time in spiritual-eschatological enthusiasm by the phrase "until he come," which so explicitly emphasizes the boundaries of time, and by the reference to the judgment yet to be. The Lord's Supper thus receives a very precise, definite *terminus ad quem*; and by anticipation of the glory of the new age it becomes a celebration between death and parousia, not beyond time and history but here on the plain of historical life together. It is just because of this that the relation between the sacrament and the church as the body of Christ, developed from *his* Lord's Supper formula (with its peculiarities), is so decisively important for Paul. This became dangerously hidden by the urgently developing interest in the elements, already indicated in the New Testament Lord's Supper texts. The congregation as the "body of Christ" is the place where the love of the Lord given in death is to be experienced, and therefore "edification" in responsibility for the brethren is the only criterion, by which even the "gifts of the spirit" are to be judged, namely as gifts of grace and service. Thus the theme of the following chapters of I Corinthians (12–14) stands in the most inward, substantive relationship to that expressed by the Lord's Supper texts which are discussed above.[76] Similarly, I Cor. 15 forbids the fanatical anticipation of the "resurrection" in Gnostic spirituality and makes a theme of "until he come" in a new way.

The eschatological dimension is not removed from the Lord's Supper by Paul. On the contrary, it has only now actually received this dimension, for he who is present and gives himself in the Lord's Supper is the Crucified One and as such the One who is to come.

Excursus I:

On the question of the literary integrity of I Cor. 10.1–22

The literary thesis of J. Weiss has been advocated again recently by W. Schmithals, *Die Gnosis in Korinth* (1956), pp. 14f. That gives me reason to discuss the problem of the context of I Cor. 8–10 once more, and especially whether 10.1–22 belongs to it.

In fact, we can agree with Schmithals that 10.1–22 (B) has its own complex of themes, and that 10.23–11.1 (C) again takes up the thread of the argumentation of ch. 8 (A), and indeed of ch. 9.1–23. There Paul has made clear by his own example why it is desirable, for the sake of another, in freedom to forgo an unchallengeable "right." However, the theme of B belongs completely together with A and C and is by no means a "basically different one" (Schmithals, p. 14). It certainly looks as if A and C are concerned only with the profane eating of meat offered to idols and B only with idol worship in the true sense, namely regular participation in the pagan cultic meals. However, 8.10 ("For if any one sees you, a man of knowledge, at table in an idol's temple") shows that the same question is also already in view there. Of course, it is not yet explicitly treated, but it belongs among the basic concepts characterized by the catch-words "knowledge," "love," "right". The special question of participation in the cultic meals cannot yet be treated by Paul here and requires first the more precise discussion which follows in B, because the Apostle first wants to agree broadly to the premises of the strong (there are no idols and thus also no meat sacrificed to idols) despite all the correctives, which he immediately adds to the sentences of the Gnostics which he quotes, in order not to divert attention from the real question (responsibility for the brethren). Thus Paul's argument would have been thoroughly open to misunderstanding here if he already had explained: actually there is nothing to object to in your, the strong's, practice; yet it must remain within limits; the matter begins to become dangerous if you think that by your knowledge you are able to even participate in the pagan cultic celebrations. In fact, he does come to this conclusion in 10.20f. But everything depends on the reason for it. This would have been poorly given by Paul if he had challenged the existence of idols in the profane sphere but recognized them in the cultic sphere. So he does not argue in this way in B. Rather, he challenges this conclusion explicitly by the questions in 10.19 and argues: by participating—sacrificing and eating—you first give the demons their power and become obedient to them. The matter is by no means as unperilous as you think; your Christian "freedom", apparently stated so grandly, actually leads to the devil. Only now is the way free again to take up what is decisive for Paul and to validate on the one hand the freedom of believers in their justified unconcern, but simultaneously to limit it to the harmless areas of eating meat sold at the market or of the profane meals, that is to say those that do not take place in the temple, and also to sharpen further the conscience of the "strong" in their brotherly responsibility. Even there, that is, away from the actual cultic event, he says in 10.28, it can suddenly yield a *casus confessionis* and demand renunciation.

What has been said shows that there is no compelling reason to take B out of the context of A and C. Justifiably, H. v. Soden had also already noted that a hypothetical compiler would have found this a strikingly bad place for the insertion of B. He would have done better to let 9.24–27 and 10.1–22 follow only after 11.1 (both belong together, as Schmithals has seen correctly), and not to sever the connection of A and C. However, an interruption by Paul himself is completely meaningful. It appears to me also to be clearly marked as such by the taking up again of the ideas of 9.19–22 in 10.32f. Finally, the connection of 9.24–27 to 9.23 is too close for one to attribute (with Schmithals) 8–9.23 and 9.24–27 (+10.1–22) to different letters.

EXCURSUS II:

On the events in Corinth and the meaning of the Pauline statements about the Lord's Supper in I Cor. 11

W. Schmithals (*op. cit.*, pp. 209ff.) gives an entirely different presentation of the events in Corinth from that attempted above (pp. 125ff.). According to him, the instigators of the disorder in the Lord's Supper are Gnostics, who, as representatives of a radical, spiritual Christology, want to have nothing to do with Christ "according to the flesh" and therefore with the Eucharist, whose center is the fleshly Jesus. To be sure, they take part in the celebration of the congregation, but they profane it deliberately and demonstratively in that they already hold an ordinary meal before and during the sacramental "Lord's Supper." The position of the Gnostics on the Eucharist may not have differed, according to Schmithals, from that on sacrifice to idols. Neither has any cultic meaning for them (p. 218). What Paul censors is not so much the questioning of the table fellowship but the destruction of the cult; in this sense "private meal" stands in opposition to the "Lord's Supper" (not to the common meal). Therefore, Paul does not seek to meet the unbrotherliness of the people in Corinth, but much more generally to ward off the misrepresentation of the cultic meal as a profane meal to satisfy hunger. Their own homes exist for that purpose. According to the practice introduced earlier by Paul and now commanded again, the Lord's Supper therefore has nothing in common with an "Agape."

In my view, this presentation suffers from serious difficulties:

1. If this section addresses the congregation in which the abuse of a system of cliques has gained ground (cf. also the "each" in v. 21),

not a single syllable refers to the Gnostics and their alleged attempts at sabotage, something one at least might expect in such decisive occurrences.

2. In spite of Schmithals' challenge, according to the information of the text the grievance consists in the fact that certain ones feast and others hunger, because the wealthy, who have arrived before the poor, give themselves to feasting without waiting for them (v. 21). In this Paul sees a contempt of the "church" and a shaming of the destitute (v. 22). Thus, nothing is said at all—at least up to v. 21— of a challenging of the custom of holding a fellowship-meal nor of the intention of again putting the purely sacramental meal in its place. But in that case the question in v. 22 and the admonition in v. 34a can only mean: If your concern only is to satisfy hunger, do it at home. To be sure, Schmithals is right in placing "private meal" in opposition to "Lord's Supper," but the element of fellowship for Paul is still of the greatest importance, because in the Lord's Supper is received the "body" of Christ that binds us together in the "body" of the congregation: Whoever partakes of the meal for himself "beforehand," and thereby lets the poor starve, places the Lord's Supper completely in question.

3. That the "tradition" in 11.23–25 has in mind a cultic gathering without a meal to satisfy hunger is excluded, to my thinking, by "after supper." I see no reason to regard it only as a later statement for the situation (thus Schmithals, p. 215, footnote 2). According to its original sense it designates a complete meal *between* the preceding cultic receiving of the bread and the subsequent receiving of the cup. Nor is Paul at all concerned about a liturgical order that has been changed in the meantime, but certainly the sense which Paul gives to both words of institution is to be understood only from this original order and the connection of meal and sacrament generally is still all-important for him.

Postscript: For the problems discussed in this essay cf. now the important book by P. Neuenzeit, *Das Herrenmahl. Studien zur paulinischen Eucharistieauffassung (Studien z. A u. NT,* 1960).

NOTES

[1] The essay reproduces a lecture given in July 1955, in Berlin-Weissensee, to theological students of East German universities; it first appeared in *ZTK* 53 (1956), pp. 312ff.

² Israel's sacrifice before the golden calf is always in the background as a type of idol-worshipping cult. Thus, convincingly, Hans v. Soden, "Sakrament und Ethik bei Paulus," in *Urchristentum und Geschichte* I (1951), pp. 246f.

³ Cf. J. Weiss, *Der Erste Korintherbrief* (1910⁹), pp. 210ff.; also his *Das Urchristentum* (1917), pp. 245ff. (ET, *Earliest Christianity* I, 1959, pp. 323ff.); W. Schmithals, *Die Gnosis in Korinth* (1956), pp. 14f. Most recently, E. Dinkler's "Korintherbriefe" in *RGG*³ IV (1960), col. 18.

⁴ "Paul has stripped off the materialistic 'superstition', but not yet entirely the spiritual" (J. Weiss, *Der Erste Korintherbrief*, p. 264).

⁵ *Op. cit.*, pp. 239ff., esp. 245ff.

⁶ *Op. cit.*, p. 257.

⁷ B. Reicke, *Diakonie, Festfreude und Zelos* (1951), pp. 266ff., understands the opponents of Paul in Corinth as Jewish Gnostics and explains the taking of their own meal beforehand by the "Jewish-puritanical position" of these people. For reasons of cultic purity they did not want to eat with Greek slaves. Yet I find nothing in the text to indicate this. In the Pauline and deutero-Pauline letters, such opponents always receive a sharper delineation (cf. Gal. 4.10; Col. 2.16–23; I Tim. 4.3). However, in I Cor. 11.22 the contrast is a social one. Also against the thesis of Reicke is the fact that it is the eating custom of the "weak" that has a Jewish motivation, at least according to Rom. 14.1–13. If one were to draw conclusions about the relations in Corinth from that, it would follow that the "weak" were the ones who had isolated themselves in the Lord's Supper. But that is already most improbable, because the charge of lovelessness in I Corinthians is always directly against the "strong" (i.e. Christian spiritualists).

⁸ H. Lietzmann, *Messe und Herrenmahl* (1955³), p. 254 (ET, *Mass and Lord's Supper*, 1955, pp. 207f.). Similarly J. Weiss, *Der Erste Korintherbrief*, pp. 283, 285, 292; also his *Das Urchristentum*, p. 510 (ET, II, p. 649). Cf. also K. Barth, *Die Auferstehung der Toten* (1953⁴), p. 34 (ET, *The Resurrection of the Dead*, 1933, pp. 63f.). Most recently W. Schmithals, *op. cit.*, pp. 209ff. (on this see Excursus II above in this essay).

⁹ In fact, we have to reckon with a multiplicity of different types of meal-celebrations in the Palestinian and Hellenistic areas. Here their eventual further differentiation can remain beyond consideration.

¹⁰ Cf. H. von Soden, *op. cit.*, p. 265, n. 36.

¹¹ This characteristic of Corinthian sacramental belief is to be affirmed unconditionally. H. v. Soden justifiably concludes this from I Cor. 10.1–13 (*op. cit.*, pp. 245f.), not "without support" from I Cor. 10.14–22, as Schmithals thinks (*op. cit.*, p. 218, n. 3).

¹² Namely before the poor had entered the gathering. The temporal sense in *prolambanein* may not be pushed aside (cf. Mark 14.8). Thus: "to take beforehand," not "to anticipate," as some understand. Cf. G. Delling, *TWNT* IV, p. 15 (ET, *TDNT* IV, p. 14).

¹³ The French humanist and teacher of Calvin, Faber Stapulensis, advocated it in his day, as did J. A. Bengel, and in the modern period among others G. Godet, A. Loisy, W. Heitmüller, H. Lietzmann; the latter in the following term: for Paul the Damascus revelation supposedly became the source in which everything that he had heard of Jesus before and after his conversion flowed together. Cf. *Messe und Herrenmahl*, p. 255 (ET, *op. cit.*, p. 208): "Paul knows the narrative of the last meal of Jesus from the tradition of the congregation . . . But the essential understanding of this story the Lord had revealed to him . . ."

¹⁴ *Die Abendmahlsworte Jesu* (1960³), p. 179 (ET, *The Eucharistic Words of Jesus*, 1966², pp. 127f.).

¹⁵ Cf. W. G. Kümmel in the Appendix to Lietzmann's Commentary, *HzNT* 9

(1949⁴), p. 185, with reference to E. B. Allo, *Saint Paul. Première épître aux Corinthiens* (1935), *ad loc.*

[16] O. Cullmann, *La Tradition* (1953), p. 14, formulates it relevantly: "The Lord is himself at work in the transmission of his words and of his works by the primitive community, which he accomplishes through it." On the question of tradition, see most recently K. Wegenast, *Das Verständnis der Tradition bei Paulus und in den Deuteropaulinen* (Wiss. Monogr. z. A u. NT Bd. 8, 1962).

[17] Also Heb. 13.10 is instructive, where the Lord's Supper clearly is alluded to. Yet the Old Testament text into which these allusions are woven is the ritual of the Day of Atonement in Lev. 16.

[18] G. Walther, *Jesus das Passalamm des neuen Bundes—der Zentralgedanke des Herrenmahles* (1950); J. Jeremias in *TLZ* 76 (1951), col. 547. Cf. also D. M. MacKinnon, "Sacrament and Common Meal" (*Studies in the Gospels, Essays in memory of R. H. Lightfoot*, 1955, pp. 201ff.). Against this, E. Lohse, *Märtyrer und Gottesknecht* (1955), pp. 127 and 141ff.

[19] The competing introductory formulae in Mark 14.18 and 22 show that.

[20] H. Schürmann, *Der Einsetzungsbericht Lk 22:19–20* (Part II of a source-critical investigation of the Lucan Last Supper narratives in Luke 22.7–38), 1955, produces evidence for the originality of Luke 22.19, 20a over against the text of Paul. Yet his reflections against a dependence of Luke on Mark (it is admitted only for Luke 22.20b) and his thesis that Luke 22.15–18, 19–20 supposedly is an older pre-Lucan, pre-Markan and pre-Pauline fixed literary text, which Paul has excerpted, have not convinced me. For a critique cf. E. Schweizer, *TLZ* 81 (1956), cols 217ff.

[20a] What follows is related to J. Jeremias, *op. cit.* (1949²), pp. 80ff., esp. pp. 88ff. (ET, 1955, pp. 106ff., esp. pp. 118ff.); in the 3rd ed. (1960; ET, 1966²) not inconsiderably modified.

[21] Cf. J. Jeremias, *op. cit.* (1960³), pp. 165ff. (ET, *op. cit.*, pp. 173ff.).

[22] "A noun with a pronominal suffix does not govern a genitive after it" (J. Jeremias, *op. cit.* (1949²), p. 99 (ET, 1955, p. 133); revoked, however, in the 3rd ed., pp. 186f. (ET, 1966, pp. 193f.).

[23] With W. Marxsen, *EvTh* 12 (1952/3), pp. 296ff., and E. Schweizer, *TLZ* 79 (1954), cols 577ff.

[24] Justifiably noted by W. Marxsen, *op. cit.*, p. 297.

[25] Rom. 7.3; Philad. 4.

[26] For a critique of translating *sōma* ("body") back into *bisra* ("flesh") see J. Jeremias, *op. cit.* (1960³), pp. 191ff. (ET, 1966², pp. 198f.); cf. E. Lohse, *op. cit.*, p. 125.

[27] J. Weiss, *Das Urchristentum*, p. 510 (ET, II, p. 649) wanted to deduce this from I Cor. 11.

[28] *Tract Pesach.* 10.4. Cf. StrB IV, pp. 67ff.; from more recent Judaism cf. K. Stern, *Die Feuerwolke* (1954), pp. 46f.

[29] References in J. Jeremias, *op. cit.* (1960³), pp. 50ff. (ET, 1966², pp. 55ff.).

[30] So J. Jeremias, who speaks of a double simile, *ibid.*, pp. 215f. (ET, p. 224).

[31] The latter is justifiably rejected by J. Jeremias, *ibid.*, p. 212 (ET, p. 220).

[32] *Das Evangelium des Markus* (1951), p. 306. Of course, doubts are raised against the conception of *touto* (this) as a descriptive definition, and not as subject (in Lohmeyer). Cf. J. Jeremias, *op. cit.*, pp. 211f. (ET, pp. 220f.).

[33] *koinōnia* has this sense of objective participation and is not covered by our much too subjectively colored term "fellowship." Cf. the synonym *metechein* in v. 17. On this cf. H. Seesemann, *Der Begriff koinonia im NT* (1933), pp. 34ff., and F. Hauck, *TWNT* III, pp. 805f. (ET, *TDNT* III, pp. 805f.).

[34] This explanation is not shaken by the lack of a copula in the Aramaic.

158   NOTES

³⁵ Cf. E. Lohse, *op. cit.*, pp. 138ff.
³⁶ On the understanding of this sacramental communion cf. R. Bultmann, *TNT*, pp. 146ff. (ET, *NTT* I, pp. 144ff.).
³⁷ J. Jeremias, *op. cit.*, pp. 161, 230 (ET, pp. 172, 237). Otherwise B. Reicke, *op. cit.*, p. 261.
³⁸ The eschatological word also supports this, for the phrase "I shall . . . not any more drink" includes, without expressing it, the idea: You will eat and drink further. Cf. M. Dibelius, *Formgeschichte des Evangeliums* (1961⁴), p. 209, n. 1 (ET, *From Tradition to Gospel*, 1935, p. 208, n. 1).
³⁹ Extensive references and literature in Lietzmann-Kümmel, *op. cit.*, pp. 57f., 93f. (Supplements); J. Jeremias, *op. cit.*, pp. 230ff. (ET, pp. 237ff.); B. Reicke, *op. cit.*, pp. 257ff. From the large number of references here we note only the parallel of an inscription of a grave in Nicea from the time of the Caesars: instructions of a testator to a village community about his estate of silver denarii [*epi tō*] *poiein autous ana*[*m*]*n*[*ē*]*sin mou* ("on their making remembrance of me") (B. Laum, *Stiftungen in der griechischen und römischen Antike* 2, 1914, p. 165, No. 6). Especially instructive is the use of *poiein* in the sense of "commit," "celebrate" (Reicke, *op. cit.*, p. 259).
⁴⁰ References in J. Jeremias, *op. cit.*, pp. 235ff. (ET, pp. 244ff.) and especially N. A. Dahl, "Anamnesis" (*Studia Theologica* I, 1–2; 1947), pp. 73f.
⁴¹ How far the memorial meals for the dead originally had something to do with the cult of the dead (cf. B. Reicke, *op. cit.*, pp. 259f.) may be left undecided. At least, the traces of such an origin are effaced beyond recognition.
⁴² Accordingly, later manuscripts also add the demonstrative to "the cup" in v. 26 (P 46 ℜ al sy).
⁴³ "This would be in keeping neither with the meaning of *kataggellein* ('announce') nor with the Passover and the Mystery Religions. Rather, one is to think of the words which are *proclaimed* in the celebration of the Lord's Supper: the death of the Lord is solemnly *announced*" (*TWNT* I, p. 70; ET, *TDNT* I, p. 72). Cf. also N. A. Dahl, *op. cit.*, p. 85: "The verb *kataggellein* used here seems to indicate that Paul also has a verbal pronouncement in view."
⁴⁴ Cf. N. A. Dahl, *op. cit.*, pp. 85f.
⁴⁵ This cosmic dimension belongs inalienably to the Lord's Supper. The formulation of J. Jeremias, *op. cit.*, pp. 117f. (1949; ET, 1955, p. 164) "*kataggellete* . . . does not designate the proclamation to outsiders (who indeed are not even there), but 'the proclamation of an accomplished event' (Schniewind)" is therefore wrong. His second clause annuls the negation of the first.
⁴⁶ Cf. Ps. 110.3 (LXX), to which E. Käsemann ("Anliegen und Eigenart der paulinischen Abendmahlslehre," in *Exeg. Versuche u. Besinnungen* I, pp. 21f. (ET, "The Pauline Doctrine of the Last Supper," *Essays on New Testament Themes*, 1964, pp. 120f.), justifiably points. Cf. also Ps. 44.18; 70.16 (N. A. Dahl, *op. cit.*, p. 85, n. 1).
⁴⁷ Emphatically established by B. Reicke, *op. cit.*, pp. 255ff.
⁴⁸ So J. Jeremias, *op. cit.* (1960³), p. 162 (ET, 1966², p. 169).
⁴⁹ Justifiably emphasized by E. Käsemann, *op. cit.*, p. 30 (ET, pp. 130f.).
⁵⁰ W. Marxsen, *op. cit.*, p. 297.
⁵¹ Similarly Did. 9.2; on this see M. Dibelius, "Die Mahlgebete der Didache," *ZNW* 37 (1938), p. 33; now in *Botschaft und Geschichte* II (1956), p. 118.
⁵² Cf. R. Bultmann, *TNT*, p. 295 (ET, *NTT* I, pp. 295f.); E. Lohse, *op. cit.*, pp. 131ff.
⁵³ Verse 17 first contains the actual Pauline expression; v. 16 expresses the tradition of the congregation, which Paul can presuppose. Cf. E. Käsemann, *op. cit.*, pp. 12f., 31 (ET, pp. 110, 131f.). This thesis, which is well-grounded both by

the introductory formula in v. 15 and also by the liturgical expressions in v. 16, is "strangely" challenged by Schmithals, *op. cit.*, p. 211.

⁵⁴ Thus in the sense of Did. 9.4: "As this broken bread once was scattered on the mountain and brought together, so let your church be brought together from the ends of the earth in your kingdom." In Paul, however, it concerns a real and logical result (because—therefore). But this conclusion can only be drawn because the same unity is already contained implicitly in the first clause which the second clause makes explicit. In other words: what is said about the unity of the bread stands from the beginning under the sign that this bread imparts participation in the one body of Christ and thus binds those who eat to the one body of Christ.

⁵⁵ The term *sōma* ("body") used here may have been prefigured in certain late-Jewish Adam-speculation in the history of religions. Cf. E. Brandenburger, *Adam und Christus* (Wiss. Mon. z. A u. NT 7, 1962), pp. 151ff. In this matter, that means: "The Body of Christ is the realm into which we are incorporated with our bodies and to which we are called to render service in the body, i.e. total service, service which embraces all our different relationships to the world" (E. Käsemann, *op. cit.*, p. 29; ET, p. 130).

⁵⁶ So H. von Soden, *op. cit.*, p. 263, and W. G. Kümmel in the Appendix to Lietzmann's Commentary (1949), p. 182, where to my thinking H. Lietzmann's interpretation is unjustifiably criticized. In justifiable opposition also P. Brunner, "Zur Lehre vom Gottesdienst," *Leiturgia* I (1954), p. 234, n. 179.

⁵⁷ Rom. 7.4 shows that Paul can also designate Christ's dead body as *sōma tou Christou* ("body of Christ").

⁵⁸ So also E. Käsemann, *op. cit.*, pp. 29f. (ET, pp. 130f.).

⁵⁹ Cf. R. Bultmann, *op. cit.*, pp. 148f. (ET, p. 147).

⁶⁰ H. von Soden, *op. cit.*, p. 246f., has shown convincingly that 10.18 does not have in mind the regular Jewish service of sacrifice, but the sacrifice before the golden calf in the wilderness (cf. n. 2 above).

⁶¹ Cf. v. Soden, *op. cit.*, p. 264, n. 32.

⁶² *TLZ* 79 (1954), col. 590, n. 83.

⁶³ K. Barth, *Kirchliche Dogmatik* IV, 1 (1953), p. 326 (ET, *Church Dogmatics* IV, 1, 1956, p. 296). E. Schweizer himself continues: "But, of course, in such an attestation he who himself is attested is really present."

⁶⁴ Cf. H. Lietzmann, *Messe und Herrenmahl*, p. 229 (ET, p. 186); K. M. Hofmann, *Philema hagion* (1938), pp. 23ff.; G. Bornkamm, "Das Anathema in der urchristlichen Abendmahlsliturgie," DEdG, pp. 123ff. (ET, in this volume, pp. 169ff.; here the investigation published in *TLZ* 75, 1950, cols. 227ff, is expanded by additional material). J. A. T. Robinson, "Traces of a liturgical sequence in I Cor. XVI. 20–24," *JTS* 4 (1953), pp. 38ff., independently came to largely similar conclusions. For the sacral-law stylization cf. E. Käsemann, "Sätze heiligen Rechtes im Neuen Testament," *NTS* I (1954/5), pp. 248ff. (ET, "Sentences of Holy Law in the New Testament," *New Testament Questions of Today*, 1969, pp. 66ff.).

⁶⁵ The *exo*-formula has its exact parallel in the excommunication-formula (*prorrhēsis*) transmitted by Lucian (*Alex.* 38), which was spoken in liturgical dialogue before a celebration of the mysteries in Athens.

⁶⁶ For particulars on Rev. 22.14ff. and other early Christian texts (Heb. 6.6; 10.29; 13.10; I Clem. 34 and others), in which to my thinking traces of this liturgy are to be found, see my essay cited under n. 64.

⁶⁷ *enochos estai* ("will be guilty") is also a legal term which we find only here in Paul, to which Heb. 6.6 is to be compared (cf. also Matt. 5.21f.; 26.66; Mark 14.64 on *enochos* as a term of judicial language).

⁶⁸ Cf. on v. 27, e.g., the list of prohibitions from the courtyard of the Herodian

temple: "Whoever is caught will be accountable for the death that follows." Cf. K. Galling, *Textbuch zur Geschichte Israels* (1950), p. 80, cited by E. Käsemann, "Sätze heiligen Rechtes im NT," p. 249 (ET, p. 67).

[69] This might explain the succinct formulation of v. 29, which understandably was soon supplemented and interpreted in the history of the text.

[70] The most unfortunate thesis of A. Ehrhardt, "Sakrament und Leiden," *EvTh* 7 (1947/48) pp. 99ff., will not be discussed further. His view was that the participants in the Lord's Supper, had according to v. 29, simply taken the judgment upon themselves, namely the rejection of Christ by the world, and that *mē diakrinōn to sōma* ("without discerning the body") is to be translated: "without making an exception of themselves." For a critique cf. W. G. Kümmel, Appendix to Lietzmann's Commentary, pp. 185f. E. Käsemann, *op. cit.* (see n. 46), pp. 11ff. (ET, pp. 109f.), wanted to understand it similarly to Ehrhardt, though without the linguistic misunderstanding of *diakrinein to sōma* (the absolute *sōma* cannot possibly mean "themselves").

[71] Similarly W. G. Kümmel, *op. cit.*, p. 186; J. Moffatt, *The First Epistle of Paul to the Cor.* (1938), *ad loc.*; B. Reicke, *op. cit.*, pp. 253f.

[72] If the idea that suffering is to serve the education of the devout is good Jewish understanding (W. Bousset-H. Gressmann, *Die Religion des Judentums*, 1928³, p. 385), it is still to be noted that Paul avoids the Jewish idea of the atoning power of suffering. On this cf. E. Lohse, *op. cit.*, pp. 29ff.

[73] Cf. C. F. D. Moule, "The Judgment Theme in the Sacraments," in *The Background of the New Testament and its Eschatology, Studies in Honour of C. H. Dodd* (1956), pp. 464ff., esp. 470ff.

[74] ". . . one ford, one bridge, one door, one ship and bearer, in which and through which we move from this world into eternal life" (Luther, "Vom Sakram. des Leichnams Christi und den Bruderschaften" (1519). *WA* 2; 753, 17–19 (ET, *Luther's Works*, vol. 35, 1960, p. 66).

[75] Paul himself can indeed speak in another place (II Cor. 3.6ff.) with the strongest words about "glory," "life," "spirit," "boldness" as the marks of the "new covenant."

[76] Cf. my essay, "Die Erbauung der Gemeinde als Leib Christi" in *DEdG*, pp. 113ff., on the parallelism of I Cor. 14 and 11.17ff. (ET, in this volume, pp. 161ff.).

ON THE UNDERSTANDING OF
WORSHIP

A. THE EDIFICATION OF THE CONGREGATION AS THE
BODY OF CHRIST

THE FACT THAT Paul deals with so many loosely arranged individual subjects and questions in I Corinthians, presented to him by reports and inquiries from the congregation, has frequently hidden the thematic unity that permeates the letter as a whole, despite the chance character of the individual themes and their connection. It remains the exegetical merit of Karl Barth to have worked out this inner unity in masterful fashion.[1] In what follows we shall try to establish the substantive homogeneity of two sections concerned with worship. The first applies to the desecration of the Lord's Supper (11.17–34), the second to the priority in worship of prophecy over speaking in tongues (14.1–40).[2] We begin with the latter, and in both sections forgo a discussion of all questions of detail in order to get more precisely in view the theological motivation that both have in common.

The judgment of Paul about the gifts of the Spirit stands in ch. 14, as in ch. 12, in clear, sharp contrast to the evaluation allotted to them from the side of the Corinthian enthusiasts. The point where the two differ does not lie in the understanding of worship as eschatological event. In this the whole of early Christianity is unified, even with all the recognizable and alleged differences in the shape and understanding of worship. The arrival of God's new world in the resurrection and exaltation of Jesus Christ forms the congregation into the congregation of the end-time and also determines the character of its worship. This eschatological consciousness is the basis for the rejection of all cult, which is the great theological theme of Hebrews, but is already widely announced in the gospels and no longer leaves room for holy places, holy times, and the cultic boundaries between the privileged people of God and pagans, or between priest and people. Positively, this eschatological consciousness is announced in the spiritual character of the proclamation of the word, of baptism and Lord's Supper, of confession, hymns and prayers, and in the ways in which the congregation expresses in life its relationship to the exalted, present and coming Lord.

Paul's dispute with Corinthian Gnosticism shows, however, that with all these statements the last word has not been spoken. Rather, the proper understanding of the congregation as an eschatological entity and its worship as eschatological event are now to be questioned. Apparently the Corinthian enthusiasts, filled and permeated by the miracle of the eschatological consummation, have respected most highly the irrational marks of spiritual ecstasy in its strange form of speaking in tongues. Paul passionately opposes this evaluation of speaking in tongues. Not that he denied the gift of speaking in tongues and thereby the miracle of spiritual ecstasy—he himself knows the language of the angels (I Cor. 13.1) better than all of them (I Cor. 14.18); nor is it that, shocked by the flood of the Spirit here over-flowing all dams and causing chaos, he now forces the congregation and its worship again into the preserved order and rules of a liturgical tradition which he could, for instance, take from the worship of the synagogue. Rather, he subjects all events of worship to the single and clear criterion of the "edification" of the congregation.[3] The gifts of the spiritualists (song, instruction, revelation, speaking in tongues, explanation) should have their place in worship, but Paul regulates them with a firm hand. The principle of this regulation—the gradation of gifts—is termed *oikodomē* (14.26).

The way in which prophecy is put above speaking with tongues shows particularly clearly what Paul understands by this *oikodomē*. The characteristic which distinguishes "prophesying" from "speaking in tongues" is the way in which its language can be understood. Paul does not dispute that "speaking with tongues" is a kind of communication brought about by the spirit; it is speaking with God in the spirit (14.2), a way of praying (14.13f.), but to those who hear it it remains incomprehensible talk (14.2, 11, 16), speaking into thin air (14.9). Therefore "speaking with tongues" is only appropriate in worship to the extent that it can be translated (14.27f.). For each word spoken in worship must be quite clear, a word that others can understand (the picture of the flute and the harp, 14.7). It must stir men's will like the call of the trumpet, which sets a troop of soldiers on the march and summons them to battle (14.8). Thus the true language of worship is not only speaking with God, to "edify" oneself (14.4); it also serves for mutual help and to that end demands comprehensible language. It should be noted that Paul does not except even prayer here. He shows how radically he understands this need for the language to be comprehensible by his refusal to allow the speaker to address his words only to those who already are of the same mind and have the same experience and knowledge. What about those who are still on the periphery, or even outside the congregation (14.16, 23)? They, too, must be able to understand, be convinced and have the hidden things of their hearts revealed. This must be disclosed by the truth of the gospel which they must affirm. They should find it necessary to bow and confess: God really is in your midst![4]

Paul uses the terms "edification" and "to edify" in ch. 14 no less than seven times (the former in 14.3–5, 12, 26, the latter twice in 14.4, 17). Here they need no other comment than that already given in the antithesis of "to prophesy" and "to speak in tongues." In this, the term "edification"[5] is clear in its negative and positive sense:[6] it expresses the "rejection of the self-sufficient hypertrophy of religious individualism and egoism, which exhausts itself in the production of spiritual phenomena in order to center upon itself." Positively, it expresses the helping of the other person, not only in his individuality but as a member of the "church" (14.4f., 12), since the congregation is not edified except through the word understandably addressed to another and applied to him as admonition and consolation (14.3). This other person already is a member of the congregation or should become one, as 14.16, 23f. show. This inclusion of the "outsiders" and "non-believers" in the discussion as well, and consequently their basic identification with the other person in the congregation, shows that Paul holds fast to the missionary function of the word even in the case of the word in worship. It is not by chance that for Paul the same verb, "to build," designates both his missionary activity[7] and the teaching and care of the congregations by his successors, even if the laying of the foundation is reserved to him as Apostle and they only can build on that (I Cor. 3.10ff.). But the same "to build" also designates the function one owes to the other person in the congregation (I Thess. 5.11), the "strong" in relation to the "weak" (I Cor. 8.11–23), as well as the speakers in worship in relation to the listeners (ch. 14). The "edification" of the congregation is first of all the content and task of the "authority" transferred to the Apostle from the Lord (II Cor. 10.8; 13.10; 12.19).[8] In a very definite manner, however, the prophetic speaking in worship—but not this alone (14.26)—continues the apostolic work in the congregation without detriment to the unrepeatable function of the Apostle in founding the congregation (I Cor. 4.14ff.). How closely the Apostle connects his work with that of the others is shown by the fact that in ch. 14 he nowhere brings out the peculiarity of his apostolic function, but describes his singular work in the congregation as fully parallel to the speaking that ensues in worship (14.6, 19).

The concept of "edification" as *nomen actionis* would, of course, be misunderstood if one were to infer from it that Paul subjected the congregation to the ideal distant goal of becoming God's temple some day through the common effort of apostles and charismatics. The congregation *is* the temple of God and is not to become it later (I Cor. 3.16f.). However, one could "call the 'edification of the church' the constitution to be accomplished, ever to be accomplished anew, the *creatio continua* of the church" (Vielhauer, *op. cit.*, p. 92). That happens in the practical behavior of the believers towards one another (cf. I Cor. 8–10 and Rom. 14f.), as well as in worship.

Because Paul makes the "edification" of the congregation the criterion of the gifts of the Spirit in worship, and thereby attributes to them their function as charisma only in the total structure of the body of Christ, he simultaneously gives unmistakable expression to the meaning that the eschatological character of worship has for him. This was not the meaning that Corinthian Gnosticism attached to it. For Gnosticism, the barrier against God's new aeon is taken away. In the eruption of the gifts of the Spirit it celebrates the penetration into God's new world. The perfect has come and shows itself expressly in the surging abundance of spiritual emotion. Therefore the Gnostic could never speak as Paul does:

> as for prophecy, it will pass away;
> as for tongues, they will cease;
> as for knowledge, it will pass away (I Cor. 13.8).

The Gnostic would say precisely the opposite: all these gifts of the Spirit are precisely the proof that the imperfect is at an end and the status of minority has yielded to perfection (cf. I Cor. 13.11).

But Paul's view reads the reverse: the "gifts of the Spirit" bear the mark of the perishable in contrast to love, which does not cease, and they are nothing without love. Therefore the introduction of ch. 14 reads: "Make love your aim, and earnestly desire the spiritual gifts," which is anything but a feeble connection to ch. 13, "an artificial and miserable retrogression to the theme in 12.21a."[9] In no way does ch. 13 hang, as J. Weiss thinks, loosely in the rivets; rather, the call to love is nothing other than the critical measuring of all spiritual gifts by the standard of "edification", though "love" is certainly not exhausted in this sphere. In the same letter Paul had already conveyed the connection of the two in the concise formula: "knowledge puffs up, but love builds up" (I Cor. 8.1). For Gnosticism there is no longer any "edification"; it revels in the perfection attained, in which even historical life together no longer means anything. But for Paul the consummation is still to be expected. Therefore, responsible life with one another and for one another gives meaning to the life and worship of the believers. That means the all-embracing criterion of "edification." But all "edification" still has before it the day of judgment, which alone will make known what the worth of each single deed was (I Cor. 3.12–15; 4.5).

Thus Paul pulls worship, too, back into the realm of historical existence from that imaginary region of eschatological consummation to which the enthusiasts had removed it. Does he then rob it of its eschatological sense? By no means. He only really gives it its eschatological meaning by making it the place of love's verification.[10] For with "love" Paul certainly does not proclaim a moral principle. Rather he understands it as an "aeon"[11]—to speak in the language of Gnosticism—it is the already present existence of the new age, the possibility opened to us in Jesus Christ and the reality embracing us in Jesus Christ: "For the love of Christ controls us, because we are convinced that one has died for all; therefore all have died. And he died for all, that those who live might live no longer for themselves but for him who for their sake died and was raised" (II Cor. 5.14f.). This passage, which apparently belongs to a completely different context, expresses very precisely the basis which Paul gives to the "edifying" behavior of brother toward brother. So also I Cor. 8.10ff.: Where the "strong" with his knowledge and freedom misleads the "weak" to over-exert himself and to ignore the voice of his conscience,[12] there he lets his brother perish, "for whom Christ died." No less clear is a parallel train of thought in Rom. 14f.: "Do not let what you eat cause the ruin of one for whom Christ died" (14.15). The congregation lives from the humiliation and self-giving of Christ, who has received us (Rom. 15.2f., 7). This is the law of its "edification" (Rom. 14.19; 15.2).

Paul did not need to develop the context in I Cor. 14 once more after he had disclosed it very carefully to the congregation in chs. 8–10. Not least in this way was the example of his own conduct, in which he made himself the servant of all (9.19ff.) "under the law of Christ" (I Cor. 9.21), forgoing the maintenance of his apostolic "authority." "Be imitators of me, as I am of Christ" (11.1).

If one views this context of Pauline thought, which the Apostle only needs to apply in ch. 14, it shows that his directions about worship are subject to the key word of the entire letter: "the word of the cross" (I Cor. 1.18ff.).

What we have recognized so far as the key idea in the Pauline understanding of worship over against the multiple forms of speaking in worship also guides and determines in entirely similar fashion the repulsing of abuses in the celebration of the Lord's Supper in Corinth (11.17–34).[12a] How shall we imagine the degeneration of the Corinthian celebration? In modern scholarship, as far as I can see, this question has had to retreat unwarrantably, even if understandably, behind the important question of the Lord's Supper tradition. However, it is in no way irrelevant for the Pauline understanding of the Lord's Supper. The familiar conception has been formulated by Lietzmann in this way: "The Corinthians had abolished the idea of the eating of Christ's body; the blessed bread was no longer 'body' for them, and they ate it as ordinary food."[13] Similarly J. Weiss: "they treated the meal not as a solemn religious action, but as an ordinary meal in which eating and drinking were the essential aspects."[14] Or K. Barth: "Out of this meal . . . in Corinth something apparently more refined has developed, namely a kind of festive banquet among themselves of the wealthy and probably educated on which the poor, pressed against the wall, had to look."[15] Very justifiably H. von Soden already opposed this conception with a reference to 10.14ff.,[16] where Paul can, in fact, presuppose a very crude sacramental understanding among the Corinthians. Following H. von Soden, we shall have to present the guilty in the Corinthian abuse in just the opposite way, not as spiritualists but as "really (animistic) sacramental thinking persons." But in that case, how is "the ruination of the celebration of the Lord's Supper" (K. Barth) to be understood? Apparently, because of their crude sacramental understanding, their loveless activity did not seem to be such at all.

As elsewhere in early Christianity, the Lord's Supper was celebrated within the framework of a common meal, in the course of which—certainly in Corinth, but of course not only there—the actual, sacramental action was inserted, probably with the recitation of the Lord's Supper tradition, apparently as the end of the entire celebration. The same arrangement is also to be recognized in the Didache, where after the table prayer (ch. 9) over cup and bread and the closing prayer of thanksgiving "after the satisfying of hunger" (ch. 10), formulae[17] follow with which the sacred act proper, not further described, is introduced with the exclusion of the "unholy."[18] The gospels also support this when they insert the institution of the Lord's Supper explicitly into an already existing meal, and yet as an independent act detached from it ("and as they were eating he took bread," etc., Mark 14.22; Matt. 26.26). Thus the Corinthian celebration in fact shows that the love feast and the Eucharist are not yet separated,[19] but we have to note the tendency precisely among the Corinthians to devalue the meal in favor of the sacramental act and to use the meal for their own eating and drinking, unconcerned about the poor latecomers, who were certainly not excluded from the closing sacramental celebration. Without any forcing, the expression in v. 21 is to be explained in this way: "For in eating, each one goes ahead with his own meal" (where the temporal sense of "goes ahead" is certainly to be retained).[20] "With his own meal" is not related, as J. Weiss thinks, to the period of time before the beginning of the gathering, but really to the "Lord's Supper" (v. 20). Of course, this has become an impossibility through the loveless conduct of the Corinthians, so that Paul can say: "When you meet together, it is not the Lord's Supper that you eat." That one must explain it in this way is shown, to my thinking, by the reference of the Apostle to the words of institution (11.23ff.), which he explicitly presupposes to be known among the Corinthians, and known as a customary sacramental formula (v. 23).[21] J. Weiss has rightly noted that it is not immediately apparent "how far the appeal to the Lord's words and the explanation of the meaning of the celebration is to serve to fight the Corinthian abuse."[22] But he obscures understanding by his assumption that the Corinthians had made an "ordinary meal" out of the sacrament. However, Paul's reference does not have the intention of moving the Corinthians again to a "sacramental" understanding of the celebration; it is to show them the meaning of this sacrament which they so scandalously take for granted. What was understood by it in Corinth may perhaps be related to the formula of Ignatius. For them the Lord's Supper was a "medicine of immortality,"[23] through which the communicants received the heavenly powers of the Resurrected One. They believed themselves transferred into the eschatological consummation through the sacrament and thought that they had a share in the redeeming destiny of their cult-god, Christ, as this was experienced in the mystery religions everywhere (10.17–20 explicitly recalls this analogy).

Paul expresses himself against this very thing with extreme pungency and interprets formula and celebration in a fully new sense. To be sure, the sacrament is concerned with redemptive participation in the "body" of Christ, given "for you" (I Cor. 11.24; 10.16) and in the new "covenant" (order of salvation). But the body of Christ given in death, which we receive, makes us, the recipients, into the "body" of the congregation (I Cor. 10.17).[24] The formulation "without discerning the body" is to be understood from that perspective (11.29). It refers not only in general terms to a recognition of the "sacramental" sense of the food (in this, as we saw, the Corinthians had pushed it perilously far), but also to a correct perception of the sense of the sacrament, correctly understanding the body of Christ as the body of Christ given for us, which binds the recipients into the body of the church and thus makes them responsible for one another.

Only in this way will the sacrament be received "worthily" (v. 27), and only so does its celebration have an eschatological meaning in the genuine sense.

However, for Paul that means that it is not already an anticipation of the eschatological meal, "but something established for the church and therefore bound to the church's time, which reaches from Jesus' death to his parousia."[25] Thus the inclusion of the congregation in the doctrine of the sacrament in the term "body" has become clear as the real scope of the Pauline idea. But that means at the same time that for him Cross and Parousia, here as in the entire letter, destroy the basis of Corinthian Gnosticism and its sacramental understanding. As Käsemann (p. 275) remarks, both facts actually move quite close to each other in the sacrament. Therefore, the interpretation that Paul gives to the Lord's Supper (in dependence on the "Our Lord, come" of the eucharistic liturgy) has supreme importance: "For as often as you eat this bread and drink this cup, you proclaim the Lord's death until he comes" (11.26). In view of the Lord's death, he calls the congregation to responsibility for one another;[26] in view of the judgment, which is already announced in the sacrament for those who eat unworthily, he calls the believers to self-examination with words which the congregation again must have known[27] from the liturgy of the Lord's Supper.

The exegesis of 11.17–34 has shown that Paul is also guided by the same motivation in his elaboration on the Lord's Supper as in the treatment of the spiritual gifts in worship in ch. 14, even if the two sections touch on each other very little terminologically. In any case, he gives the worship of the congregation its place, not behind time and history but on the plane of historical life together, which still has the consummation before it. At the same time, in the subordination of all spiritual gifts to the criterion of "edification" and thus in the responsibility for the brother in worship of which ch. 14 speaks, concern for the proclamation of the Lord's death until he comes is present in a very definite sense. Paul had no need to explain it further. Therefore in both places his teaching about right worship is a piece of his "theology of the Cross."

B. THE ANATHEMA IN THE EARLY CHRISTIAN LORD'S SUPPER LITURGY*

Paul closes I Corinthians with a series of liturgical formulae: (1) the summons to the holy kiss, (2) the Anathema on those who do not love the Lord, (3) the Maranatha, (4) the promise of the grace of the Lord Jesus, which clearly stands in contrast to the closing assurance of the Apostle's personal love (I Cor. 16.20–24). The formulae listed stem, as one may say more precisely, from the Lord's Supper liturgy, which according to the convincing conjecture of R. Seeberg, H. Lietzmann and others, was attached to the reading of the Apostle's letter in the meeting of the congregation.[1] Apparently the summons to the holy kiss[2] is the introduction to the holy meal. Since Justin, it has been a definite part of the eucharistic ritual, where it has maintained its place for centuries in East and West.[3] For I Cor. 16, the origin of the phrases from the primitive Christian Lord's Supper liturgy is definitely assured and is also supported by the context: Anathema and Maranatha, both in characteristic connection. A parallel text to I Cor. 16.22 is the Lord's Supper formula of Didache

* Expansion of an essay that appeared in *TLZ*, 1950, columns 227ff.

10.6. Both texts are closely related, in view of their sacral-juristic style and their content:

I Cor. 16.22	Did. 10.6
If anyone has no love for the Lord, let him be accursed. Our Lord, come!	If anyone is holy, let him come; if anyone is not, let him repent; Our Lord, come; amen.

Without doubt, Lietzmann has correctly recognized the character of the saying in Did. 10.6 in the oldest Lord's Supper liturgy, when he classifies it as a dialogue between the leader and the congregation and makes the leader first speak the initial words, "Let grace come and this world pass," to which the congregation responds, "Hosanna to the son of David." The leader speaks the invitation-formula cited as far as the Maranatha; finally, the congregation again confirms the call they have heard with "Amen." Lietzmann has, of course, without adequate reason undertaken to place 10.6 before 10.1. The formulae close the preceding meal and lead to the actual and contrasted eucharistic act, not further described.[4] The summons to exchange the kiss of peace, the Anathema and Maranatha, and with them the pronouncement of grace in I Cor. 16, also belong in the same place as Did. 10.6. The Anathema has the purpose of excluding the unworthy at the beginning of the celebration of the meal from sharing the sacrament.[5] Peterson already conjectured that Paul did not coin this Anathema himself, but has cited an older liturgical formula.[6] This is, in fact, to be accepted, for the sentence contains nothing specifically Pauline; "to love the Lord" is found only here in Paul, and the verb "to love", as related to God or Christ, found also elsewhere in Paul, is a general early Christian summary of the attitude of faith expressed in confession (Rom. 8.28; I Cor. 2.9; 8.3; Eph. 6.24; II Tim. 4.8; I Clem. 29.1; 59.3).[7]

The summons to confession is implicitly contained in the negative thrust of the Pauline formula in I Cor. 16.22. By analogy with Did. 10.6, the liturgical sentence, used and shortened by Paul, may therefore have read: "If anyone loves the Lord, let him come; if anyone does not love the Lord, let him be accursed. Maranatha." E. Peterson wanted to understand the Maranatha of Did. 10.6 and of I Cor. 16.22 itself as an Anathema and the Amen as an exorcistic reinforcement.[8] But here he has gone too far—his documentation from inscriptions for the apotropaic use of Maranatha do not support his thesis. However, the Maranatha certainly may have been appealed to as confirmation of the Anathema on those who deny love to the Lord, whether one understands it as the invocation of the coming Lord or as proclamation of his presence in the congregation.[9] In any case, the Maranatha appeals to the heavenly judge and lends threatening emphasis to the Anathema. Thus the formula belongs in the sphere of sacral law. It contains no disciplinary direction for any kind of human initiative (the congregation or a college of judges) to practice the office of the keys against this or that unworthy person, to ban this or that person. Rather, it expresses the decision as coming from God for the given situation and leaves the transgressor to the judging punishment of God. In this the responsibility falls entirely on the one addressed and the Anathema represents the summons to self-examination.

I Cor. 16.22, as well as Did. 10.6, does not draw boundaries between the baptized and unbaptized. According to Did. 9.5 (cf. also Justin, *Apol.* I.66.1), the right to participate in the Lord's Supper belongs only to the baptized,[10] and it is to be understood that this limitation became an established order in the following period. However, the directions expressed clearly presuppose that this regulation was not self-evident.[11] Did. 10.6 also says nothing about it, and the Pauline letters in no way give reason to see baptism from the first as a *conditio sine qua non* for participation in the celebration of the Lord's Supper. Naturally, in general those participating would have been baptized. But that does not mean that the "outsiders" or "unbelievers" (I Cor. 14.16 and 24f.), who shared in the worship of the congregation and who, convicted by the power of the proclamation, worshipped and confessed: God really is among you (I Cor. 14.25), were denied participation in the Lord's Supper. Apparently, the attitude of these convicted by the Word indicates precisely what Did. 10.6 describes as conversion and sanctification. Even if the accomplishment of "repentance" soon could and had to be connected with a church-ordered catechumenate, which prepared people for baptism and thus indirectly for participation in the Lord's Supper, it is nevertheless not to be doubted that the pair of liturgical injunctions of Did. 10.6 presupposes earlier conditions than the criteria for admission of Did. 9.5; and that in the time of the apostles the Anathema on the unbelievers stood in the place where later the congregation drew the boundary between the baptized and unbaptized.

The same connection between invitation and refusal in the oldest liturgy of the Lord's Supper can also be recognized in the final chapter of Revelation. Lohmeyer rightly maintained that behind

22.17–19 and 20 there is the perspective of a liturgical occurrence.[12] However, it may be accepted that even beyond this general character- istic the end of Revelation is permeated by reminiscences of the eucharistic liturgy. The "Come, Lord Jesus" (v. 20) (translation of Maranatha) stems from the liturgy of the Lord's Supper. The word of invitation "Let him who is thirsty come, let him who desires take the water of life without price" (v. 17) recalls the Lord's Supper liturgy, as also does the last occurrence of the wedding-motif (v. 17), which according to 19.9 includes the idea of the messianic meal. Perhaps so also does the self-designation of v. 16: "I am the root and offspring of David . . ." We may place it next to the phrase in the Lord's Supper prayer of Did. 9.2: "We give thee thanks, our Father, for the holy vine of David, thy servant," whose origin from the prayers of the Hellenistic synagogue and original relation to Israel as a saved people has been demonstrated by M. Dibelius.[13] It is not by chance that in Rev. 22.16, too, in the self-designation of Jesus, a corresponding Christianization of Jewish views occurs in the context of formulae that point to the early Christian celebration of the meal. This section is also introduced by a promise of salvation to those who have a claim on the tree of life and who may enter the heavenly city (v. 14), and by an exclusion-formula against the un- godly ("outside are the dogs," etc., v. 15).[14] The preceding sentence, "See, I come soon, and my reward is with me, to pay each according to his work" (v. 12), documents with complete clarity that the near- ness of the Lord, and thus the basis of the last judgment and the origin of sacred justice, dominates worship and eucharistic celebra- tion.

One can, I think, discover further traces of this liturgy in still other places. The eucharistic text of Did. 10 is followed by well-known directions about teachers, apostles and prophets, that is, warnings about false teachers, parasites and lying prophets (ch. 11–13). Chapter 14 then continues with the directives about the Eucharist. What at first seems an obscure connection immediately becomes clear when one observes that the warning about the false teachers occurs in the immediate context of the Lord's Supper texts. If the perspective that sees a reminiscence of the Eucharist in Rev. 22.17ff. is correct, then one may find it also in the promise of the messianic meal in 2.7: "To him who conquers I will grant to eat of the tree of life" (cf. Rev. 22.14, 19), as well as in the phrase "To him who conquers I will give some of the hidden manna" in 2.17 (cf. John

6.48ff.), both of which follow a word of judgment on the false teachers. Of course, this concrete mention of false teachers is missing in the letter to Laodicea, and the depicting of apostasy and the call to repentance is thought of more generally, but the promise and the victor's word, which have a special weight here at the end of all seven letters, are therefore formulated even more clearly in dependence on the picture of the messianic meal ("Behold, I stand at the door and knock . . ." Rev. 3.20f.).[15]

If one still remains in a certain uncertainty with regard to the peculiar pictorial language of Revelation, the connection of the warning about false teachers with the Eucharist is fully clear in the letters of Ignatius. The admonitions of Ignatius, in which a sacramental fellowship under the leadership of the one bishop occurs, are again and again surrounded by warnings about the heretics, who with their attack on the "flesh" of Christ also excluded themselves from partaking of his flesh and blood in the sacrament (*Magn.* 7–8; *Smyrn.* 5–7; *Trall.* 6–11; *Philad.* 2–4). Already in Ignatius this connection is stereotyped: the defense of the Incarnation of Christ against the docetic Gnosis occurs alongside the defense of the sacrament. In spite of *Smyrn.* 7.1, one sees from *Smyrn.* 8.1; 9.2, that even the heretics must have arranged their own cultic meals, but apparently without wanting to partake in them of the "flesh and blood of Christ." Therefore, I think, it is permissible to connect the fact that in Gnostic circles there were, even with the refusal of wine, various meal-celebrations, especially water-eucharists.[16] The avoidance of wine in the meal by no means always points with certainty to Gnosticism—it can also be a question of old meal customs. In any case, however, in Ignatius the emphasis on the sacramental presence of the "flesh" and "blood" of Christ (*Trall.* 8.1; *Rom.* 7.3; *Philad.* 4) plays a noteworthy role in repulsing a docetic Gnosticism.

One may well ask whether this background explains the obscure passage of I John, which is closely related to Ignatius in its anti-docetic tendency: "This is he who came by water and blood, Jesus Christ, not with the water only but with the water and blood . . . There are three witnesses, the Spirit, the water, and the blood; and these three agree" (I John 5.6ff.). The usual interpretation of this passage with reference to the sacraments, simply by its kinship to John 19.34f.,[17] appears to me to be undoubtedly correct. The explicitly polemical formulation of vv. 5, 6f. best allows, I believe, a reference not only to baptism but to a Gnostic water-eucharist, which, as the Mandaean sacramental texts show, has a meaning similar to baptism, namely the reception of the heavenly water of life. Indeed, it is characteristic of John that he only draws on the terminology from the sacrament and does not make it a theme *expressis verbis*, though without disputing the sacramental origin of the idea. Again, it is clear that the anti-Gnostic polemic of I John also remains in an environment of sacramental ideas even in his closing warning: "Little children, keep yourselves from idols" (5.21).

If the warning about the false teachers and their schisms already had a connection with the liturgy of the Lord's Supper in the earliest period, we may also set the same abrupt warning occurring in Rom. 16.17ff. in this context. Again and again, its position here has been reason for surprise. However, its placement is to be explained by noting that the introductory formula of the Lord's Supper liturgy directly precedes it: "Greet one another with a holy kiss" (Rom. 16.16). In the phrase in 16.20, Paul also uses a traditional formula.

A further passage which seems to me to belong in our context is I Cor. 11.27f. The sacral-juristic, stylized warning about unworthy eating and drinking[18] and the summons to self-examination (v. 28) initially have a general character. Paul formulates it apparently in connection with these or similarly expressed formulae of the liturgy, which in Corinth itself he can presuppose just as he can the Lord's Supper "tradition" (vv. 24f.). They would have corresponded in meaning to the Anathema of I Cor. 16.22, the rejection of the unholy and the call to repentance of Did. 10.6, and the repulsion of the ungodly in Rev. 22.15. Only in I Cor. 11.29 ("for anyone who eats or drinks," etc.) does the Apostle give an actual and concrete interpretation to the general formula. The eschatological motif, missing in none of the passages cited, is not difficult to recognize in I Cor. 11.26; "until he comes" is clearly a reshaping of the Maranatha invocation. The peculiarity of I Cor. 11 is that Paul uses paraenetically the warning and exclusion formula of the liturgy addressed to the unbelievers against the participants in the Lord's Supper in Corinth, that is, against those who believe they are entitled to participation in the meal as a matter of course.

One also may find reminiscences of the Anathema of the Lord's Supper liturgy in the Letter to the Hebrews. The "is guilty of profaning the body and blood of the Lord" of I Cor. 11.27 occurs again in variant form in Heb. 6.6: "since they crucify the Son of God on their own account and hold him up to contempt." The connection of the phrase with the Lord's Supper celebration is supported by the immediately preceding reference to baptism and the Lord's Supper ("those who once have been enlightened, who have tasted the heavenly gift," 6.4). We can also recognize in 10.29, behind the phrase, "who has spurned the Son of God, and profaned the blood of the covenant," the threat-formula from the introduction to the eucharistic liturgy. The refusal of a second admission to repentance has its basis in the fact that for the disloyal the one they have encountered in word and sacrament as savior has become their avenger and judge. As in I Cor. 11, Heb. 6 and 10 also use original liturgical formulae paraenetically, of course without slavish dependence. Finally the exclusion-formula of the Lord's Supper liturgy also stands, I believe, behind Heb. 13.10: "We have an altar from which those who serve the tent have no right to eat." Indeed, for Hebrews, as the context shows, the main concern is to show that the "altar" of Christians has its place beyond all cultic spheres, beyond the "camp," where Jesus completed the sacrifice of reconciliation on the cross. From the rich use of Lord's Supper terminology in 13.10–15 it is to be noted, however, that here Hebrews thinks simultaneously of the Lord's Supper.[19]

The use of liturgical motifs in early Christian admonition, to be noted in I Cor. 11 and in Hebrews, is perhaps most clearly to be recognized in I Clem. 34. There the admonition to be zealous in accomplishing good works is placed in the surprisingly large framework of the liturgy. This is the life situation of the congregation, where the coming of the Lord as judge of the world is proclaimed,[20] and the congregation joins in the "Holy, Holy, Holy" of the ministering angels in order to share in "the great and glorious promises" of God.[21] If we do not note the intended admonitory scope of I Clem. 34, then in view of the progress of the chapter we may candidly ask whether a phrase such as "receive bread with boldness" of I Clem. 34.1, which here is focused on the reward of the faithful worker, may not have stood verbatim or in quite similar form in the liturgy that hovers before the mind of the author. But nothing depends on this detail; the connection between admonition and liturgy is assured by the context all the same.

Finally, one last conjecture. It is well known that in Luke's Gospel the mention of the betrayer at the Lord's Supper is rearranged. It does not precede the institution of the meal but follows it (Luke 22.21–23).[22] Hillmann sought to explain this fact by a literary dependence of the Evangelist on I Cor. 11.[23] He thinks that behind the Lucan account of the institution stands the Pauline Lord's Supper text. Behind the discussion about the "dispute" of the disciples that follows in Luke, the Corinthian strife over the Lord's Supper again is to be recognized. And the mention of the betrayer after the meal is to be explained from the warning, not to become guilty of the body and blood of the Lord, added by Paul to the "tradition." Such a literary dependence of the Lucan pericope on I Cor. 11 does not appear to me to be acceptable even for the words of institution themselves—the Pauline text is more strongly stylized liturgically than the full text in Luke.[24] Both merely go back to the same tradition. Furthermore, the vague analogy between I Cor. 11 and the disciples' discussion in Luke does not support Hillmann's thesis. Thus the peculiar placement of the mention of the betrayer in Luke is to be explained in another way, namely by the admonitory use of the original threat-formula belonging to the Lord's Supper liturgy as recognized in I Cor. 11 and Hebrews. If, then, one substitutes the hypothesis of a literary dependence of the Third Evangelist on Paul by the hypothesis of a dependence on a primary liturgical and secondary admonitory tradition valid for both, it is true that Luke wants to describe Judas as one who—to use I Cor. 11—is guilty of the body and blood of the Lord, or in the words of Hebrews, crucified the Son of God on his own account, held him up to contempt and trampled him under foot, and thus forfeited his claim to be admitted once more to repentance.

X

NOTES

A. *The Edification of the Congregation as the Body of Christ*

[1] K. Barth, *Die Auferstehung der Toten* (1953⁴; ET, *The Resurrection of the Dead*, 1933); on this see R. Bultmann, *Theol. Blätter* 5 (1926), cols 1ff., now in *Glauben und Verstehen* I, 1954², pp. 38ff. (ET, *Faith and Understanding*, 1969, pp. 66ff.).

[2] From the course of I Corinthians one does not get the impression that the preaching service and the celebration of the Lord's Supper were separate events in Corinth. Both are apparently elements of the one worshipping assembly. The directions, valid for both, alternate with each other; cf. already 10.14ff. (Lord's Supper); 11.2ff. (veiling of women in prophetic speaking); 11.17ff. (Lord's Supper); 12.1ff. (the gifts of the Spirit, chiefly the spiritual gifts appearing in the preaching service); 14.1ff. (prophecy and speaking in tongues). The *terminus technicus* of the gathering in both is "to come together" (11.17, 20; 14.23, 26). The connection of the celebration of the Lord's Supper and the preaching service is well documented also elsewhere (Acts 2.42; 20.7ff.; Justin, *Apol.* I. 67). O. Cullmann's thesis of the co-ordination of both elements can be supported by these

passages, *Urchristentum und Gottesdienst* (1950²), pp. 29ff. (ET, *Early Christian Worship*, 1953, pp. 26ff.). It was already advocated emphatically by A. Schweitzer, *Die Mystik des Apostels Paulus* (1954²), pp. 246ff. (ET, *The Mysticism of Paul the Apostle*, 1955, pp. 253ff.). However, it is impossible to erect a universally valid law. Cf. also R. Bultmann, *TNT*, p. 143 (ET, *NTT* I, pp. 144f.). For Paul, the assumption of the connection between the Lord's Supper and the preaching service appears to contradict the participation of "outsiders" and "unbelievers" (I Cor. 14.16, 23). However, this objection is not sound. On this cf. the following essay on "The Anathema in the Early Christian Lord's Supper Liturgy".

³ On this see the excellent monograph by P. Vielhauer, *Oikodomē* (1939), esp. pp. 90ff. Cf. also O. Michel, *TWNT* V, pp. 142ff. (ET, *TDNT* V, pp. 140ff.)

⁴ In my judgment it is to be translated in this way, and not "in you." Adoration and acclamation apply to the epiphany of God in the congregation, not only to the confirmation of the inspiration of the speaker. Moreover, Paul clearly formulates the confession of the vanquished in dependence on Isa. 45.14 (cf. also Zech. 8.23). Without wanting to ignore the peculiarity of the speaking in tongues, we will have to see in this passage the passionate attack of Paul on all irresponsible speaking in worship that does not concern itself with those on the fringe and those outside, and that with self-satisfied skill makes use of an esoteric language or even a Christian "jargon," by contrast with which a stranger must feel himself hopelessly on the outside. To be sure, the speaking in tongues can be designated as a sign of judgment for unbelievers (14.20ff.), which in its strangeness manifests their strangeness in contrast with the Spirit of God, but the real working of the word is that it brings to light the truth about man ("convicts") and opens to him God's will.

⁵ For Paul, *nomen actionis* here as elsewhere (with a few exceptions).

⁶ On this cf. Vielhauer, *op. cit.*, pp. 91f.

⁷ I Cor. 3.5ff.; II Cor. 10.8; 12.19; 13.10. Cf. Vielhauer, *ibid.*, pp. 83ff.

⁸ Thus this does not have for him the character of a formal qualification and authority; rather, its content is filled by its origin. So Gal. 1.8 is valid.

⁹ J. Weiss, *Der Erste Korintherbrief* (1910⁹), pp. 311 and 321.

¹⁰ Cf. the essay, "The More Excellent Way," in this volume.

¹¹ E. Käsemann, *Leib und Leib Christi* (1933), pp. 171ff.

¹² Note the ironic sound in 8.10: "his conscience, because he is weak, will be 'encouraged',—to eat food offered to idols" (translation from the German).

¹²ᵃ Cf. my essay, "Herrenmahl und Kirche bei Paulus," in *SzAuU*; ET, "Lord's Supper and Church," in this volume.

¹³ H. Lietzmann, *Messe und Herrenmahl* (1955³), p. 254 (ET, *Mass and Lord's Supper*, 1955, pp. 207f.).

¹⁴ J. Weiss, *Das Urchristentum* (1914), p. 510, n. 1 (ET, *Earliest Christianity* II, 1959, p. 649, n. 57).

¹⁵ K. Barth, *op. cit.*, p. 34 (ET, pp. 68f.).

¹⁶ H. von Soden, "Sacrament und Ethik bei Paulus" in *Urchristentum und Geschichte* I (1951), p. 265, n. 36.

¹⁷ Concerning this formula cf. the essay that follows.

¹⁸ That *Didache* 10.6 stands in the right place, M. Dibelius has recognized in "Die Mahlgebete der Didache," *ZNW* 37 (1938), pp. 40f. H. Lietzmann, *op. cit.*, p. 236ff. (ET, pp. 192ff.), differs; he wanted to place the verse before 10.1.

¹⁹ Cf. J. Weiss, *op. cit.*, p. 510, n. 1 (ET, p. 649, n. 57).

²⁰ Against Bachmann, *Der Erste Brief des Paulus an die Korinther* (1921³), *ad loc.*; but also W. Bauer, *Wörterbuch zum NT* (1958⁵), col. 1404 (ET, *A Greek-English Lexicon of the NT*, 1957, p. 715).

²¹ There is no proof that the Corinthians had gone over from this "Pauline" type of celebration to that of Jerusalem, which had no sacramental character, as

Lietzmann thinks (*op. cit.*, p. 254; ET, 207f.). The tendency of their celebration is in exactly the opposite direction.

[22] *Op. cit.*, pp. 509f. (ET, pp. 648f.).

[23] Correctly so E. Käsemann, "Anliegen und Eigenart der paulinischen Abendmahlslehre," *EvTh* (1948), p. 270; *Exegetische Versuche und Besinningen* I (1960), p. 18 (ET, p. 116). Cf. this study also with what follows.

[24] We are not to understand "*koinōnia tou sōmatos*," following H. von Soden, *op. cit.* p. 263, as "participation in the body, in the spiritual life of Christ, and therefore in the (spiritual) body of Christ." This explanation, conveyed first by v. 17, is, rather, a specific Pauline interpretation of the tradition recognizable in v. 16. That is shown clearly by E. Käsemann, *op. cit.*, p. 265 (ET, pp. 109f.). Von Soden has otherwise worked out the tendency of Pauline ideas in excellent fashion.

[25] E. Käsemann, *op. cit.*, p. 273 (ET, p. 121).

[26] Thus the "social" and the "sacramental" directions, about whose unity J. Weiss (*op. cit.*, pp. 509f.; ET, pp. 648f.) justifiably asks, are joined to each other.

[27] On this cf. the following essay.

B. *The Anathema in the Early Christian Lord's Supper Liturgy*

[1] R. Seeberg, "Kuss und Kanon," in *Aus Religion und Geschichte* I (1906), pp. 118ff.; H. Lietzmann, *Messe und Herrenmahl* (1955[3]), p. 229 (ET, *Mass and Lord's Supper*, 1955, p. 186); K. M. Hofmann, *Philema hagion* (1938), pp. 23ff.

[2] Rom. 16.16; I Thess. 5.26; II Cor. 13.12; I Peter 5.14.

[3] Hofmann, *op. cit.*, pp. 94ff.

[4] H. Lietzmann, *op. cit.*, pp. 236ff. (ET, pp. 192ff.); correctly M. Dibelius, *op. cit.*, (see n. 18 in the preceding essay).

[5] An exact parallel to the invitation and exclusion formula recognizable from I Cor. 16.22 and Did. 10.6 is offered by the exclusion formula (*prorrhēsis*) and act of exclusion (*exelasis*) before the celebration of the mystery religions, mentioned by Lucian, *Alex.* 38, which, as Lucian explicitly notes, stem from Athens (i.e. Eleusis) (reference from J. Leipoldt). The formula reads: "If there be any atheist or Christian or Epicurean here spying upon our rites, let him depart in haste; and let all such as have faith in God be initiated and all blessing attend them" (translated by H. W. Fowler and F. G. Fowler in *The Works of Lucian of Samosata*, 1905, Vol. II, p. 229). In the exclusion Lucian lets the pagan liturgist cry: "Out Christians," and the throng responds with "Out Epicureans". For further particulars see in my article *musterion* in *TWNT* IV, p. 811, n. 17 (ET, *TDNT* IV, p. 804); F. J. Dölger, *Antike und Christentum* (1932), pp. 132f.; J. Leipoldt, *Reallexikon für Antike und Christentum* I, pp. 260f., under "Alexander von Abonuteichos".

[6] E. Peterson, *EIS THEOS* (1926), pp. 130f.

[7] The love toward the Father and the Son is a main theme above all in the Johannine writings (John 8.42; 14.15, 21ff., etc.). I John 4.20 formulates the confession explicitly: "If anyone says, 'I love God'." The connection between love toward God (or Christ) and confession is illuminated from I Cor. 8.3 and 8.6. Because the love toward God expresses itself in confession, there is a possibility of loving him with the lips (I Clem. 15.4: "they loved him with their mouth"). It is not necessary here to go into the Old Testament origin of this term.

[8] *Op. cit.*, pp. 130f.

[9] On the translation of Maranatha and a critique of Peterson's thesis cf. K. G. Kuhn, under *Maranatha* in *TWNT* IV, pp. 470ff., esp. pp. 474f. (ET, *TDNT* IV, pp. 466ff., esp. pp. 471f.).

[10] Did. 9.5: "But let none eat or drink of your eucharist except those who have been baptized in the Lord's name" (with reference to Matt. 7.6).

[11] "Thus the unbaptized were occasionally admitted to the celebration of the meal, which is forbidden here," R. Knopf, *HzNT* 16 (1953[2]), pp. 181ff.

[12] E. Lohmeyer, *Die Offenbarung des Johannes, HzNT* 16 (1926), p. 179.

[13] M. Dibelius, *Botschaft und Geschichte* II (1956), pp. 117ff.

[14] That it deals with a liturgical *prorrhēsis* is shown by the pagan parallel in Lucian, *Alex.* 38 (see n. 5 above). *hoi kunes* ("the dogs") is a familiar Jewish characterization of the cultically unclean, the pagan (Matt. 7.6; 15.26f.; Phil. 3.2. Jewish references in StrB I, pp. 724ff.). It is well known that Did. 9.5 refers the logion of Matt. 7.6, "do not give what is holy to the dogs," to the Eucharist.

[15] E. Lohmeyer, *op. cit.*, pp. 39f., correctly maintained the connection of 3.20f. to the "Lord's Supper" with a reference to Luke 22.29f.

[16] Cf. the abundant references in W. Bousset, *Hauptprobleme der Gnosis* (1907), pp. 305ff.; L. Fendt, *Gnostische Mysterien* (1922), pp. 29ff.; Lietzmann, *op. cit.*, pp. 238ff. (ET, pp. 195ff.).

[17] Against Bultmann, *Das Evangelium des Johannes* (1959[16]), p. 535.

[18] Cf. "Whoever . . . will be guilty. . .," v. 27. Only here in Paul is *enochos* ("guilty") a legal term.

[19] Lord's Supper terms in Heb. 13.10ff. are: "eat," "blood . . . for sin," "body" (Heb. 13.11 makes clear the meaning of the sacrifice, from which those gathered for the Lord's Supper live, by the contrasting picture of the expiatory sacrifice). In the Lord's Supper the hymnic praise (13.15) sounds as "sacrifice of praise," cf. my essay: "Das Bekenntnis im Hebräerbrief," *Theol. Blätter*, 1942, cols. 6of.; now in *SzAuU*, pp. 199f. The similarity in terms between Heb. 13.10ff. and Rev. 22.14 (*exousia* as a claim to and sharing in the sacrament; in addition the motif of the future *polis*, into which the believers enter, Heb. 13.14; Rev. 22.14) should also be noted.

[20] I Clem. 34.3 = Rev. 22.12.

[21] On the origin and use of the individual motifs of I Clem. 34 in the eucharistic liturgy cf. R. Knopf, *HzNT, Erg.-Bd.* 1 (1920), pp. 102f.

[22] The oldest form of the prediction of the betrayal is probably contained in Luke 22.21. Matthew and John are the first to offer the explicit designation of Judas as the betrayer. And John is the first to allow Judas to be excluded from the circle of the twelve before Jesus begins his last revelatory speech to his own. Cf. Bultmann, *Die Geschichte des synoptischen Tradition* (1961[5]), pp. 284f. (ET, *The History of the Synoptic Tradition*, 1968[2], p. 264).

[23] Cf. W. Hillmann, *Aufbau und Deutung der synoptischen Leidensberichte* (1941), pp. 235f.

[24] I shall not enter into the details. In the judgment that the shortened text of Luke (D) is secondary I follow M. Dibelius, *Die Formgeschichte des Evangeliums* (1959[3]), pp. 210ff. (ET, *From Tradition to Gospel*, 1935, p. 209ff.). Now also J. Jeremias, *Die Abendmahlsworte Jesu* (1960[3]), pp. 133ff. (ET, 1966[2], pp. 139ff.).

Additional literature relevant to this and the preceding essay: Cf. the commentary by J. Héring on I Corinthians (1949). Also W. Bauer, *Der Wortgottesdienst der ältesten Christen* (1930); G. Delling, *Der Gottesdienst im Neuen Testament* (1952) (ET, *Worship in the New Testament*, 1962); C. H. Hunzinger, *Die jüdische Bannpraxis im neutestamentlichen Zeitalter*, Göttingen Dissertation (1954); H. Schlier, "Die Verkündung im Gottesdienst der Kirche," *Die Zeit der Kirche* (1956), pp. 244ff.; J. A. T. Robinson, "Traces of a Liturgical Sequence in I Cor. 16.20–24," *JTS* 4 (1953), pp. 38ff.; H. Schlier, "Über die Einheit der Kirche im Denken des hl. Paulus," *Catholica* 90 (1954), pp. 14ff.; W. Schmithals, *Die Gnosis in Korinth* (1956); G. Bornkamm, "Herrenmahl und Kirche bei Paulus," in *SzAuU* (ET, "Lord's Supper and Church in Paul" in this volume, pp. 123ff.).

XI

THE MORE EXCELLENT WAY

I Corinthians 13*

I. THE VANITY OF ALL VALUES WITHOUT LOVE

ON THIS NOTE Paul begins the praise of love, which as "the way far above," the *via maxime vialis* (Bengel), leaves all human values in the depths beneath it like an ascent to the summit:[12]

1 If I speak in the tongues of men and of angels,
  but have not love,[13]
  I am a noisy gong or a clanging cymbal.
2 And if I have prophetic powers,
  and understand all mysteries and all knowledge,
  and if I have all faith, so as to remove mountains,
  but have not love,
  I am nothing.
3 If I give away all I have,
  and if I deliver my body to be burned,
  but have not love,
  I gain nothing.

* First published in *Jahrbuch der Theol. Schule Bethel* (8) (*Friedrich von Bodel-schwingh zum 60. Geburtstag*), 1937, pp. 132ff. The essay, except for a few changes (on I Cor. 13.13) and additions, remains unchanged. From more recent literature on "clanging cymbal" in 13.1 I add the articles by E. Peterson, *alalazō* (*TWNT* I, p. 228, ET, *TDNT* I, pp. 227f.) and K. L. Schmidt, *kumbalon* (*TWNT* III, pp. 1037f.). Cf. also H. Riesenfeld, "Note supplémentaire sur I Kor. 13" (*Coniect-anea Neotest.* X (1946), pp. 1ff., and XII (1948), pp. 50ff.). Further material in W. G. Kümmel in the Appendix to H. Lietzmann, *An die Korinther* I, II (*HzNT* 9, 1949), pp. 188f.—The English translation omits sections I and II of the original essay, and what appears here as I and II were III and IV. In the omitted sections the author challenges the position of W. Jaeger, "Tyrtaios über die wahre Arete", *Sitzungsberichte der Berliner Akademie* 1932, Phil.-hist. Kl., pp. 537ff. He makes reference also to W. Jaeger, *Paideia* I (2nd ed. 1936) and to H. Heyses, *Idee und Existenz* (1935). For purposes of comparison the original numbering of the foot-notes has been retained.

The form and content of these moving sentences correspond exactly. The stipulating protases of the sentences begin similarly five times. They roll along like waves, swelling to three parts in the second verse[14] and shattering three times on the same "and have not love." And the last part of the sentences express this futility of the onset with impressive symmetry: "I am nothing"—"I gain nothing."

All that Paul enumerates in vv. 1–3 describes man—and, indeed, the *homo religiosus Christianus*—in his highest possibilities.[15] We shall recall it in paraphrase: If I spoke the wonderful language of the Spirit (as it occurs in the worship of the congregation); even if I joined in the heavenly praise of the angels, in the "new song" that no man can learn (Rev. 14.2f.), in inexpressible words (II Cor. 12.4) which resound in another world, it would be vain, meaningless noise if I did not have love. If I had the gift of prophecy and the knowledge of those to whom the hidden counsels of God are opened and who explore the "depths of divinity," and if I had the gracious gift of faith that works miracles (I Cor. 12.9; Mark 11.23) and had not love, I would be nothing. And if I gave my possessions and goods to charity—that would be doing what surely everyone holds as love—and if I courageously and sacrificially plunged into martydom,[16] it would be a vain beginning and God's reward[17] would remain denied to me.

That is the major movement which runs through these first verses. There is an end to human achievement and human deed, even to the gifts of grace[18] in the congregation, because all these possibilities become vain and shatter in the presence of love if they have not become one with it.

These first verses gave *Jaeger** immediate cause to understand "love" (*agapē*) as a definition of the highest virtue (*aretē*). Actually, however, these very first verses already show that "love breaks out of the circle of enumerated heroic achievements, not only in view of its worth but in view of its origin. Tyrtaios left the circle of protecting fields open until he named the force that closes them. For Paul, love does not lead to a new field of activity—the threefold "and have not love" has no parallel in Tyrtaios—but back into the multiplicity of human activity. Verses 4–7 speak precisely about this.

* See asterisk footnote at the beginning of article.

II. THE NATURE AND REIGN OF LOVE

4 Love is patient and kind;
  love is not jealous;
  love is not boastful or arrogant;
5 It is not rude nor does it insist on its own way;
  it is not irritable or resentful;
6 It does not rejoice at wrong,
  but rejoices in the right.
7 Love bears all things, believes all things,
  hopes all things, endures all things.[19]

Here, too, the style and rhythm of the sentences are more than mere marks of external form. The extended, symmetrical threading of one member of a sentence to another, progressing with special transitions and connections—fifteen verbs in these three verses![20]—allow the calm and untiring character of love to become visible, until in the last verse its all-embracing power is expressed and the entire train of thought is closed by the simple and explicit fourfold repetition of "all things."

That here everything is affirmed about love—and not about man—is surely not just poetic expression. Rather, it corresponds to the profound contrast of all that is the essence of the natural man.[21] The positive expressions at the beginning and end frame eight negative parts of the sentence. Thus the miracle of love's nature and reign, its patience and goodness, becomes visible in what it is not. It is patient, it has "the long breath,"[22] it exercises patience, it waits in kindness on the other and gives him time where the tendency would be to be "done" with him. It does not boil up in unbridled passion that breaks all ties. It does not boast and puff itself up. That also destroys the fellowship, because the boaster—no matter whether he deceives with what he is not or proudly displays what he is—lets his brothers feel the disparity; he is really too good for them.[23] Love does not place itself beyond the limits and ordinances of custom. For example, the conduct of the Corinthian Gnostics[24] shows that the breaking of custom stems from the same motivation as a scorn of the "weak" and a proud puffing-up. It happens when a man seeks to present the values of his own knowledge and the extent of his own freedom by publicly differentiating himself from the conduct of the retarded weak and cuts himself off from the natural connections and ordinances of the human fellowship. Alongside all coarser forms, that is the finer "spiritual" form of self-seeking. But love does not seek its own way. And bitterness remains far from it. Even if unbelief, lies, evil and scorn could provoke one to anger and provide sufficient reason "to reckon evil" to the other, the evil is left standing as an unresolved matter, an uncanceled guilt between us. Where one retains evil toward the other person, there one abandons him; but love abandons evil and retains the other person; it is the power of fellowship, because it remits guilt and therefore does not let the brother go.[25] The destruction of fellowship occurs when one gains on the guilt of the other. The wrong of one upholds the right of the other. Alongside the tax collector arises the Pharisee, and with him the sinister, Pharisaic joy that perhaps hides itself with loud and moving lamentation. But love does not rejoice over unrighteousness, no—it rejoices mutually in the truth. This mutual rejoicing assumes that the truth gives benefit to the other person;[26] that is what makes love glad.

The last short sentences, formulated with impressive symmetry and ending the long row of negatives, also show the power of love in relation to the other person. Its life-power lies in indestructible trust —it believes all, it hopes all—and it works in the twofold manner of patience: the patience which does not let the other person fall ("bears all things") and therefore covers what he does to the brother with silence (I Peter 4.8),[27] and the patience through which the one who loves guards himself from falling ("endures all things").[28]

III. THE IMMORTALITY OF LOVE

8 Love never ends;
  as for prophecy, it will pass away;
  as for tongues, they will cease;
  as for knowledge, it will pass away.
9 For our knowledge is imperfect,
  and our prophecy is imperfect;
10 but when the perfect comes,
  the imperfect will pass away.
11 When I was a child,
  I spoke like a child,
  I thought like a child,
  I reasoned like a child;
  when I became a man,
  I gave up childish ways.

12 For now we see in a mirror[29] dimly,
   but then face to face.
   Now I know in part;
   then I shall understand fully,
   even as I have been fully understood.
13 So faith, hope, love abide, these three;
   but the greatest of these is love.

Again, the form and content of the section correspond to each other
exactly. The division of the sentences corresponds to the movement of
the ideas. The positive thesis, which expresses the theme of vv. 8–13,
stands at the beginning (8a) and is taken up again in the close (v. 13).
Three shortened, similarly constructed sentences formulate the contrast (8b–d) and receive their basis in vv. 9 and 10. In this the contrast
has become visible initially as that between the transitory imperfect
and the perfect, but simultaneously as the contrast between Now and
Then, on which all that follows depends. It is conveyed by the double
comparison: child and man (v. 11: three times the same "as a child,"
after the "when I was a child") and the mediated indirect view
through a mirror and the future direct view. While of course v. 11
entirely preserves the limits of the picture and illustrates the destruction of the imperfect (the verb "pass away" in 8–11 four times!), the
second comparison points immediately beyond itself; for the view
"from face to face" is at the same time a description of the perfect
knowledge. Thus the idea in v. 12 becomes more flexible and is
expressed in the double antithesis "Now"—"Then." Then comes the
movement of the ideas in the last sentence in which "love," the theme
of the whole, stands as the last word, pointing back to the beginning
(v. 8) and simultaneously to the goal.

The perfection of love, which is demonstrated by comparison with
the highest gifts of grace and the deeds of Christian life (negatively in
1–3) and by the simple portrayal of its constant and unconquerable
power in the troubles of common life (positively in 4–7), is presented
in the last major section of the chapter by the praise of its immortality.
The permanence of love is the miracle which can be measured in the
face of the passing character of all other gifts of grace. Characteristically, Paul confirms the transient character of even the highest
possibilities and powers of the life of faith not by reference to the in-
security and uncertainty of human ability—it is indeed "gifts of
grace" of which he speaks and not natural, human capacities—and
therefore not on the foundation of skeptical judgment, but on the

foundation of what is to come: "but when the perfect comes." "Because the sun rises, all lights go out."[30] Because "the prize of the upward call of God in Christ Jesus" is near (Phil. 3.14), because the Lord is at hand (Phil. 4.5), the "power of his resurrection" (Phil. 3.10)[31] and the being "at home with the Lord" (II Cor. 5.8), therefore all, even the highest, spirit-effected human possibilities, are preliminary and transient.[32] They are similar to the speaking, striving, thinking of the child that is moved by dreams and wishes. Only the man recognizes the extent of reality and detaches himself from illusions and dreams. The second picture means the same thing, only its meaning is limited to the contrast between the preliminary and indirect knowledge and what is perfect and direct (see above).[33]

In what does the perfection of this final knowledge exist? Paul surprisingly does not follow "now I know in part" with "then I shall know perfectly," but rather "then I shall know fully, even as I have been fully known."[34] The consummation consists in the fact that the cleft between knowing and being known by God is abolished. "Even as I am fully known": the divine gracious will of election reaches into the eternal pre-temporality before my knowledge begins, before I am born.[35] Thus "I shall know fully": the certain expectation reaches into the coming eternity when the transient things are put away. How will it happen that knowing and being known stand in harmony? We must answer with Rom. 8.29: "For those whom he (God) foreknew he also predestined to be conformed to the image of his Son" (cf. also Phil. 3.21; II Cor. 3.18). Thus the certainty of hope is based on the certainty of election in which the believers are destined for resurrection and glory.[36]

The attempt has repeatedly been made to derive the correspondence between knowing and being known from the concepts and terminology of Hellenistic mysticism.[37] It actually offers striking parallels for this change of "to know" and "to be known." Thus supposedly the expression in I Cor. 13.12—like the similar passages in I Cor. 8.2 and Gal. 4.9—means the inner mystical union of the knower with God. "*Gnosis* (knowledge) is the union with God" (Lietzmann on I Cor. 8.2). But if Paul could speak in this way of *Gnosis* it would not be justifiable to say that he attributed so low a value to it. Moreover, it is precisely the purpose of I Cor. 8.2 to show love toward God (and not knowledge) as the relationship that corresponds to being-known-by-God. However, the second passage (Gal. 4.9), which dutifully and shamingly reminds the Galatians of their conversion, has nothing else in mind than that the preaching of the gospel had encountered them and that they had believed. Finally, I Cor. 13.12 simply says that a real correspondence of knowing and being known is for the time being denied to us (II Cor. 5.7; 4.18). Thus nowhere is there an indication that knowledge—as Hellenistic mysticism understands it—leads to deification. For this reason the Pauline passages, not by chance, differ from the mystical ones in the simple fact that, as far as I am aware, mysticism always describes knowing and being known in the same tense, while for Paul everything depends on the pre-temporality of being known, i.e. "to be known" has the sense of election. Thus all the cited sentences of Paul describe the prevenient grace of God that first makes the faith, love and hope of the congregation possible at all.[38]

"But now[39] faith, hope, love abide,"[40] that is to say "when the perfect comes and the imperfect will pass away" (v. 10). In them the perfect, the new coming aeon, already is present, the eternal in the midst of the transitory, the "incorruptible" in the "corruptible" (I Cor. 15.42). That Paul also names faith and hope alongside love is at first surprising, for the expectation is that—as in v. 8—eternal permanence will be expressed only about love. The question then is how faith and hope can be spoken of in this way, since they are surely to find their end in seeing (II Cor. 5.7; Rom. 8.24).

Reitzenstein has investigated the first question[41] in particular, and has given it an illuminating answer: Paul speaks here, as so frequently in I Cor., to ward off the reveling enthusiasm for redemption that threatens the faith of the Corinthians, weakens love and destroys hope, because it tempts the believers to put the wisdom of the world in the place of the message of the cross (1.18ff.; 3.18ff.), to seek the proud perfection of the individual instead of the building up of the congregation in love (8.1ff.), and to exchange the necessity and trouble of waiting for the luxuriant riches of religious experiences (4.8ff.; ch. 15, and others). All of these marks belong to Gnosticism, a clear picture of which we are able to make for ourselves from pagan and Christian witnesses. Gnosticism also used the kind of formulae in which the divine, basic powers of the redeemed man were listed in its teaching about the world and redemption. These teachings were apparently known to the Corinthians, and it is legitimate to suppose that they had known a formula similar to I Cor. 13.13, which spoke of the redeeming might of God's four powers: knowledge, love, hope, and faith.[42]

These formulae, in which the divine powers of redemption were listed in this or similar fashion, did not arise at all from an abstract trifling, but from a striking and widespread faith: These powers of God—so goes the Gnostic doctrine—belong to the original, un-destroyed creation; they are dispersed in the unredeemed world; man suffers from the chaos of this undone creation and is himself torn apart, as is the creation. But in the redemption the gathering of the powers of God occurs; they join themselves together as the members of a new man, returned to his divine nature.

However we may answer the question of a connection between I Cor. 13.13 and the Gnostic formulae, in any case Paul's word runs completely counter to the speculation of the Corinthian Gnostics, and an eventual dependence on a Gnostic formula can only under-score the contrast; for with the addition "(only) these three," faith in the eternal permanence of knowledge[43] is averted and thereby the contrasting Gnostic view is undone.[44]

When Paul says of faith, hope and love that they remain beyond the end of this aeon, he means that they are more than human impulse and human behavior; yes, more also than the gifts of grace given to one and denied to another. They have their essence from what is beyond and will be revealed with the coming of the Lord. It is striking that Paul can speak also of faith and hope in this way. In II Cor. 5.7 he in fact places faith and sight in contrast and simi-larly faith and hope in Rom. 8.24. How can he also say here of "faith" and "hope" that they "abide"? If the difference of both expressions in contrast to I Cor. 13.13 is unmistakable, our passage still shows with complete clarity that Paul can also understand man in the consummation only as one dependent on God and unendingly open to him, constantly a recipient who does not have the basis of his life in himself ("faith"), constantly one who hopes, who waits for God ("hope").[45]

In the coordination of faith and hope (not as a "value" in itself), love also remains. If faith is based on what God has done and hope directs itself to what God will do, then love—from God, to God and thus simultaneously love toward the brother (cf. I John 4.7ff.)—is the permanent presence of salvation, the "bond of perfection" (Col. 3.14).[46] As such it is the greatest.[47]

IV

I Corinthians 13 is permeated from beginning to end by a single deep contrast that remains singular in all of its variations. It is the contrast between what man is in his highest natural and supernatural possibilities and the nature of love. "There is no reason to make this chapter into a great sentimentality,"[48] if one takes seriously the unflinching antithesis in what it says: the tongues of men and angels, all mysteries, all knowledge, all faith, all my possessions, everything of myself—empty, rumbling nothingness, I am nothing, nothing is of use to me. Hence the eight negatives in 4–7 and the incalculable contrast between what will be destroyed and what remains, between now and then in 8–13. "There is no chapter (except 15) in the entire letter in which Paul could have expressed so radically and sharply what he had to object critically to in the Corinthian Christians."[49] "Is it not true that the descriptions heaped on love here simply abolish the subject, man . . .?"[50] And yet it would be wrong to understand love here only as the distant ideal, derived in contrast—only as the antithesis to impatience, evil, boasting, etc., an unreachable, radiant idea of enticing and yet deathly brightness in the pure and starry heaven of values. No—Paul can speak of it so extollingly, movingly, completely, because it is a reality so living, concrete and variedly effective in detail, as it is described in 4–7, and at the same time it is the all-embracing power of God, put into force in the midst of this world as the love of God in Jesus Christ: "The love of Christ holds us bound," controls us (II Cor. 5.14). "But God, who is rich in mercy, out of the great love with which he loved us, even when we were dead through our trespasses, made us alive together with Christ" (Eph. 2.4), "that Christ may dwell in your hearts through faith; that you, being rooted and grounded in love, may have the power to comprehend with all the saints what is the breadth and length and height and depth, and to know the love of Christ which surpasses knowledge, that you may be filled with all the fulness of God" (Eph. 3.17ff.).

From this love and in this love the church has its life—I Cor. 13 does not stand where it does by chance, as an "excursus" between chs. 12 and 14. "Love" is related to the multiplicity of the "gifts of grace" as Christ is to the many members of his body (I Cor. 12.12); indeed, we may not speak of an analogy at all, but must understand the relationship between Christ and love as being still closer: love is the new aeon already present now; that is, the presence of Christ himself in the congregation.

Thus love is the realm of God's grace that embraces the believers, a power of life which in a certain sense is there before the believers.

From it they receive their life, and surrounded by it they live. It makes the church into a new creation in which the old has passed away (II Cor. 5.17), separated from the world in its fleshly existence and yet precisely in this way, as Eph. and Col. especially say, really a "world-wide" creation.[51] It has its essence from Christ's act of love (Eph. 5.22–32), and lives its essence in the love, the "bond of perfection" (Col. 3.14), in concrete and historical life together.[52]

From what has been said it follows that theologically there is no possibility of including love, whose greatness is praised in I Cor. 13, as a new definition of the highest "virtue" in the history of ancient ethics—whereby it makes no difference whether this evaluation of "love" is viewed as a worthy contribution in the history of the ancient idea of virtue or as a contribution to the great work of destruction brought into the world by Christianity. It is not only that the term "virtue" is completely missing in the New Testament[53]—furthermore, the essential content of the term is of no use in determining the nature of love or in receiving its own definition from love. Every description of love as a value, virtue, ideal, makes of it a superior—human or superhuman-divine—possibility of consummation,[54] but does not recognize it as the reality of a new world decided and begun in Jesus Christ. Because when I Corinthians refers to love it is not the self-perfection of man that is praised[55] but the redemption accomplished in Jesus Christ, the present power of God's grace and the glory of the coming consummation proclaimed in immortal love, the designation of love as "virtue" is a wrong beginning from the outset.

We could even say that every understanding of love as virtue and deed turns the gospel of I Cor. 13 into law[56], in that it directs itself to the striving and duty of man, instead of to the grace of God. It leads the believer to look to himself when he should look to what God has done;—and in that case, how is I Cor. 13 not to become a fatal law?[57]

It hardly needs to be said that with all this no apology for Christian love is given, in contrast with the manifold attacks which apply to it today along with the gospel. Perhaps at first the opponent will justifiably assert: yes, our attack is directed to this very basis of Christian existence shown here. But how else can a defense of love be made unless it remains unassailed in the midst of attacks—not in the sense of a Stoic equanimity that holds the other person at a distance and does not allow him to come close, but in maintaining the way given to it: "Love is patient, kind . . ., it does not let itself be em-

bittered, imputes not evil . . ." There is no other defense for it any
more than there can be a defense of the love of God for the world in
Jesus Christ, a defense of the Holy Spirit, of the new creation and the
congregation of the Lord.

If we want to support it in any other way, we fall into hopeless error,
as if we were his defender and not those defended by him; as if we
and not the Holy Spirit were God's advocate before the world, the
comforter and counselor of the believers; as if he would become victor
only through the fervent love of his believers and it did not hold true
that "in all these things we are more than conquerors through him
who loved us" (Rom. 8.37).

NOTES

[12] The following translation does not seek to give the impression that I Cor. 13 is
a poem; it sets out only to allow the division of ideas and the rhythm of the sentences
to be recognized. The position of the individual words also belongs to this. In the
exegesis I have limited the discussion of individual questions and am content to
refer to the most important commentaries by J. Weiss, Lietzmann, K. Barth,
Bachmann, Schlatter, H. D. Wendland. In addition, A. Harnack: "Das Hohe
Lied des Apostels Paulus von der Liebe (I Kor. 13) und seine religionsgeschichtliche
Bedeutung", *Sitzungsberichte der Kgl. pr. Akademie der Wissenschaften* (1911), pp.
132ff. (cites Harnack); H. Scholz, *Eros und Caritas* (1929); A. Nygren, *Eros und
Agape I* (1930), pp. 113ff. (ET, *Agape and Eros*, 1953, pp. 133ff.). On K. Barth,
Die Auferstehung der Toten (1953[4]; ET, *The Resurrection of the Dead*, 1933), cf. R.
Bultmann, *Glauben und Verstehen I* (1954[2]) pp. 38ff., esp. pp. 49ff. (ET, pp. 66ff.,
77ff.). Further literature later.

[13] It is good to retain the phrase of Luther familiar to us; it keeps a fine difference
between the "I" and "love" through the use of the article of separation, corresponding to the nature of the *agapē* and the formulation: "but have not love"
(and not "but I love not")·

[14] J. Weiss, *Der Erste Korintherbrief* (1910[9]), p. 314, gives a careful stylistic analysis
of the entire chapter. Cf. also Harnack, *op. cit.*, p. 153, n. 4.

[15] Cf. K. Barth, *op. cit.*, pp. 38f. (ET, p. 71).

[16] Lietzmann (*ad loc.*) counters the reading of the best Egyptian manuscripts,
"that I may glory," recommended by Harnack, *op. cit.*, pp. 139ff.: "The *hina*
('in order that')—sentence is equivalent to the *hōste* ('so as')—sentence in v. 2:
The statement of a purpose of the agent would destroy the parallelism" and
"anticipate the contrasting *agapēn de mē echō*."

[17] Cf. among others Matt. 5.10–12 and the promises of the commissioning speech;
on this H. von Campenhausen, *Die Idee des Martyriums in der alten Kirche* (1964[2]), p. 8.

[18] Therefore it is wrong to call love a *charisma*. No charisma is excluded from being
active in love, but none have any value if love is missing. Differently, H. Scholz,
op. cit., p. 107.

[19] In vv. 4–6 two substantively correlated members of the sentence are each time
bound together with one another; the translation seeks to express that through the
resumption and omission of the subject.

[20] "Here the use of the characterizing and descriptive adjective is totally disregarded. All emphasis is put on the verb" (Harnack, *op. cit.*, p. 154).

[21] K. Barth, *op. cit.*, p. 48 (ET, pp. 85f.).

[22] F. von Bodelschwingh, *Das Geheimnis und die Fülle Christi nach dem Kolosserbrief* (1936), p. 32.

[23] The *gnōsis* tempts the believers to this solitary, brilliant, vain dimension; cf. I Cor. 8.1.

[24] The section 11.2–16 shows how seriously Paul takes also this question.

[25] That is indeed the sense of *aphesis* and *aphienai* ("forgiveness" and "to forgive").

[26] "Giving thanks with joy" (Bengel). It is possible that the composite is there only for the sake of rhythm and coincides in meaning in the simple form (Harnack, *op. cit.*, p. 147).

[27] Harnack, *ibid.*

[28] Thus these last sentences lead back to the beginning: Love is patient, kind (v. 4)—". . . In I Cor. 13.7 hoping and loving apparently are thought of as something directed toward men, even if for Paul such behavior is based in the corresponding behavior toward God, as here the obviousness of the transition from one to the other (v. 13) shows." Bultmann, in the article *elpis*, *TWNT* II, p. 527 (ET, *TDNT* II, p. 530). Similarly Schlatter, *Paulus der Bote Jesu* (1956), p. 360.

[29] The "in a mirror" means the manner of seeing: we have only the unclear image, the knowledge is an indirect one. The translation "through a mirror" can be misunderstood as though we could see the thing itself through the picture; here that is just what Paul wants to deny. Cf. also Harnack, *op. cit.*, p. 150, 3, and J. Behm, "Das Bildwort vom Spiegel I Kor. 13.12," *Reinhold-Seeberg-Festschrift* I (1929), pp. 314ff.

[30] K. Barth, *op. cit.*, p. 44 (ET, p. 81). Melanchthon uses a similar picture in his commentary, but in a deviating sense. He finds from v. 9f.: "Let not these good things be destroyed, which were here formerly: but throw away imperfections and add to these former things greater strength." And thus he says: "that this bright light, which was in darkness, may remain bright, even grow brighter, as the sun now rides higher over the earth." (Corp. Ref. XV, 1146). "Faith, hope, love, (only) these three" in v. 13 show that Paul may not be understood in this idealistic sense but knowledge and prophecy will be destroyed.

[31] For the relation between I Cor. 13 and 15, cf. Barth, *op. cit.*, pp. 46f. (ET, pp. 83f.); R. Bultmann, *op. cit.* (see n. 12), p. 51 (ET, p. 79).

[32] "When he shall have arrived at the goal, then the course shall cease its aid" (Calvin, *ad loc.*).

[33] Cf. Scholz, *op. cit.*, p. 106, n. 1.

[34] *epigignōskomai* can actually be used with the same meaning as *gignōskein* (*TWNT* I, p. 703; ET, *TDNT* I, p. 703), but here it has the sense of complete knowledge. Paul places these in contrast to the simple *gnōsis* as something—really *toto coelo*—different, for the *gnōsis* will be destroyed (vv. 8f.)

[35] Being known by God is an Old Testament expression, cf. Gen. 18.19; Ex. 33.12; Amos 2.2; Hos. 13.5; Jer. 1.5. Cf. Bultmann, *TWNT* I, pp. 698, 705 (ET, *TDNT* I, pp. 698, 706).

[36] From this it can be understood once more why knowledge—as the temporal, passing contrast to the eternal, perfect knowledge—is excluded from this promise: it tempts the believers to boast (I Cor. 8.2) and brings them to circumvent the promise that the body of humiliation will be changed into the body of the glory of Jesus Christ (Phil. 3.21). The unity of change and entrance into complete knowledge is described by Clement of Alexandria in *Paedagog.* I, 6.36 (ET, *The Ante-Nicene Fathers* II, 1956, p. 218): "for with it (they say), having the face which is

like an angel's, we shall see the promise face to face." However, Clement does not interpret I Cor. 13.12 eschatologically but in idealistic and Platonic fashion (*Stromata* V, 1.7; 11.74; ET, pp. 446, 462).

[37] Cf. R. Reitzenstein, *Die hellenistischen Mysterienreligionen* (1927³), pp. 284ff.; M. Dibelius in *Botschaft und Geschichte* II (1956), pp. 3, 7, 9f. Justifiably opposed, R. Bultmann, *TWNT* I, pp. 709f. (ET, *TDNT* I, 709f.). A. Schweitzer, *Die Mystik des Apostels Paulus* (1954²), pp. 297f. (ET, *The Mysticism of Paul the Apostle*, 1955, p. 306).

[38] The principle "like is recognized by like" (for example, *Corp. Herm* XI 20), so meaningful ontologically for mysticism, thus has no place in the exegesis of 13.12. With greater justification it may be used as a pictorial clarification—but only as a picture!—to bring to mind man's situation, who, sitting in darkness and knowing nothing of the light, does not follow the beams of light until the sun arises and awakes in him the longing for the light. So Chrysostom (in dependence on Plato's Parable of the Cave?). J. A. Cramer, *Catenae Graec. Patr.* V (1844), pp. 257f.

[39] It is well to note the difference between the now (*arti*) in v. 12 and the now (*nun de*) in v. 13; the first has the sense of "now still"; in the second the limitation is missing. Cf. Schlatter, *op. cit.*, p. 365.

[40] The triad faith, hope and love is encountered in Paul several times (I Thess. 1.3; 5.8; cf. also Gal. 5.5f. and Col. 1.4f.) and apparently is already appropriated by him as a formula expressing the essence of Christian existence. For its influence in early Christian literature, cf. M. Dibelius, *HzNT* II (1937³), on I Thess. 1.3.

[41] On a discussion of the question cf. especially R. Reitzenstein: *Historia Monachorum* (1916), pp. 100ff.; *Nachrichten der Göttinger Gelehrten Gesellschaft* (1917), pp. 130ff.; *Die hellenistischen Mysterienreligionen* (1927³), pp. 383ff. Against this, von Harnack: *Preuss. Jahrbücher* (1916), pp. 1ff. Cf. also A. Brieger: *Die Trias Glaube, Hoffnung, Liebe.* Heidelberg Dissertation, 1925; Stauffer, article *"agapē"* in *TWNT* I, p. 52 (ET, *TDNT* I, p. 51f.); Bultmann, article *"gignōskō"* in *TWNT* I, p. 710 (ET, *TDNT* I, p. 710).

[42] It is referred to in *Porphyrius ad Marcellam* c. 24. Further material on the passages and discussion of the question also in Lietzmann, *op. cit.*, in the excursus on I Cor. 13.13.

[43] It is instructive to see how difficult it was even for Christian theology to bear this judgment on *gnōsis*. Cf. with the passages cited from Clement of Alexandria especially *Quis dives salvetur* c. 38, where I Cor. 13.8 is cited with the omission of "as for knowledge, it will pass away." Melanchthon also includes knowledge again in the list of what abides: "Neither is enumeration out of order: for many other virtues can be included in this grouping. (But) in whatever enumeration of virtues, the first and foremost thing is knowledge" (CR XV, 1147f.).

[44] W. G. Kümmel in the Appendix on I Cor. 13.13 (Lietzmann, *op. cit.*, p. 189) disputes the assertion that the sentence has a polemical ring to it. But one may not ignore it in "the three things," especially since 13.8–11 is formulated in clear antithesis to the Corinthian over-valuation of the charismata. On this cf. the essay, "Die Erbauung der Gemeinde als Leib Christi," in *DEdG*, p. 117 (ET, in this volume, pp. 161ff.). In what way the formula-character of the triad is supposed to tell against the theses of Reitzenstein and Lietzmann, I do not understand.

[45] Cf. A. Schlatter, *op. cit.*, p. 366; R. Bultmann, *Das Urchristentum im Rahmen der antiken Religionen* (1954²), pp. 207f., 233 (ET, *Primitive Christianity in its Contemporary Setting*, 1956, pp. 186, 208).

[46] On the understanding of this passage and I Cor. 13.13 cf. E. Käsemann, *Leib und Leib Christi* (1933), pp. 151ff. and 171ff.

[47] With this explanation, the meaning of I Cor. 13.13 given in the first version

of my essay, justifiably doubted by W. G. Kümmel in Lietzmann, *op. cit.*, p. 189, is corrected.

48 K. Barth, *op. cit.*, p. 47 (ET, p. 83).

49 *Ibid.*, p. 47 (ET, p. 84).

50 *Ibid.*, p. 48 (ET, p. 86).

51 Cf. E. Käsemann, *op. cit.*, pp. 156ff., 183ff.

52 *en Christo* and *en agapē* become in similar fashion a definition "of the individual historical life of the believer, who lives not from himself but from the divine deed of salvation" (Bultmann, TNT, pp. 323f., 340f., ET, *NTT I*, pp. 328f., 344f.). Cf. also A. Schweitzer, *op. cit.*, pp. 125 and 249ff. (ET, pp. 124f. and 303ff.).

53 Cf. O. Bauernfeind, article *aretē* in *TWNT* I, pp. 457ff. (ET, *TDNT* I, p. 457ff.).

54 The *erōs* can be so praised (cf. *Maxim. Tyr. Philos.* XX, 2), which should not be confused with the *agapē* of I Cor. 13. Lehmann and Fridrichsen offer an attempt at a Stoic-ethical interpretation of I Cor. 13, connected with a hypothesis of interpolation that is in no way convincing. "I Kor. 13. Eine christlich-stoische Diatribe," *Theol. Stud. u. Krit.* 94 (1922), pp. 55ff. On the difference between the Stoic *aretē* and *agapē*, cf. also Harnack, *op. cit.*, pp. 159f. On the difference between *erōs* and *agapē*, see especially H. Scholz.

55 Thus I Cor. 13 is a message about Jesus Christ and not a self-presentation of the Christian, or a presentation of the ideal Christian. If one wants to feel justified so to understand I Cor. 13, perhaps from the approved life of the Christian according to vv. 4–7, then Paul would answer: and if I had all patience, kindness, humility, etc.—and had not love, I would be nothing.

56 Thus clearly Harnack, *op. cit.*, p. 162: "the plain uncolored moral is thereby revealed as the essence of religion itself."

57 Because the Reformers are concerned for the acknowledgment and acceptance of God's love, they therefore fight the Roman doctrine of justification occurring through love. That the *caritas* of Catholic doctrine, in spite of its sacramental character, in fact remains in the system of values established by the Greek ethic, is already shown by the combination of the four ancient cardinal virtues with the three exalted above them and thus from below to the theological virtues leading into heaven. The justifying power of love, therefore, is also derived from a general value-concept applied to I Cor. 13: "The greatest virtue justifies all the more; love is the greatest virtue: Therefore love justifies all the more" (cited by Melanchthon, CR XV, 1155.) Similarly in Calvin, who notes on this: "What are we to say to this kind of argument?. . . According to that way of thinking, a king will plough the land better than a farmer, and will make a better job of a shoe than a shoemaker, because he is a man of nobler birth than both of them together . . . But we do not teach that faith justifies because it is more valuable, or holds a more honored place, but because it receives the righteousness which is offered freely in the Gospel" (on I Cor. 13.13, ET by John W. Fraser in *The First Epistle of Paul to the Corinthians* (Calvin's Commentaries, 1960, pp. 283f.) Cf. also Melanchthon, *ad loc.* and *Apolog.* IV. 111ff., 122ff., 225ff. and others.

Additional literature: Cf. the commentary by J. Héring on I Corinthians (1949). Also J. Dupont, *Gnosis* (1949), esp. pp. 483ff.; V. Warnach, *Agape* (1951), esp. pp. 111ff., here also extensive bibliographical material; T. G. Bunch, *Love, a Comprehensive Exposition of I Cor. 13* (1952); G. v. Rad, "Die Vorgeschichte der Gattung von I Kor. 13:4–7," *Festschrift für A. Alt* (1953), pp. 154ff., and *Gesammelte Studien zum Alten Testament* (1958), pp. 281ff.; C. Spicq, "L'agape de I Kor. 13," *Ephemerides Theologicae Lovanienses* 31 (1956), pp. 357ff.